"In *Ernie McClintock and the Jazz Actors Family: Reviving the Legacy* Cizmar excavates the practices of Black Arts Movement activist and acting teacher Ernie McClintock's groundbreaking acting techniques which de-centered Stanislavski based approaches to actor training to combine African and African American experiential aesthetics with voice work centered in jazz music, yoga, karate, and African movement. Cizmar deftly explores McClintock's "common sense" or "jazz acting" methods to illuminate his powerful social justice agenda used in many regional black theatres across the country during the Black Arts Movement and beyond. Cizmar's beautiful book makes McClintock's archive feel urgent and resonant in the twenty-first century as Black theater artists around the world ask for accountability and legibility within the mainstream theater landscape. Cizmar's descriptive prose and archival research are coupled in a fascinating account of twentieth-century Black acting methods that challenged the American actor training repertoire. Cizmar's thoughtful analysis leaves the reader asking how McClintock's work could be erased from the history of American actor training. The book is a must read for any artist, scholar, or theater enthusiast interested in the early practices of anti-racist theater and the struggles for equity and representation of Black artists in the American theater."

Nicole Hodges Persley, *Associate Professor of American Studies and African and African American Studies, University of Kansas*

ERNIE MCCLINTOCK AND THE JAZZ ACTORS FAMILY

Ernie McClintock and the Jazz Actors Family is a critical biography examining the life and work of Ernie McClintock, the founder of the Jazz Acting Method and 1997 recipient of the Living Legend Award from the National Black Theatre Festival, whose inclusive contributions to acting and actor training have largely remained on the fringes of scholarship and practice.

Based on original archival research and interviews with McClintock's students and peers, this book traces his life from his childhood in Chicago to Harlem in the 1960s at the height of the Black Arts Movement, to Richmond, Virginia in 2003, paying particular attention to his Black Power–influenced, culturally specific acting theory and versatile Black theatrical productions. As a biographical study, this book establishes McClintock as a leading figure of the Black Theatre Movement, proven by the Jazz Acting technique, his critically acclaimed productions, and his leadership positions in organizations such as the Black Theatre Alliance. *Ernie McClintock and the Jazz Actors Family* explores how the Jazz Acting technique was applied in productions such as N.R. Davidson's *El Hajj Malik*, Derek Walcott's *Dream on Monkey Mountain*, Cheryl West's *Before It Hits Home*, Endesha Mae Holland's *From the Mississippi Delta*, and many collectively-authored pieces. The book also investigates why he has been excluded from dominant theatre histories, especially considering how, as a gay Black man, he persistently defied the status quo, questioning practices of administrators of theatres and mainstream theatrical standards.

Ernie McClintock and the Jazz Actors Family is situated at the intersection of Black acting theory, Black Arts Movement history, and Black queer studies, and is an illuminating study of an important figure for actors, acting teachers, acting students, and cultural historians. This is an essential resource for readers who are seeking histories and approaches outside of a white, straight, Eurocentric framework.

Elizabeth M. Cizmar is an assistant professor of acting and directing and Affiliate Faculty of African American and Diaspora Studies at Vanderbilt University. She holds an M.F.A. from the Actors Studio Drama School/The New School and a Ph.D. in Drama from Tufts University.

ERNIE MCCLINTOCK AND THE JAZZ ACTORS FAMILY

Reviving the Legacy

Elizabeth M. Cizmar

NEW YORK AND LONDON

Designed cover image: From the Private Collection of Geno Brantley

First published 2023
by Routledge
605 Third Avenue, New York, NY 10158

and by Routledge
4 Park Square, Milton Park, Abingdon, Oxon, OX14 4RN

Routledge is an imprint of the Taylor & Francis Group, an informa business

© 2023 Elizabeth M. Cizmar

The right of Elizabeth M. Cizmar to be identified as author of this work has been asserted in accordance with sections 77 and 78 of the Copyright, Designs and Patents Act 1988.

All rights reserved. No part of this book may be reprinted or reproduced or utilised in any form or by any electronic, mechanical, or other means, now known or hereafter invented, including photocopying and recording, or in any information storage or retrieval system, without permission in writing from the publishers.

Trademark notice: Product or corporate names may be trademarks or registered trademarks, and are used only for identification and explanation without intent to infringe.

Library of Congress Cataloging-in-Publication Data
Names: Cizmar, Elizabeth M., author.
Title: Ernie McClintock and the Jazz Actors Family : reviving the legacy / Elizabeth M. Cizmar.
Description: New York, NY : Routledge, 2023. | Includes bibliographical references and index.
Identifiers: LCCN 2022033801 (print) | LCCN 2022033802 (ebook) | ISBN 9781032034713 (hardback) | ISBN 9781032034669 (paperback) | ISBN 9781003187448 (ebook)
Subjects: LCSH: McClintock, Ernie. | African American theatrical producers and directors—Biography. | African American theater—History—20th century
Classification: LCC PN2287.M125 E76 2023 (print) | LCC PN2287. M125 (ebook) | DDC 792.02/33092 [B]—dc23/eng/20221103
LC record available at https://lccn.loc.gov/2022033801
LC ebook record available at https://lccn.loc.gov/2022033802

ISBN: 978-1-032-03471-3 (hbk)
ISBN: 978-1-032-03466-9 (pbk)
ISBN: 978-1-003-18744-8 (ebk)

DOI: 10.4324/9781003187448

Typeset in Bembo
by codeMantra

To Geno Brantley who opened up his home to me and has provided unconditional love and support over the past eight years. Thank you.

CONTENTS

List of Figures   *xi*
Acknowledgments   *xiii*

    Introduction: Explicit Images and Inclusive Practices   1

1   Afrocentric Roots in Chicago's Blackbelt (1937–1964)   26

2   Shaking Up Harlem (1965–1972)   51

3   Canonizing the Contemporary Black Classics (1973–1981)   81

4   Quaring the Black Theatre Movement (1981–1986)   109

5   Rebel in Richmond (1987–1993)   136

6   The Persistence of a Living Legend (1994–1997)   161

7   To See Another Day (1998–2003)   187

    Conclusion: Beyond the Biography   219

Index   *227*

FIGURES

1.1	Ernie McClintock's Parents, Ella Wade Mason and Wade Mason	28
1.2	Portrait of Young Ernie McClintock, age unknown	31
1.3	Signed Original Playbill of *A Hatful of Rain* at the Selwyn Theatre	35
1.4	Vivian Blaine, Steve McQueen, and Frank Silvera in *A Hatful of Rain*, 1955	36
1.5	McClintock in Stage Makeup	39
1.6	Gossett Academy of Dramatic Arts (GADA) Course Offerings Pamphlet	44
1.7	Letter of Recommendation from Louis Gossett Jr., June 1, 1966	45
2.1	"Perspective on Black Acting," *Black World* May 1974	52
2.2	Logo of the Afro-American Studio for Acting and Speech. L to R: Joan Green, Carl Ajaye	52
2.3	Sign Hung in the Afro-American Studio for Acting and Speech	53
2.4	Candid Photo and Description, Marcus Hemphill, Glenda Dickerson, and Ernie McClintock following *Atreus Aegyptus* at NYU, December 1980	57
2.5	Brochure for the Afro-American Studio for Acting and Speech, fall 1971	59
2.6	Physical Warm-Up Exercises at the Afro-American Studio for Acting and Speech	62
2.7	*Where It's At* flyer	67
2.8	Newspaper Clippings About *Where It's At*	69
2.9	Production Candid, *El Hajj Malik*. Center: Helmar Cooper, Down R: Joan Green	73
2.10	Display ad 31, *New York Times*, December 3, 1971	74

xii Figures

3.1	Company Members from the 127th Street Repertory Ensemble	82
4.1	127th Street Repertory Ensemble's 1982 Season Poster	111
4.2	127th Street Repertory Ensemble's 1982 AUDELCO Award Nominations	112
4.3	Ernie McClintock and Amiri Baraka, indoors	116
4.4	Ernie McClintock and Amiri Baraka, outdoors	116
4.5	Denzel Washington and Gregory Wallace at the 1982 AUDELCO Awards	127
4.6	Ensemble of Horses in *Equus*	128
5.1	Invitation for Harlem Jazz Theatre Showcase	137
5.2	Still of Jazz Actors: Top Row L to R: Mia Burdie, Cheryl Sullivan, dl Hopkins, Linwood Jones, Ed Broaddus, Jakotora Tjoutuku, Mary Hodges Bottom Row L to R: J. Ron Fleming, Toni McDade-Williams, Derome Scott Smith	143
5.3	Letter from Ernie McClintock to S. Allison Baker June 8, 1993	148
6.1	The Living Legend Award 1997	162
7.1	Ronald Walker Standing in Front of His Artwork	188
7.2	Entry from Ernie McClintock's Journal	188
7.3	Clip from a pamphlet for Richmond's Second Annual Black Theatre Festival, 2002	189
7.4	Helen Butler, Joan Green, and Tanya Tatum backstage at the Barksdale Theatre	195
7.5	Tupac Shakur, Ronald Walker, and Ernie McClintock Stand Before a Poster for a Production of N.R. Davidson's *El Hajj Malik*	201
7.6	*Ndangered* Flyer	204
7.7	Back of Program for "Hold Fast to Your Dreams," March 10, 2001	207
7.8	Ernie McClintock's Red Chaise	212
7.9	Cast Photo of *Miss Evers' Boys*	212

ACKNOWLEDGMENTS

I am so grateful for those who have directly and indirectly supported my research.

Thank you to the Vanderbilt Department of Theatre including Christin Essin, Phillip Franck, Liz Haynes, Krista Knight, Leah Lowe, Alex Sargent-Capps, Emily Stewart, and Kristyl Tift for their support and willingness to include Ernie McClintock's work as part of the curriculum. I also thank all my current and former students for their curiosity, questions, and sense of play in the rehearsal hall and the classroom.

Many thanks to the archivists at Dartmouth's Rauner Special Collections Library for their assistance, not just through providing materials in a timely fashion, but for cheerleading this project from the start. Geno Brantley provided the access to dive deep into the lives and work of Ernie McClintock and Ronald Walker. I will be eternally grateful.

I feel incredibly blessed to have the support of friends, mentors, and peers in the field, who have championed my research and provided guidance along the way. Thank you, Candice Amich, Anna Castillo, Nicole Rose Brandon, Iggy Cortez, Matt DiCintio, Brian Healy, Amy Klewitz, Olympia Lettry, Barry Long, Khalid Yaya Long, Amina McIntyre, Adeana McNicholl, Detra Payne, Jennifer Smolos, Hesam Sharifian, and Billy Wheelan. Thank you to my Tufts professors, Natalya Baldyga, Tom Connelly, Barbara Grossman, Noe Montez, Heather Nathans, and Laurence Senelick who all laid the foundation for my scholarship. Special thanks to Monica White Ndounou—my earliest mentor in academia who believed in me from the start. I've been so lucky to make connections with senior scholars and artists across disciplines who champion my work including Joe Bandy, Rosevelt Noble, Nicole Hodges Persley, Kevin Powell, and Tracy Sharpley-Whiting.

This book's very existence is due to the generosity and time spent from Ernie McClintock's students and colleagues who took the time to be interviewed over the past eight years: Alaundra Douglas, Sharalyn Bailey, Jerome Preston Bates, Geno Brantley, Cindy Burroughs, Woody Carter, Diana Carver, Antonio Charity, Breena Clarke, Helmar Cooper, Thaddeus Daniels, Shantell Dunnaville, Bolanyle Edwards, Indira Etwaroo, J. Ron Fleming, Jr., Joan Green, Gwendolen Hardwick, Mary Hodges, dl Hopkins, James de Jongh, Lola Louis, Dorian Missick, Al Suavae Mitchell, Onaje Muid, Donna Pendarvis, Marc Primus, Pemon Rami, Iman Shabazz, Levy Lee Simon, Hazel Rosetta Smith, Derome Scott Smith, Christel Temple, Gregory Wallace, and Sheldon Woodley.

And, to my family: Mom, Papa, Katherine, Natalie, Maria, Jason, Jeff, Trevor, Ella, Eulalia, Jude, Amelia, Stephan, Anabel, Julia, and Sabrina, I'd be lost without you. Thank you for having my back, picking me up when I am down, celebrating my accomplishments, and helping me laugh along the way.

INTRODUCTION

Explicit Images and Inclusive Practices

On February 17, 1972, Ernie McClintock, wearing a denim suit and matching denim hat, addressed state and city officials in a New York City town hall meeting. Legislators were discussing the repeal of laws governing the sale of theatre tickets, city financial aid to selected companies, a national playwriting contest, and free buses to the Broadway theatre area. McClintock was vice president of the Black Theatre Alliance (BTA), an organization that unified African American theatres to combine resources and write grants for federal funding. He made quite an impression on his audience by asserting that these proposed changes were racist.

> For many listeners, the highlight of the day came when Ernie McClintock, director of the Afro-American Studio for Acting and Speech, took the podium to denounce the Black Report as 'an overt act of prejudice against the Black community' for failing to take into account the spread of neighborhood Black and Spanish theatrical productions.[1]

He proclaimed that Joe Papp, the artistic director of the Public Theatre, had "no more right to be funded to produce Black theatre than I do to produce Yiddish theatre."[2] McClintock insisted the administrators of Consumer and Cultural Affairs listen to his colleagues—who were not scheduled to speak—despite the meeting running over time. Shouts of support erupted from the standing-room-only audience. Hazel Bryant, BTA secretary and founder of the Afro-American Total Theatre, took the floor and began singing the Black spiritual "Done Made My Vow and I'll Never Turn Back." This incident, reported by the *New York Times*, demonstrates McClintock's leadership role in the Black

2 Introduction: Explicit Images and Inclusive Practices

Arts Movement, his eccentric and unorthodox style, and his deeply held belief in representing the Black Theatre Movement with a multitude of voices.

Ernie Claude McClintock, born February 19, 1937, on the South Side of Chicago, grew up in a racially and politically charged post–World War II environment. His home life was filled with cultural arts. McClintock was exposed to both mainstream theatre and popular culture, but as an African American born in Chicago, his lived experience were grounded in Black art and music, such as the blues and jazz. While pursuing his associate degree in medical technology at Crane College (now Malcolm X College), he witnessed Frank Silvera in *A Hatful of Rain*. This performance inspired him to take theatre classes and attend as much theatre as he could. Even while enrolled in the United States Armed Forces Institute from 1960 to 1961, he found his way on stage. Upon returning to Chicago, he studied acting at the Helen Espie Fine Arts Institute until 1964. In the early 1960s, he met Ronald Walker, who soon became his life partner and would be his creative collaborator until Walker's passing in 2001. McClintock founded the Afro-American Studio for Acting and Speech in Harlem in 1966, and was the artistic director of the 127th Street Repertory Ensemble in 1973, and the Harlem Jazz Theatre in 1986. By 1991, the couple moved to Richmond, Virginia, where McClintock established the Jazz Theatre of Richmond in 1991 followed by the Jazz Actors Theatre in 1993. On August 26, 2003, McClintock made his transition[3] in Richmond.

Throughout his career, McClintock pioneered a genre of actor training initially called "common sense acting," which in the early 1990s became known as Jazz Acting. McClintock's numerous productions included stories from Black women, Caribbean voices, South African stories, queer experiences, and Black revolutionaries. Reviving his legacy profoundly alters misconceptions about the Black Arts Movement, which is commonly misunderstood to be associated with militant activism, laden with homophobic and misogynistic rhetoric. This book excavates McClintock's legacy by answering two primary questions: Why is Ernie McClintock an important figure of the Black Theatre Movement? And why has he been left out of the narrative of the Black Arts Movement?

The Emergence of Theatre in the Black Arts Movement

This book explores McClintock's productions and methodologies through the lens of jazz aesthetics, but first it is important to understand the historical context of the Black Arts Movement. The revolutionary theatre of the 1960s sprang from the civil rights movement, which advocated for self-governing institutions and organizations from, by, about, and for Black people. Diplomatic efforts to attain equality—for example, for Black and white folks to be able to drink from the same water fountains—yielded a slow-burning progress.[4] In the throes of assassinations, racial segregation, and discrimination, frustrations mounted in Black communities and exploded with a provocative movement that brought America's attention to the dehumanization, incarceration, and oppression of Black bodies. In the post–World War II era, the American dream faltered as Black soldiers returned home with the realization that they had fought for a democracy they were not afforded, spurring Black people to claim space and citizenship without relying on white participation or cooperation.

In the early to mid-1960s, Black communities in the African Diaspora experienced moments of hope riddled with death and devastation. In 1961, the assassination of the first democratically elected prime minister of the Democratic Republic of the Congo, Patrice Lumumba, exposed US hypocrisy. Lumumba had called on the United States and United Nations to help suppress rebel uprisings backed by Belgian forces. The United States did not find it economically or politically beneficial to engage with the newly formed democratic nation, which led to rebels murdering Lumumba.[5] It is widely believed that the US CIA was involved and facilitated the assassination. According to historian Peniel Joseph, Lumumba's assassination ignited up-and-coming activists, Black nationalists, and radicals. The common struggle of being a person of African descent culminated in action-based revolutionary initiatives in the United States, such as African Americans' reclamation of self-defining and self-determining language. Thus, the Black Power and Black Arts Movement reflected a global diasporic effort. On February 15, 1961, activists of African descent surrounded the United Nations headquarters in New York in protest and proclaimed that they were no longer Negroes but Afro-Americans.[6] Another assassination—of Malcolm X on February 21, 1965—catapulted the demand for civil rights to the forefront of US politics. Stokely Carmichael rallied Black communities, calling for unity, and in his 1966 address to Black folks, he proposed the initiation of Black Power—a construct of political, economic, and cultural self-determination—as a vehicle to achieving radical democracy in the United States.[7]

The late 1960s were riddled with watershed moments in American history, with events suggesting that the fight for civil rights was over where the focus of the country shifted abroad coupled with assassinations of two civil rights leaders. Specifically, these events include the carnage of the Vietnam War, along with the assassinations of Martin Luther King Jr. and Robert F. Kennedy. As well as opposing the war in Vietnam, King had shifted his agenda in 1967 to focus on connecting the economic system with racial inequalities. At the same time, J. Edgar Hoover, the first director of the FBI, sought out Americans considered disruptive to federal institutions, including King, who was targeted throughout the 1960s for calling into question problematic policies at home and abroad. King's unwavering anti-war stance and primary focus on the intersection between class and race led to his murder in Atlanta on April 4, 1968.[8]

Following his brother's assassination in 1963, Robert F. Kennedy, first as US attorney general and then as a US Senator and presidential candidate, had become increasingly focused on America's underclass. With his presidential run, Kennedy unified Americans from all ethnicities in his desire to fight for underrepresented people in government. But Kennedy's assassination—which occurred after his California Democratic Party primary win on June 6, 1968—dashed these hopes for change; historian William Chafe argues that his murder silenced the last echo of civil rights in the political arena.[9]

These assassinations were, essentially, a defeat for all who were fighting for equality based on peace, social justice, and efforts to reform the system from the inside out. Richard Nixon took advantage of racial tensions and found his constituency—white lower- and middle-class Americans—who propelled him into the presidency. Nixon appealed to this demographic which fed racism in the economic sphere. In 1969, a *Newsweek* poll reported that most white Americans believed that African Americans had improved chances of getting a job, a house, and an education.[10] Nixon's campaign therefore took advantage of whites' dissatisfaction with the job market where they felt victimized, ultimately condoning racist attitudes.

Against this background, Amiri Baraka and Larry Neal emerged as leaders of the explosive and revolutionary Harlem-based Black Arts Movement. A well-known anecdote regarding the movement holds that after Malcolm X's assassination in 1965, Baraka divorced his Jewish wife, moved from his Lower East Side home, and established the Black Arts Repertory Theatre and School (BART/S) in Harlem, creating a theatre of revolution.[11] Setting aside the simplified (or perhaps exaggerated) story of Baraka's pilgrimage to Upper Manhattan, the unabashed marriage of radical politics and theatre as a site of revolution reveals the significance of bold action-based initiatives to ignite cultural revolution in theatrical realms. Before BART/S, Baraka was an integral poet in the Umbra Writers' Workshop on the Lower East Side, a protonationalist community that embraced a radical Black identity, including the poetry of Baraka and Sonia Sanchez, yet lacked concrete action initiatives.[12] After these assassinations and the resulting rise of the Black Arts Movement, Baraka became more action-oriented. He promoted militant radical "terror tactics to forge unity in the community, wanted to reject individualism and emphasize community and community action."[13] Although BART/S lasted only a year, it demonstrated how Black theatre could serve the community and spark a cultural revolution.

As Larry Neal outlined in his 1968 article "The Black Arts Movement," the movement complemented Black Power's economic and political goals by focusing on aesthetic and cultural goals to radically alter institutional racism and identify a Black Aesthetic.[14] In broad terms, Black Power and the Black Arts Movement centered on empowering Black communities and creating political and social change. Neal asserted that the mainstream white Western cultural aesthetic had to be restructured because there were in fact two Americas: one white, one Black. Therefore, "the Black artist takes this to mean that his primary duty is to speak to the spiritual and cultural needs of Black People."[15] The Black Aesthetic assumes that an African American cultural tradition already exists. Further, it can be traced back to the African continent, or an Afrocentric viewpoint, and its main goal is the "destruction of the white thing, the destruction of white ideas, and white ways of looking at the world."[16] Neal's influential essay extends to literature, poetry, visual art, and the performing arts. With Baraka as an artist and Neal as a theorist, the artistic community began to concretize their own criteria, but not without heated debates about how the Black Aesthetic should be realized.

By the time BART/S closed its doors in late 1965, the Black Theatre Movement was gaining traction. Theatres rooted in the liberation of people of African descent sprang up across Harlem. The movement included a multitude of opinions about what sort of theatre would ignite social change.[17] Harlem residents were economically depressed yet politically advanced in that they were painfully aware of discrimination in various institutions, including commercial theatre. Because they experienced racism daily, they created a theatre for, by, about, and near them. Theatres established performance and artistic spaces that would empower their communities to rally together and demand social change.

Each theatre had a unique philosophy and practices regarding funding, separatism, genre, and rhetoric. Finding sources of income is critical in maintaining a theatre, and several private organizations (i.e., the Ford Foundation) provided financial resources. However, issues arose when wealthy white philanthropists controlled or withheld funds on the grounds of ideology. Some Black theatre organizers worried that funding from white people meant their donors' opinions about programming could overshadow the goals of their respective theatres. Regarding federal funding, in 1965, despite political turmoil at home and abroad, Congress created agencies to support the arts and humanities for the first time since the New Deal.[18] The National Endowment for the Arts and the National Endowment for the Humanities began awarding federal money directly to artistic endeavors. It was certainly a positive shift to have federal and private funding for Black artists. In Baraka's case, BART/S was initially funded by the HARYOU Act (Harlem Youth Opportunities Unlimited), in which the federal Office of Economic Opportunity provided $110 million to Black educational programs. However, following an evening of Baraka's one-act plays, BART/S lost funding because of its unabashed aim to destroy governmental institutions.[19] Thus, many artists opposed accepting financial support out of fear that they would have to compromise their work to appease the white hegemonic powers.

In the early 1970s, when the Nixon administration slashed federal funding for the arts, many theatres were shut down, but companies rallied.[20] Moreover, the Watergate scandal and Nixon's impeachment and resignation eclipsed efforts for social justice as the media instead was focused on presidential abuses of power. These cuts in the arts in the 1970s were part of a broader attack on

Black and Brown communities, as well as queer folk—and this is what, in part, McClintock was responding to with his Afrocentric technique and organizational efforts.

Because of the paucity of funding, the Black Theatre Movement's New York companies unified under the BTA, of which McClintock was initially the vice president and later president, fully explored in Chapter 3. Between 1971 and 1984, the BTA provided resources and institutional support to more than 60 member companies across the country. In addition to publishing a yearly directory of theatres, writers, technicians, and industry contacts, the BTA sponsored the annual Black Theatre Alliance Festival at the Brooklyn Academy of Music.[21]

Although Black theatre companies supported one another through organizations like the BTA, they were divided on the question of whether they should be separatist spaces on stage and off. Being a separatist space meant that the theatre would be primarily composed of people of African descent. To develop an authentic Black Aesthetic, separatists believed, there needed to be a purely Afrocentric space, free from the white gaze. Proponents of separatism argued that artists should not have to define their Blackness or Black art in relationship to whiteness or white art. This is also why the theatres (including the New Lafayette Theatre, the Afro-American Studio for Acting and Speech, and the National Black Theatre) were based in Harlem, surrounded by a Black community.

The theatres that emerged in the Black Arts Movement illustrate that the Black experience is not monolithic, as evidenced by a versatility of genres, including revolutionary drama, realism, devised work, and ritualistic theatre. The genre of performance correlated to the strategies of a company's theatrical aesthetic and rallied communities to unify and, ultimately, to achieve social justice. A prime example of the separatist philosophy applied includes Barbara Ann Teer's National Black Theatre (est. 1968). She was interested not in commercial success but in redefining the process of theatre making, with a focus on rituals derived from West Africa. Entertainment was immaterial; in fact, the group repudiated conventional theatre and basic concepts of Western art.[22] Teer developed an acting technique dedicated to improving the cultural and intellectual lives of Black people outside the structure of white paradigms and trajectories. Specifically, white theatrical norms held that a play going from off-Broadway to Broadway was considered a definition of success. The technique focused on "God-conscious" art, guided by the creative impulse that emanates from within. Teer referred to her company members as "liberators" rather than actors.[23] Hence, the National Black Theatre aligned with the separatist philosophy of Baraka and Macbeth but focused on healing and community building rather than the violent rhetoric of revolutionary theatre.

In contrast, the Negro Ensemble Company (est. 1967) was situated in New York's East Village, surrounded by a more racially diverse community and audience. Black journalist Clayton Riley of the *New York Times* accused the company of being "a new form of White art in blackface," perhaps because they accepted a sizable contribution from the Ford Foundation.[24] At the Negro Ensemble Company, which was physically distant from the epicenter of Black theatre in Harlem, the presence of mixed audiences could suggest that these works were not geared toward Black folks but instead had commercial goals. Despite criticism from Black Aesthetic purists, the socially and politically stirring work of Douglas Turner Ward grabbed the attention of Black and white audiences alike. Notably, Ward's one-act plays *Happy Ending* (1965) and *Day of Absence* (1965), which opened at the Negro Ensemble Company, were absorbed by the mainstream and ran off-Broadway, earning positive reviews from mainstream critics. During this time period, there was an emphasis on what would be the most authentic Black theatrical aesthetic through the lens of a Black Aesthetic. However, the contribution of Ward's work and the prominence of *Day of Absence* in theatre history shows that there is not one way to produce "legitimate" work. There can be multiple spaces, separatist or more integrated, where Black artists make profound contributions to the theatrical landscape.

BART/S workshopped revolutionary themes that emerged in some of Baraka's most well-known works including *Experimental Death Unit #1* (1969), *Madheart* (1969), *A Black Mass* (1969), *Great Goodness of Life* (1969), and the Obie Award–winning *The Dutchman* (1964). As he was a poet who produced striking and sometimes disturbing images, Baraka did not base his characters in realism. His works defy the typical Aristotelian model of beginning, middle, and end with a structure of rising action, climax, and falling action. Aristotelian tragedy and realism, as well as naturalism in the twentieth and twenty-first centuries, are based in white Western storytelling. Topically, Baraka's plays were visceral in terms of the traumas experienced by Black communities, but his revolutionary plays assaulted Eurocentric theatre and motivated his audiences to pursue social justice.

Similarly, the New Lafayette Theatre (1967–1972), led by artistic director Robert Macbeth and playwright Ed Bullins, embraced a revolutionary spirit and focused on realism in the context of street life. "Street life" describes life in urban areas of the United States in which the population is at the lowest echelon of the capitalist socioeconomic structure. Pejorative labels associated with Black communities in lower-income neighborhoods include "welfare parasites" and "junkies," stereotypes that still appear today. Macbeth believed it was pretentious to say that one was bringing cultural enlightenment to the disadvantaged; he intended to create a community of artists and an audience who were equal participants in the theatrical event.[25] Some emblematic performances from this genre produced at the New Lafayette Theatre include Bullins's *In the Wine Time* (1968), *The Electronic Nigger* (1968), *Goin' A Buffalo* (1968), plays that examine Street Life communities. For example, in *Goin' A Buffalo*, the characters belong to a low socioeconomic class and may seem unrefined but on closer examination are full of depth and humanity. Bullins's plays capture the musicality of street culture, and his characters express their struggles through a distinctive rhythm and language.

Some companies belonging to the Black Theatre Movement created their own work, such as Vinnette Carroll's Urban Arts Corps (1967-1983). Carroll aimed to find a way to end the alienation of artists of color, including Latinx representation, by ushering them into the mainstream and putting them in touch with their communities. The Urban Arts Corps began as a summer arts program in which Black and Puerto Rican artists developed their own performance material. Carroll's efforts resulted in numerous plays and musicals, such as *Don't Bother Me, I Can't Cope* (1971), co-written by Micki Grant, which graced the Broadway stage in 1972. Carroll's mission diverged from that of New Lafayette and BART/S in that her original pieces were structured to allow actors and musicians to gain commercial and financial success, ultimately increasing diversity and representation in the mainstream, which was a departure from the separatist perspective.

The genre and organizational versatility of the Black Theatre Movement reveal what playwright and scholar Paul Carter Harrison refers to as the kaleidoscopic character of African diasporic memory.[26] The kaleidoscopic character encapsulates the multitude of identities and experiences of people of African descent, countering the myth that Blackness is monolithic. Although the theatres might have disagreed on whether to accept sizable donations from white organizations versus rubbing two pennies together to keep the doors open, assault-based tactics versus healing approaches, and commercial goals versus activist aims, they were connected in their efforts to raise the profile of Black theatres and create art that was culturally rooted in Afrocentric ideals and practices. Although Baraka is the most well-known figure of the Black Theatre Movement, McClintock, who had already moved to Harlem and begun conducting classes before Baraka left the Lower East Side in search of Black theatre, deserves greater recognition as one of its pioneers.

Ernie McClintock: Inclusive Approach, Excluded from the Narrative

What distinguished McClintock from his contemporaries? McClintock developed an innovative acting technique and included scripted and unscripted work in his 200-plus productions. Most companies sat in *either* the scripted *or* the unscripted camp. For example, the National Black Theatre focused on work generated by the company, while the New Lafayette Theatre primarily produced the work of Ed Bullins. However, McClintock included published and new plays as well as collectively-authored poetry theatre, demonstrating his and his actors' versatility. These productions range from a women's poetry theatre to Baraka's *Four Black Revolutionary Plays* (1969). I argue that McClintock is distinctive among his contemporaries because of this inclusive programming, which was grounded in his Afrocentric acting theory. I define inclusivity in McClintock's theatre as his creation of space for many Black experiences, including but not limited to Black revolutionaries, womanists, and queer Black men.

One way McClintock championed womanism was in founding the women's poetry theatre, where five womanist actors asserted themselves in everyday spaces on the streets of Harlem, empowering women throughout all five boroughs of the city. Womanism was first named by writer Alice Walker in her 1983 book *In Search of Our Mothers' Gardens: Womanist Prose*. Layli Philips defines womanism as

> a social change perspective rooted in Black women's and other women of color's everyday experiences and everyday methods of problem solving in everyday spaces, extended to the problem of ending all forms of oppression for all people, restoring the balance between people and the environment/nature, and reconciling human life with the spiritual dimension.[27]

Bolanyle Edwards, an early member of the Afro-American Studio's poetry theatre, still remembers her piece "Pussy Poem":

> Shit. The world is full of pussies.
> Black pussy, white pussy, yellow pussy.
> Pussy, pussy, pussy.
> All you got to do is be cool.
> Pussy even stinks.
> Pussy eats. Pussy drinks. Pussy laughs. Pussy cries. Pussy even dies.
> From overuse, underuse, old age, and abuse.[28]

Although Edwards contends "it's not a nice poem," the performance made a lasting impression on audiences.[29] She recalls that after the performance became popular, many New York fans learned the poem by heart and recited it along with her. "Pussy Poem" illustrates McClintock's ability to open a space for women to express even taboo subjects. Actor self-acceptance, a foundational component of his technique (discussed in Chapter 2), could be a painful process, but it led to liberation in performance and from the patriarchal gaze.

McClintock also created space for queer self-expression in, for example, one of his most well-known productions (discussed in detail in Chapter 4), Peter Shaffer's *Equus* (1973). The 127th Street Repertory Ensemble's production of this play was an unlikely choice insofar as the call to destroy Western storytelling techniques was concerned in that the play was written by a British white man and the story about a British white teenager. But in the jazz tradition, McClintock revised this story in the context of Black queer sexuality. In 1982, few plays explored Black queer sexuality, so McClintock appropriated

Schaffer's successful Broadway play and transformed it through Jazz Acting. *Equus* is the story of Alan Strang, a British teenage boy, who after blinding six horses is treated by psychiatrist Dr. Martin Dysart. Through the therapy sessions, Strang's repressed sexuality contends with his upbringing by a religious mother and an atheist father. In an interview, cofounder of the Afro-American Studio and historian Marc Primus recalled with delight, "My god, I remember *Equus*. It was an interesting story. But by the time Ernie got to it, it was a different story entirely."[30] In McClintock's staging, *Equus* became a story about repressed Black sexuality, at times showing audiences the beauty of queer male sexuality.[31] A Black teen in a fundamentalist religious household discovering his sexuality with six muscular, barely clothed, dark-skinned Black men created an image that titillated many and frightened others.

Queer sexuality does not fit in with traditional notions of heteronormative Black masculinity. One of the most striking ways McClintock's ideology conflicted with Baraka's relates to the attempt by Black militant groups to affirm Black masculinity and dominance, distancing the Black Aesthetic from femininity and homosexuality. In Baraka's "Babylon Revisited," he infamously wrote, "The bitch killed a friend of mine named Bob Thompson a Black painter, a giant, once she reduced him to a pitiful imitation faggot."[32] As E. Patrick Johnson notes, this strategy employing a homophobic slur worked to signify that Black masculinity and heterosexuality are authentic, whereas Black homosexuality is trivial, ineffectual, and inauthentic.[33] There are differences in opinion over what constitutes Black masculinity (gay/straight, masculine/feminine), but Baraka[34] and McClintock shared certain goals: community building, art for social change, Black pride, and reaching people who were denied access to theatre and education. Efforts to reduce the Black Arts Movement to a homophobic monolith perpetuate stereotypes and half-histories, thereby erasing divergences. So why has McClintock's legacy been overlooked in Black Arts Movement scholarship? In sum, his erasure can be attributed to his incredibly inclusive aesthetic and his sexual orientation.

McClintock's aesthetic did not fit into tidy theatre genre categories: revolutionary, ritualistic, street theatre, or realist. Not only did McClintock welcome a variety of genres from Black writers, he was distinct in his training and aesthetic because the primacy was on the development of the actor and the inclusion of actors and collaborators who playwright and jazz actor Levy Lee Simon referred to as the misfits of Harlem.[35] His inclusive aesthetic did not conform perfectly to the prescription of art from Black revolutionary thinkers such as Larry Neal, who demanded that Black art destroy "the white thing."[36] In his essay "The Black Arts Movement" Neal famously quoted Don L. Lee to illustrate the need for a new, separate Black arts in which "we must destroy Faulkner, dick, jane [sic], and other perpetuators of evil. It's time for Du Bois, Nat Turner, and Kwame Nkrumah. As Frantz Fanon points out: destroy the culture and you destroy the people."[37] Like a jazz musician, McClintock subverted the "white thing" and created an innovated acting technique infused with the Afrocentric ideals of community and self-determination.

An Afrocentric Framework: Community and Self-Determination

McClintock's training and aesthetic were rooted in an ensemble dynamic and artistic autonomy tied to Afrocentric notions of community and self-determination. This places McClintock within the larger African continuum, and his approach resonates with the work of Harlem Renaissance thinkers Alain Locke (1885–1954) and W. E. B. Du Bois (1868–1963). The Afrocentric lens is critical to the development of Jazz Acting and in analyzing McClintock's repertoire. Molefi Kete Asante defines "Afrocentricity" as placing African ideals at the center of any study that involves African culture and behavior.[38] Asante also "offer[s] Afrocentricity as a moral as well as an intellectual location that posits Africans as subjects rather than objects of human history."[39] To position Black bodies as subjects rather than objects, McClintock's theatre implemented programming created exclusively for Black actors, as did other institutions like BART/S. This separatist approach in actor training addresses sociologist Ron Eyerman's question regarding the effects of cultural trauma: "How is the past to be represented in the present, to individuals, and more importantly in this context, to and for a collective?"[40] In African American communities, Eyerman contends that the "memory of slavery has been tinged with some strategic, practical, and political interest by the hegemony," which "can lead to a distorted identity-formation."[41] Specifically, when thinking about the entertainment industry and films like *12 Years a Slave* (2013), actors of African descent put on powerful performances, yet the "good slave owners versus bad slave owners" narrative is perpetuated, when in truth there was no such thing as a "good slave owner." In academic spaces (fully explored in Chapter 3), textbooks like *History of the American Nation* (1919) minimized the slave trade and its impact on African Americans. In McClintock's school, where Black history was a fundamental course (discussed in Chapter 2), students were able to study their collective history in the diaspora. Moreover, the theatre is a space of identity formation through imagination and representation, linking the past and the present. "Linking the past and present" means that although students may not have known their direct lineage, they were able to connect to their ancestors and collective history.

Mainstream acting techniques such as the Method, the Meisner technique, and Practical Aesthetics are all based on Russian teacher Konstantin Stanislavski's acting theories, which are also culturally rooted. As Shonni Enelow suggests, "all methods have histories, are connected to cultural practices, and depend on axiomatic ideologies. The technical aspects of acting are even more directly linked to their histories and ideologies than those of other art forms."[42]

McClintock responded to community needs by establishing a space in which Black bodies were subjects rather than objects, refuting distortions of Black identities perpetuated by white-centric practices.

Community is a critical aspect of Afrocentricity; for McClintock's theatre, this first principle is reflected in the ensemble dynamic as well as the actor–audience relationship. By the time McClintock was established in his career as a teacher and director, the concept of ensemble related not just to the current company members but to the familial community. Specifically, the elders of the Afro-American Studio for Acting and Speech mentored (and continue to mentor) Jazz Actors across the country. *Community* also suggests the relationship with the local community, the geographical locations, and the actors on stage. Significantly, within Afrocentric live performance, "call and response" acknowledges the collective experience of the onstage participants and the audience.[43]

Audiences are always an important part of a theatrical experience, but in the context of McClintock's theatre and his contemporaries in Harlem, the performance's impact on the audience was a form of social change. Arguably, the Black Theatre Movement centered on a reciprocal dynamic between the actor and spectator in which "the idea is to open dialogue between the arts and the people, rather than between the artists and the dominant White society."[44] In creating dialogue with the audience, Jazz Acting puts the actors in the forefront of productions to directly connect with the spectators, with limited sets and theatrical effects. Actors must accomplish this without resorting to the common tactic of blocking the audience out of their conscious awareness. Instead, the actor must be able to perceive and respond to the audience's reactions throughout a performance.[45]

In white western theatre, realism—and subsequently naturalism—introduced the performance convention known as the fourth wall to create a sense that the spectators are voyeurs peering in on the characters' private lives.[46] The fourth wall concept has been popular with traditional Eurocentric playwrights and directors into the twenty-first century. In terms of acting theory, the convention relates to actors who are meant to create naturalistic characters that mirror human behavior and psychology. By contrast, African American theatres trace their roots to African storytelling, which rarely considers an actor–audience division. In the spirit of jazz riffing, McClintock's technique highlights the blurred lines between actor and spectator and echoes call and response, allowing for improvisational moments.

Jazz Acting, like its musical namesake, requires discipline and ensemble building for artists to riff in performance, allowing a play between a collective sound and individual artistic expression. The technique is rooted in multiple Black identities and experiences, and it effectively equips actors to portray roles in contemporary plays, classical works, and collectively -authored[47] pieces. Jazz riffing in music refers to the musicians diverging from the base melody and finding improvisational and conversational moments based on the other musicians in the ensemble or even responses from the crowd. With Jazz Acting, actors stay true to the script and never deviate in language but find performative riffs, meaning reactions, physicality, and interactions can vary from night to night. The improvisation or riffing happens through the dynamic of the actors on stage rather than by going off-script.

The second foundational principle in McClintock's theatre was self-expression, which links to Malcolm X's notion of self-determination, a demand that African Americans actively assert themselves in daily social and political life. In 1968, Malcolm X proclaimed, "We assert that we have the right to direct and control our lives, our history and future rather than have our destinies determined by American racists."[48] Holistically, self-determination works to challenge white ideology without needing to define Blackness in relation to it. In other pockets of the Black Arts Movement, cultural efforts reclaimed Afrocentric holidays, heroes, institutions, and organizations to celebrate Black identities across the diaspora. Likewise, McClintock's theatre invited performers and spectators to engage in this reclamation of Black culture.

As part of the African continuum, McClintock is connected to his African ancestors. I argue that his focus on actor training and the unearthing of a Black actor's individuality and authenticity echoes Alain Locke's work from the Harlem Renaissance. The theories of McClintock and Locke connect in their emphasis on the artist's self-expression. In other words, as Locke advocated in "The Negro and the American Theatre" (1927), "A race of actors can revolutionize the drama quite as definitely and perhaps more vitally than a coterie of dramatists."[49] Locke and McClintock's synergy lay in the agency of the actor; the performers are not just there to serve a playwright or director but to bring interpretations of the text and characters to a live performance.

Hence, what distinguished McClintock from Amiri Baraka was his development of the actor rather than his production of an oeuvre of plays and poetry. I am not suggesting that one is better than the other—both the development of the individual actor as well as the repertoire of plays that came out of the Black Theatre Movement are equally significant. Perhaps more significantly, Baraka aligned with prolific historian, sociologist, and writer W.E.B Du Bois in terms of his use of the theatre as a site of protest and reverse "double consciousness [...] this sense of always looking at one's self through the eyes of the others, of measuring one's soul by the tape of the world, that looks on in amused and pity." He continues: "One ever feels his two-ness—an American, a Negro; two souls, two thoughts, two unreconciled strivings; two warring ideals in one dark body, whose dogged strength alone keeps I from being torn asunder."[50] Baraka's work created a space to protest double consciousness by upending it and establishing a separatist theatre. McClintock aligns with the notion of Black actors freeing themselves from double consciousness, but his approach alludes to Locke's advocacy of self-expression.

Alain Locke and W.E.B Du Bois debated whether the aim of Black arts should be rooted in propaganda.[51] In his essay "Art or Propaganda?" (1928), Locke wrote: "propaganda perpetuates the position of group inferiority even in crying out against it."[52] I propose that McClintock's work is more aligned with Locke's stance than Du Bois's, because it was fundamentally about Black artists' healing and self-expression. In this framework, William J. Harris articulates that the jazz aesthetic is "a procedure that uses jazz variations as paradigms for the conversions of white poetic and social ideas into black ones... Art in the best sense is rooted in self-expression and whether naïve or sophisticated is self-contained."[53] The idea of the "self-contained" speaks to McClintock's establishment a Harlem-based studio and his recruitment of actors of African descent.

Broadly speaking, my research reveals that McClintock promoted Locke's assertion that Black actors had the agency and power to revolutionize theatre, and he put the theory into practice through Jazz Acting in training and performance. McClintock's method and aesthetic were consistently underpinned by the Afrocentric concepts of community and self-determination. Therefore, his technique and production history—in which Black actors subverted white Western approaches and narratives—created a space for positive identity formation for performers and audiences. As such, the theoretical framework used throughout this book understands McClintock's approach in training and directing as a construct that fostered an actor's self-expression (self-determination) and simultaneously promoted a larger collective voice—the ensemble (community).

Methodology

Uncovering and reviving McClintock's legacy requires interdisciplinary engagement in the fields of performance studies, Africana studies, and acting theory, along with interviews and McClintock's archive, which is in transition from a private home to a public archive. I combed existing collections along the Eastern Seaboard, piecing together material from Emory University's Robert W. Woodruff Library, the Library of Virginia, Dartmouth College's Rauner Special Collections Library, the Schomburg Center for Research in Black Culture, the New York Public Radio Archives Collection, and the Billy Rose Theatre Division Collection. To establish a comprehensive view on McClintock's ever-developing training practices and production aesthetic and the breadth of voices represented in his theatre, I interviewed around 50 of his pupils and associates.

My quest to unearth McClintock's legacy began when I was preparing for my doctoral oral comprehensive exams at Tufts University, where my primary area of research was the Black Arts Movement of the 1960s and 1970s. I was awestruck by the explosion of politically and socially motivated theatre focused on a radical demand for equality and justice. Playwrights, actors, poets, directors, and designers of this time are exemplary models for artists who want to create socially conscious theatre. My oral exam focused on Macbeth and Bullins's New Lafayette Theatre, simply because there was a healthy amount of secondary research on it. The New Lafayette Theatre reflected much of what I had initially learned about the Black Arts Movement. As I prepared for my exams, McClintock's name repeatedly appeared in anthologies such as James Hatch and Errol Hill's *A History of African American Theatre* and Mance Williams's *Black Theatre in the 1960s and 1970s*. McClintock's name reverberated in my mind, and two questions haunted me: Who was this enigmatic figure who established an acting technique for Black actors but whom I had never heard of? And why have no scholars written about him beyond listing his company and a few productions, or in passing in footnotes? My inquiry led me to find his pupils on Facebook, and after three years of gaining their trust, in 2018, Geno Brantley (McClintock and Walker's surrogate son) granted me access to the Jazz Actors' collection of materials. We are now collectively working to appraise McClintock's personal papers and transfer the archive to a permanent home.

While my research includes aspects of ethnography, the paradigm I applied is more aligned with interpretive research. I make this distinction because in ethnographic studies, analysis is composed of both observation and participation. Although McClintock expanded his student base to include white actors, my research focuses on his Afrocentric approach created for Black actors. Specifically, his technique and productions connect to an African-based culture and spirituality, a collective past in the African Diaspora that traces back to African ancestry, symbolism, and mysticism. As a cisgender white female practitioner and scholar, I believed an ethnographic approach would not serve my project. I consciously avoid the notion of being a "white savior" responsible for reviving McClintock's legacy. McClintock's presence is always felt among his students, and his technique has continued to be practiced after his death in 2003. Throughout the research and writing process, I have checked myself to avoid overshadowing the Afro-American Studio for Acting and Speech and the Jazz Actors Theatre with my white positionality. This book aims to excavate McClintock's legacy and privilege the experience of the actors under his tutelage.

I employ the term *queer* to identify McClintock's sexual identity and his way of seeing the world as a gay Black man. The term is not without controversy, and it can be interpreted as problematic, especially considering it was initially a slur for nonheteronormative folk. Yet as E. Patrick Johnson argues, "To embrace 'queer' is to resist or elide categorization, to disavow binaries (that is, gay versus straight, Black versus white) and to proffer potentially productive modes of resistance against hegemonic structures of power."[54] Ernie McClintock and his partner, Ronald Walker, resisted these hegemonic structures in their lives and in their professional work.

In this book, I refer to McClintock as both queer and gay. Within the context of his lifetime and his generation, *queer* was not regularly used because of its pejorative connotations. Thus, I presume the term *gay* is what he used during his lifetime. Specifically, as his associate and cofounder Marc Primus proclaimed during an interview with me in 2015, "We were a gay theatre!"[55] Further, as scholar Cathy Cohen argues, "queer theorizing which calls for the elimination of fixed categories seems to ignore the ways in which some traditional social identities and communal ties can, in fact, be important to one's survival."[56] These fixed categories (gay, lesbian, bisexual) also have a history, and people who fought during the gay liberation movement have ushered in current and progressive thinking, expanding notions of gender fluidity and those across a sexual spectrum who perhaps fall in "unfixed" categories. Therefore, I do not want to eliminate the fixed category of gay or the gay community when analyzing and understanding the successes and challenges McClintock, Walker, and Primus experienced in their lived moment.

Other individuals interviewed for this book, who studied in the first decade of the studio, did not necessarily see the studio as gay or straight; they did not even consider McClintock and Walker's sexuality as part of the company's identity. Yet there were whispers both inside and outside the studio about McClintock and Walker's relationship and sexuality. Primus, McClintock, and Walker held a meeting with the students, facetiously called "the great homosexual trial." At this meeting, Primus recalls:

> I got up and lectured them on homosexuality and what it was and how we were not going to lie about who or what we were. We didn't care what they thought. And everybody just kind of accepted it and just went right on. We discussed it once and that was it and everybody went right on doing what they were doing. Very interesting. If you face things on.[57]

McClintock's sexuality and the challenges he faced are certainly not the only important aspect of his theatre, nor should they eclipse the various identities within the school and company. However, his sexual identity does matter. It matters for understanding his inclusive vantage point from the mid-1960s on, and it matters for future generations of students and actors who can identify with queer people of color in history. Therefore, I employ the term *queer* as a theoretical framework and identifier to draw connections to current practices and companies in the African continuum that are building on McClintock's legacy, as well as the legacies of queer folk who came before him.

Chapter Outline

This book argues that in addition to being marginalized because of his Black queer positionality, McClintock has been left out of the traditional narrative because he insisted on including a multitude of voices in his theatres. The chronological structure of the book provides McClintock's biography alongside scholarly analysis of his innovative aesthetic, which is tied to Afrocentricity. McClintock's career spans four decades and approximately 200 productions of scripted work and collectively-authored pieces. This book does not aim to be an exhaustive account of every production but rather an introduction to an extraordinary and unorthodox artist whose life story and artistic aesthetic can inspire more conversations about overlooked artists. The choice of productions analyzed was based on the availability of materials (interviews, archival findings) and to showcase the range of perspectives McClintock invited into his creative space.

The first three chapters establish McClintock's assessment of American theatre and actor training and how he developed his technique and aesthetic. Despite heteronormative standards in his community and throughout the country, he pursued the creation of an Afrocentric institution within the gestalt of the Black Theatre Movement. Chapter 1, "Afrocentric Roots in Chicago (1937–1964)," traces McClintock's childhood on the South Side of Chicago and identifies the influences that shaped his aesthetic. McClintock grew up in a post–World War II society imbued with sociopolitical tensions, and his home life was filled with the arts. He listened to the blues with his father, played piano with his mother and sisters, and frequently attended the Regal Theater to listen to the music of Sarah Vaughan, Dinah Washington, Ella Fitzgerald, and Cab Calloway.[58] McClintock was exposed to mainstream theatre and popular culture, but his lived experience and immediate surroundings were grounded in Afrocentric art, emphasizing local and diasporic community building. After he began training as an actor, he concluded that white mainstream techniques produced Black actors imitating white lived experiences: "Most Black actors had been trained through white approaches, white techniques. What happened on the stage for them was a kind of imitation of white people and sometimes imitating themselves rather than BEING themselves. Imitating the imitation."[59] Moreover, these techniques were geared toward heteronormative storytelling in the classical (white) canon. When McClintock moved to New York in 1962, he trained with Louis Gossett Jr., building the foundation of his acting technique before moving to Harlem and creating his own studio among Black revolutionary artists.

Chapter 2, "Shaking Up Harlem (1965–1972)," chronicles the development of the Afro-American Studio for Acting and Speech, in which McClintock and Walker created a healing environment and taught students to bring their identities into the rehearsal space, focusing on self-expression and ensemble building. Framing the studio along the lines of Black Power philosophy engendered an inclusive performance technique and dynamic aesthetic. At the Afro-American Studio, the training uplifted students rather than leading them to access traumatic memories to drum up emotions, a practice often perpetuated in the mainstream. In Black history and culture classes taught by Marc Primus at the studio, part of this healing was a specific practice that contextualized African-inspired values and the rehabilitation of dislocation and subjugation, beginning with the Middle Passage.[60] Students learning about their history connects to the a collective historical memory of trauma and the response of healing in a ritualized environment (the rehearsal hall). Primus asserted that for the students to heal, they had to understand their roots and establish a sense of self.[61] The courses were carefully chosen to build community and foster the actors' self-expression, departing from Stanislavski-based approaches dominant at the time. Chapter 2 analyzes two productions: *Where It's At* (1969) and N.R. Davidson's *El Hajj Malik: The Dramatic Life and Death of Malcolm X* (1969). The former was a collectively-authored production filled with music, dance, and poetry, and the latter a scripted ensemble piece about the slain leader. They are case studies in how theory was put into practice, demonstrating the efficacy of Jazz Acting across multiple genres and in varying contexts.

Chapter 3, "Canonizing the Contemporary Black Classics (1973–1981)," highlights the formation of the 127th Street Repertory Ensemble where, in addition to formalizing a professional company reflective of jazz aesthetics, McClintock established what he called the Contemporary Black Classics. This genre is situated within the 1970s conversation about the Black Aesthetic, a controversial topic that risked purporting monolithic notions of Blackness. For McClintock, the Contemporary Black Classics were an ever-evolving inclusive canon in which the criteria for what was considered a "Classic" could change based on the cultural and political context of a given historic moment. Chapter 3 highlights two Contemporary Black Classics that embody Jazz Acting in performance: Amiri Baraka's *Slave Ship* and James de Jongh's *Do Lord Remember Me*. This chapter also describes how McClintock occupied leadership positions in the BTA and the Audience Development Committee, Inc. (AUDELCO), demonstrating his influence on the movement. Despite McClintock's innovative training, in which actors generated noteworthy performances in scripted and unscripted work, he and his company were regarded as "freaks" in the Harlem community.[62] Yet despite rumors and whispers meant to keep McClintock on the fringes, his tenacity and commitment to Black theatre prevailed.

Chapter 4, "Quaring the Black Theatre Movement (1981–1986)," explores the historical context of the early 1980s and how McClintock included distinct Black experiences in season planning and, despite shifts in the political ecosystem, created groundbreaking theatre in Harlem. It further investigates how McClintock's queer positionality created a pathway for diversity and inclusion, with Black actors from varying backgrounds working together within the walls of the 127th Street Repertory Ensemble. This chapter applies E. Patrick Johnson's quare theory to analyze McClintock's decision-making process in season selection, allowing him to be even more inclusive in his school and company. In 1982, McClintock directed Ntozake Shange's *Spell #7* (1979), Peter Shaffer's *Equus*

(1973), and Dereck Walcott's *Dream on Monkey Mountain* (1970) at the Renny Theatre in Harlem, respectively, about womanist, queer, and Caribbean stories. This program exemplifies McClintock's inclusivity with three distinct storytelling perspectives. By remaining steadfast in his principles, aesthetic, teaching, and identity, McClintock broadened the landscape of inclusion in Harlem.

The final three chapters detail how McClintock innovated Richmond, Virginia, theatre by identifying a gap in Black actor training, contended with incumbent administrators to establish a Black theatrical presence, and invited voices from overlooked demographics in the Black community. Chapter 5, "Rebel in Richmond (1987–1993)," chronicles McClintock and Walker's last years in New York, when the 127th Street Repertory was renamed the Harlem Jazz Theatre, acknowledging a deeper connection to jazz aesthetics. While McClintock gained national recognition, the country faced the AIDS epidemic, which was initially labeled the Gay-Related Immune Deficiency and thus stigmatized gay men nationwide. Ultimately, McClintock and Walker left New York in 1990, seeking change because of a sharp decline in funding for Black theatres and because they were devastated by the deaths of 57 company members from AIDS.[63] They identified Richmond as a town in need of Black theatre leadership for a diverse population. They revised their training technique to meet the needs of a younger student population but maintained the core of McClintock's approach. Chapter 5 analyzes the development of the technique in Richmond, as well as how McClintock's unorthodox ways shook up administrators and producers while inspiring a new generation of Black artists.

Against the backdrop of the sociopolitical context of the 1990s, Chapter 6, "The Persistence of a Living Legend (1994–1997)," focuses on two Jazz Actors Theatre productions: Richard Wesley's *The Mighty Gents* (1979) and Cheryl L. West's *Before It Hits Home* (1993). By drawing on critical race theory, this chapter argues that these productions examined those "left behind" by the Black Arts Movement. McClintock incorporated these characters in his production season, continuing to include narratives that brought visibility to populations often stigmatized and stereotyped, specifically queer folks and former gang members. Through these productions that represented two divergent communities, McClintock's technique yielded impactful performances that both supported and educated his community. From the 1960s, his revolutionary spirit remained steadfast; he subverted theatrical practices and raised the profile of his ancestors.

Chapter 7, "To See Another Day (1998–2003)," chronicles the last years of McClintock's life, as he produced original work and direct theatre until his final days. The chapter analyzes how he continued to create new work that spoke to the concerns of his community and discusses his establishment of the Richmond Black Theatre Festival. He maintained the jazz aesthetic throughout his work and produced Black theatre, including Dr. Endesha Mae Holland's *From the Mississippi Delta* (2005), a womanist autodrama, hip-hop theatre pieces such as *The Rose that Grew from Concrete* (2002) and *Ndangered* (1999), and David Feldshuh's *Miss Evers' Boys* (1989), a fictional account of the Tuskegee Study. The 2002 theme of the second and final installment of the Richmond Black Theatre Festival, "To See Another Day," reflected his intention for Black actors to continue his work for an inclusive and Afrocentric theatre community. In addition to historical context, the chapter engages with womanism and hip-hop scholarship to understand the nuances and complexities of McClintock's Jazz Acting in performance.

Even though the Richmond Black Theatre Festival discontinued after McClintock's death, this book's conclusion, "The Legacy Lives On," acknowledges how his legacy persists, both on and off the stage, in the work of his students. It also acknowledges how artists and educators can understand McClintock's life and legacy for contemporary practice. It argues for that excavating McClintock's legacy can be an effective tool for teachers, students, and companies to rethink progressive EDI strategies and incorporate lost narratives in the classroom and on stage. McClintock is embedded in the ecosystem of Black acting methods, and he is a model of a queer artist rooted in the principles of Black Power who found his jazz subversion of the white mainstream and cliques within Black theatre. Institutions that want to be more inclusive of artists, students, and educators from historically marginalized groups can find inspiration in his model.

Time for a New Beginning

At first glance, inclusivity within a socially progressive movement may seem intuitive and to align with the goals of activist art. However, each Black Theatre Movement company had its own ideological goals that determined their genres and artistic processes. For Baraka, theatre was a weapon of the revolution, and his oeuvre reflects the theatre of assault. Conversely, Teer aimed to create a ritualistic home in which Black artists could heal and make changes in their communities. McClintock was a visionary because a theatre including a multitude of Black perspectives (militaristic, womanist, and queer) made a great impact, unifying a community connected through a collective memory and Afrocentricity. McClintock is a significant figure in the Black Theatre Movement because his acting theory and production aesthetic covered a wide range of genres, from devised poetry theatre to scripted revolutionary drama.

McClintock's erasure from theatre scholarship can be attributed to his inclusivity, because his work cannot be categorized according to strict definitions of genre or process. Further, as a Black gay man producing activist theatre in the 1960s, his identity did not fit with traditional notions of heteronormative Black masculinity. Even in the early years of the Afro-American Studio for Acting and Speech, McClintock was pushed to the fringes by militant factions of Black Power. In particular, portions of the Harlem community viewed him as apolitical, even though his play selections included work by Bullins and Baraka, the fathers of Black revolutionary drama.[64] Marc Primus remarked:

> The Afro-American Studio was formed and created by gay people, it was a gay place. It was certainly not acceptable to the radicals of the Black Arts Movement. Of course it was political. It was more political than they ever hoped to be.... We didn't even talk about it but we all agreed that we were going to create a Black cultural system.[65]

With McClintock and Walker's leadership, the identity of the Afro-American Studio and 127th Street Repertory Ensemble was formed from the resolve to include many Black voices and experiences.

The significance of McClintock's biography is twofold: It challenges monolithic understandings of the Black Arts Movement, and it offers a model for contemporary activist–artists amid social and political turmoil. Since the establishment of the Black Aesthetic, a palpable tension has existed between the limitations of a single aesthetic, which is meant to identify the essence of Black artists. In the early years of the Black Arts Movement, poet Amiri Baraka, scholar Larry Neal, and activist Ron Karenga were known to privilege a heteronormative Black male experience, resulting in misogynistic and homophobic rhetoric. Baraka and Karenga later retracted their discriminatory statements, but dominant narratives still reduce the Black Arts Movement to exclusionary beliefs. Conversely, situating Black art as reflective of multiple perspectives provides a more inclusive and comprehensive exploration of artists and performers. From its inception, McClintock's progressive and innovative acting technique reconciled the inherent conflict between the singular Black Aesthetic and multiple aesthetics from queer and female voices. By identifying his contributions and calling out the biases in theatre and scholarship, his narrative can further nuance the political and social power of the Black Arts Movement. It can serve as a model for current and future activist–artists.

Reviving McClintock's legacy presents the Black Arts Movement in a new light, and his tenacity and strategies can inspire socially conscious artists. For teachers and scholars of acting, including multiple perspectives and exploring Afrocentric techniques offers students from diverse backgrounds ways to develop their craft beyond predominant Stanislavski-based approaches. For young folks who have been ostracized in their communities, McClintock is an exemplary figure of someone who forged ahead with unorthodox practices, challenged those around him to bring out powerful performances, and inspired communities. To understand his pedagogy and artistic development, we need to start at the beginning. From the time he was a little boy living in Chicago in the 1940s, he was surrounded by Black culture, art, music, and community. As a young adult, after seeing one production of Frank Silvera on stage, he was awakened to a theatrical calling.

22 Introduction: Explicit Images and Inclusive Practices

Notes

1. Lichtenstein, "'Black Report' Gets a Mixed Review."
2. Lichtenstein, "'Black Report' Gets a Mixed Review."
3. I employ the term "transition" to refer to McClintock's transition from life to death into the spiritual world.
4. Chafe, *Unfinished Journey*, 294.
5. Joseph, *'Til the Midnight Hour*, 38.
6. Joseph, *'Til the Midnight Hour*, 40.
7. Joseph, *Stokely*, 115–16.
8. Chafe, *Unfinished Journey*, 355.
9. Chafe, *Unfinished Journey,* 357.
10. Chafe, *Unfinished Journey*, 400.
11. Molette and Molette, *Black Theatre*, 26.
12. Smethurst, *Black Arts Movement*.
13. Hay, *African American Theatre*, 78–133.
14. Neal, "The Black Arts Movement."
15. Neal, "The Black Arts Movement," 29.
16. Neal, "The Black Arts Movement," 30.
17. For an overview of the theatres from the Black Arts Movement, see Williams, *Black Theatre in the 1960s and 1970s.*
18. President Franklin D. Roosevelt's New Deal (1933–1939) was an initiative of public works programs and financial reforms designed to kickstart the economy after the Great Depression (1929–1933).
19. Neal, "The Black Arts Movement."
20. Vassar, "Nixon, the Supreme Court, and Busing."
21. The Black Theatre Alliance (BTA) was an organization founded by playwrights Hazel Bryant, Delano Stewart, and Roger Furman. The BTA (1971–1984) unified Black theatre companies based in New York City and provided resources for companies, artists, and touring companies. For more detailed information about the companies, refer to the Helen Armstead-Johnson Theater Collection, the Schomburg Center for Research in Black Culture. Lichtenstein, "'Black Report,'" 20.
22. Harrison, "Praise/Word," 5.
23. Williams, *Black Theatre in the 1960s and 1970s.*
24. Riley, "We Will Not Be 'A New Form of White Art in Blackface," 1.
25. Hatch, "From Hansberry to Shange," 393.
26. Harrison, "Praise/Word," 7.
27. Womanism differs from feminism. As Layli Philips articulates, womanism's link to gender is that "race/class/gender matrix that is Black womanhood, serves as the origin point for a speaking position." Conflating womanism and feminism, or asserting that womanism is a version of feminism, detracts from the particular positionality of Black women and their autonomy. Philips, "Introduction," xxi.
28. Edwards, interview.
29. Edwards, interview.
30. Primus, interview.
31. The representation of queer Black bodies as muscular, able, and fit is certainly a moment for critique in thinking about how queer bodies are represented in contemporary culture. Therefore, there limitations in McClintock's inclusivity when it comes to representations of queer beauty.
32. Baraka, "Babylon Revisited."
33. Johnson, "Appropriating Blackness, "74.
34. It is important to acknowledge that Baraka's views on queer folk drastically changed over time. His evolution as a thinker and writer especially shifted when he learned his daughter was queer.

35 Simon, interview.
36 Neal, "The Black Arts Movement," 30.
37 Neal, "The Black Arts Movement," 30.
38 Asante, *Afrocentric Idea*.
39 Asante, *Afrocentric Idea*, xii.
40 Eyerman, *Cultural Trauma*, 9.
41 Eyerman, *Cultural Trauma*, 2.
42 Enelow, *Method Acting and Its Discontents*, 5.
43 "Call and response" is a succession of two distinct phrases derived from sub-Saharan African dialogue in rituals and songs. The form developed into gospel music, which is most visible today in the Pentecostal Baptist church. Ndounou, "Early African American Theatre."
44 Sell, "Blackness as Critical Practice," 238.
45 Molette and Molette, *Black Theatre*, 99.
46 Naturalism as a late nineteenth-century movement developed by novelist Émile Zola. It aimed to re-create everyday life on stage in terms of sets, acting style, and limited theatricality. Refer to Zola's "Naturalism on the Stage" for an in-depth study.
47 I refer to McClintock's original pieces in which actors would contribute to generating the content, text, movement, as collectively authored-pieces, not "devised." I have chosen the term collectively-authored to privilege McClintock's Afrocentric aesthetic.
48 Quoted in Eyerman, *Cultural Trauma*, 2.
49 Locke, "The Negro and the American Theatre," 263.
50 Du Bois, *Souls of Black Folk*, 8.
51 Du Bois, "Criteria of Negro Art," 328.
52 Locke, "Art or Propaganda?," 334.
53 Harris, *Poetry and Poetics of Amiri Baraka*, 13.
54 Johnson, "Queer Theory," 166.
55 Primus, interview.
56 Cohen, "Punks, Bulldaggers, and Welfare Queens," 450.
57 Primus, interview.
58 Watson, "McClintock," 9.
59 McClintock, interview.
60 Primus, interview.
61 Primus, interview.
62 Simon, "The Ernie McClintock and Nathan George Experience."
63 Primus, interview.
64 Bailey, "New York: Afro-American Studio for Acting and Speech."
65 Primus, interview.

Bibliography

Asante, Molefi Kete. *The Afrocentric Idea,* Rev. ed. Philadelphia, PA: Temple University Press, 1998.

Bailey, A. Peter. "New York: Afro-American Studio for Acting and Speech." *Black Theatre*, 1, n.d.

Baraka, Amiri. "Babylon Revisited." *Poetry Foundation*, n.d. Accessed September 15, 2015. https://www.poetryfoundation.org/poems/42559/babylon-revisited.

Bogle, Donald. *Toms, Coons, Mulattoes, Mammies and Bucks: An Interpretive History of Blacks in American Films*, 4th ed. New York: The Continuum International Publishing Group, 2001.

Chafe, William. *The Unfinished Journey*. New York: Oxford University Press, 1995.
Cohen, Cathy. "Punks, Bulldaggers, and Welfare Queens: The Radical Potential of Queer Politics?" *GLQ: A Journal of Lesbian and Gay Studies* 3, no. 4 (1997): 437–65.
Du Bois, W. E. B. "Criteria of Negro Art." In *Call and Response: Key Debates in African American Studies*, edited by Henry Louis Gates Jr. and Jennifer Burton, 328–33. New York: W. W. Norton, 2001.
Du Bois, W. E. B. *The Souls of Black Folk*. Oxford: Oxford University Press, 2007.
Edwards, Bolanyle. Interview by Elizabeth Cizmar, August 25, 2015, Atlanta, GA.
Enelow, Shonni. *Method Acting and Its Discontents: On American Psycho-Drama*. Chicago, IL: Northwestern University Press, 2015.
Eyerman, Ron. *Cultural Trauma: Slavery and the Formation of African American Identity*. New York: Cambridge University Press, 2003.
Fleming, J. Ron. Interview by Elizabeth Cizmar, September 18, 2015, Richmond, VA.
Giovanni, Nikki. "Black Poems, Poseurs, and Power." In *Call and Response: Key Debates in African American Studies*, edited by Henry Louis Gates Jr. and Jennifer Burton, 711–75. New York: W. W. Norton, 2001.
Glover, William. "White Imitations Dropped by Acting School in Harlem." *Times-Picayune*, December 24, 1972, 1.
Harris, William J. *The Poetry and Poetics of Amiri Baraka*. Columbia, IN: University of Missouri Press, 1985.
Harrison, Paul Carter. "Praise/Word." In *Black Theatre: Ritual Performance in the African Diaspora*, edited by Paul Carter Harrison, Victor Leo Walker II, and Gus Edwards, 1–10. Philadelphia, PA: Temple University Press, 2002.
Hatch, James. "From Hansberry to Shange." In *A History of African American Theatre*, edited by Errol G. Hill and James V. Hatch, 375–409. Cambridge: Cambridge University Press, 2003.
Hay, Samuel. *African American Theatre: An Historical and Critical Analysis*. Cambridge: Cambridge University Press, 1994.
Horne, J. W. Robinson. "Aspects of the Arts: 'The Blacks' Ensemble 'Tour de Force'." *Richmond Afro-American and the Richmond Planet*, May 22, 1993, B3.
Johnson, E. Patrick. *Appropriating Blackness: Performance and the Politics of Authenticity*. Durham, NC: Duke University Press, 2003.
Johnson, E. Patrick. "Queer Theory." In *The Cambridge Companion to Performance Studies*, edited by Tracy C. Davis, 166–81. Cambridge: Cambridge University Press, 2008.
Jones, LeRoi/Amiri Baraka. "The Revolutionary Theatre." *Liberator*, July 1965, 1–3.
Joseph, Peniel. *'Til the Midnight Hour: A Narrative History of Black Power in America*. New York: Henry Holt, 2006.
Joseph, Peniel. *Stokely: A Life*. New York: Basic Civitas, 2014.
Lichtenstein, Grace. "'Black Report' Gets a Mixed Review." *New York Times*, February 18, 1972, 20.
Locke, Alain. "Art or Propaganda?" In *Call and Response: Key Debates in African American Studies*, edited by Henry Louis Gates Jr. and Jennifer Burton, 333–35. New York: W. W. Norton, 2001.
Locke, Alain. "The Negro and the American Theatre." In *The Black Aesthetic*, edited by Gayle Addison, 263–71. Garden City, NJ: Doubleday, 1971.

McClintock, Ernie. Interview by Robert Wilson, June 13, 1973, New York, NY: Countee-Cullen Harold Jackman Memorial Collection, Archives Research Center, Atlanta University Center.

Molette, Barbara J., and Carlton W. Molette. *Black Theatre: Premise and Presentation*. Bristol: Wyndham Hall Press, 1986.

Ndounou, Monica White. "Early African American Theatre." Lecture, Tufts University, Medford, MA, October 25, 2012.

Neal, Larry. "The Black Arts Movement." *Drama Review* 4, no. 12 (Summer 1968): 28–39. https://doi.org/10.2307/1144377.

Philips, Layli. "Introduction." In *The Womanist Reader: The First Quarter Century of Womanist Thought*, edited by Layli Philips, xx–xxi. New York: Routledge, 2006.

Primus, Marc. Interview by Elizabeth Cizmar, August 25, 2015, Atlanta, GA.

Riley, Clayton. "We Will Not Be 'a New Form Of White Art in Blackface'." *The New York Times*, June 4, 1970, 1.

Sell, Mike. "Blackness as Critical Practice." In *Avant-Garde Performance and the Limits of Criticism*, 217–42. Ann Arbor: University of Michigan Press, 2008.

Simon, Levy Lee. "The Ernie McClintock and Nathan George Experience." In *Odyssey Towards the Light*. Unpublished manuscript, last revised 2015.

Smethurst, James Edward. *Black Arts Movement: Literary Nationalism in the 1960s and 1970s*. Chapel Hill: University of North Carolina Press, 2005.

Vassar, Evan. "Nixon, the Supreme Court, and Busing." *Nixon Foundation*, April 2, 2015. https://www.nixonfoundation.org/2015/04/nixon-the-supreme-court-and-busing.

Watson, Jamantha Williams. "McClintock." *Black Masks*, August/September 1996, 9.

Williams, Mance. *Black Theatre in the 1960s and 1970s: A Historical-Critical Analysis of the Movement*. Portsmouth, NH: Greenwood Press, 1985.

Zola, Emile. "Naturalism on the Stage." In *Modern Theories of Drama*, edited by George W. Brandt, 80–88. Oxford: Oxford University Press, 1998.

1
AFROCENTRIC ROOTS IN CHICAGO'S BLACKBELT (1937–1964)

Ernie Claude McClintock was born on February 19, 1937, in Chicago, Illinois, two years before World War II. Although there is a dearth of primary evidence on the details of McClintock's childhood, adolescence, and early adulthood, clues to these periods are embedded in firsthand interviews with him, newspaper articles quoting him, and photographs. Using the clues offered in primary sources, this chapter draws strong connections between the sociopolitical context of the United States and McClintock's primary influence of being entrenched in Black cultural expression in the 1940s and 1950s in Chicago's Blackbelt, also known as Bronzeville. The factors that led to the Black Power Movement are also critical to understanding the impetus for the creation of Black Theatre in the 1960s that was free from the white gaze. The shift in African American theatre focusing on a theatre of revolution is related to the subversion of commercial theatre itself, but theatre does not exist in a vacuum and can be considered a microcosm of the culture wars, racism, and discrimination of the United States as a whole.

To gain a full understanding of McClintock's work, life, and trajectory in the Black Theatre Movement in the mid-1960s, one must understand his upbringing, including the adversity he faced and the rich cultural arts that filled his childhood and adolescence. Often, narratives about African American history and the figures therein solely focus on struggle, pain, and suffering. While struggle is an important part of building resilience and a propulsion to change an unjust society, it is possible for joy, music, art, and community—in short, a celebration of people—to exist alongside it. Arguably, the tenacity of Americans of African descent is not just about the fight against oppression but also the development of an African American culture that is reflected in art, music, literature, and aesthetics. Hence, the purpose of this chapter is to highlight the

DOI: 10.4324/9781003187448-2

world that McClintock grew up in, the focus on community in the Blackbelt, and his witnessing of artists who were engaged in self-determination in places like the Regal Theater. Simultaneously, McClintock was part of the generation that emerged in the post–World War II era who became increasingly frustrated by the slow burn of progress in the 1950s. By the mid-1960s, the Black Power Movement urged African Americans to claim space; McClintock and his peers in the Black Theatre Movement inhabited performance spaces to ignite a cultural revolution.

The methodology of this chapter geographically locates McClintock in critical moments of his early life to unpack the sociopolitical context of his childhood, adolescence, and early adulthood. From these touchstones, the chapter traces connections to the political gestalt of the time, the artists he witnessed firsthand, and the foundation of his political consciousness. To make those connections to the sociopolitical moments of McClintock's life, this analysis is in conversation with the scholarship of William Chafe, Mark H. Haller, Clovis E. Semmes, Peniel Joseph, Harry Elam Jr., Bruce McConachie, and Melissa Barton. From a theoretical perspective, the importance of the Afrocentric concept of community was introduced to McClintock at an early age and became a fundamental component of his aesthetic. This chapter argues that McClintock's early years in the midwestern Blackbelt influenced his desire to create a separatist theatre that was free from the white gaze and provided the foundation for his Afrocentric aesthetic. The social and political state of society unequivocally affected how McClintock, like many of his contemporaries, saw the injustices of the world and, more important, how he would gain strength from his community, which would ultimately shape his inaugural institution in 1966.

Growing Up in Chicago's Blackbelt in the 1940s and 1950s

McClintock was born in Chicago during the period known as the Chicago Black Renaissance. Although there is scholarly debate over the exact dates of this renaissance, with the period said to span between 1928 and 1960, "there is little disagreement that Chicago was a major, if not *the* major urban locus for African-American art, theater, poetry and fiction, blues and jazz, and intellectual energy during the 1930s 1940s, and 1950s."[1] Although the period saw a robust outpouring of African American art and culture, working-class Black Chicagoans contended with unstable labor conditions and crowded living quarters. Researching the historical context of Chicago during McClintock's adolescence provides a way of viewing McClintock's close-knit community and the realities of being Black in the United States in the segregated post–World War II society.

In the late 1930s, Ella Mae Mason and Wade Mason adopted Ernie Claude McClintock; McClintock lovingly referred to them as Ma and Pa (Figure 1.1). He had two siblings, Earl and Felicia, who were the Masons' biological

FIGURE 1.1 Ernie McClintock's Parents, Ella Wade Mason and Wade Mason. *Credit*: Private collection of Geno Brantley.

children. Although there is not much archival information available about his family and the exact living conditions of the household, extensive research and scholarship enables us to envision his upbringing in a working-class family on Chicago's South Side. Although the Great Depression (1929–1939) marked a worldwide economic plummet, according to historian Gareth Canaan,

> research may reveal that the relationship between economic and social struggle with African American political protests, so often associated with the Great Depression and the 1930s, had its roots in the economic and social conditions of Black Chicago during the 1920s.[2]

Essentially, the Great Depression exacerbated already-downtrodden living and working conditions. Although between 1924 and 1929 Chicago saw a rise in employment for Black folk, it did not necessarily "guarantee economic security for African American workers and their families,"[3] especially in relation to wages and promotion opportunities to support families. That was the environment in which McClintock's parents lived in the 1920s, prior to his birth. The working conditions were poor, and Black folks were exposed to even more hazardous conditions than their white counterparts in places like packinghouses, laundries, and upholstery factories. Regarding living conditions, the majority of Black Chicagoans faced high rents, overcrowding, dilapidated buildings, and poor sanitation.[4] Additionally, Chicago was segregated via its infrastructure that separated whites from Blacks.

Although the deep segregation meant that white folks and people of color lived in two separate worlds, both mentally and physically, Black Chicagoans were not deterred from creating art and nurturing the community—the Blackbelt became a hub of live performance and Black culture. Starting in the 1920s, Black entertainers found jobs on Chicago's north side, a predominantly white part of the city, but they were still not welcome as customers. The speakeasies, cafés, and nightclubs on Rush Street on the northside were run by white community leaders and often financed by white bootleggers. Another district on the Southside, known as "The Stroll," became famous from 31st to 39th Streets: "The cafes, dance halls, black and tan cabarets, and gambling houses... nurtured the careers of black artists, attracted white and black customers, and received protection from the emerging black political leaders."[5] One leader, Oscar De Priest, became the first African American to be elected to Congress, in 1929. De Priest was a successful businessman prior to his political career and his controversial protection of gambling became less important than his robust political career that established him as an important symbol of Black achievement.[6] During Prohibition, the South Side of Chicago became one of the most significant centers of jazz and other forms of popular Black entertainment in the country. Many entertainers who McClintock saw perform in the 1950s, including Cab Calloway, got their start in Chicago's South Side in the 1920s.

By McClintock's eighth birthday (Figure 1.2), World War II had ended, ushering in a new era of consumerism and development in the infrastructure of the United States. After the war, American consumerism eclipsed social progress. According to historian William Chafe, "the 1950s represented more a time of transition than solidity. During the immediate aftermath of World War II, the possibilities for massive social change in the condition of workers, blacks, and women had been snuffed out."[7] On the surface, the US economy was booming and the country saw technological advancements in infrastructure. Between 1947 and 1960, highways were built to connect cities, and suburban neighborhoods were developed. Sixty percent of the residents of the United States owned homes in these suburbs, and in this postwar period, incomes increased as much as they had in the previous half century.[8] Concurrently, the idealistic myth of global democracy was debunked,[9] in that when soldiers returned from war, institutionalized systems of racism remained intact. Further, the civil rights movement had rested on the assumption that the basic economic and social structure of America was sound, yet poverty increased while "the rich increased their share of the nation's wealth."[10] Black soldiers who had fought for democracy side-by-side with white soldiers returned to a country that was entrenched in racism, thus revealing the sanctioned inequality of the United States.

In 1955, when McClintock was 18 years old, Chicago native Emmett Till was lynched in Mississippi. Till's murder, a national tragedy, was a turning point and the 14-year-old posthumously became a symbol for civil rights. In summer 1955, Till was visiting family in Mississippi when Roy Bryant and J. W. Milam beat, shot, and discarded the boy's body in the Tallahatchie River. Till had apparently whistled at Bryant's wife, Carolyn; historian Elliott J. Gorn posits that "it was the classic Southern tale of a black male accused of violating the region's taboo against interracial intimacy."[11] Till's mother, Mamie Till, insisted on an open casket funeral in Chicago, with her son's mutilated body on display for the world to see. She said, "I think everybody needed to know what had happened to Emmett Till."[12] More than 50,000 people lined the streets of Chicago to see Emmett Till. Following the funeral, *Jet* magazine published photos of Till lying in his coffin.

It is unclear whether McClintock and his family were among the 50,000 mourners paying their respects to Till and his family. However, the lynching would have had an impact on every American, especially those who lived in Chicago's Blackbelt. Emmett Till became an avatar of the civil rights movement and brought the ugly, true side of racism in the United States to the fore. For McClintock, who became a leader of the Black Theatre Movement and a self-proclaimed Black nationalist, one can only imagine the impact of the lynching of a boy close to his age and from the same Chicago community.

The popularization of television further changed the sociopolitical climate in the United States, in that news programs broadcast blatant acts of violence and discrimination. Specifically, in 1957, following the *Brown v. Board of Education* (1954) decision that ruled that segregated schools were unconstitutional, the NAACP (National Association for the Advancement of Colored People) registered nine Black students at Little Rock Central High, Arkansas. This event was broadcast across the nation. The governor of Arkansas called on the Arkansas National Guard to prevent the students from entering the school. President Eisenhower issued an executive order to federalize the National Guard and ordered the support of integration. Protests from segregationist councils ensued, and eventually Eisenhower sent troops to protect the students as they entered the school. A microcosm of America's racial climate, this sequence of events at Little Rock brought blatant discrimination against people of color into family living rooms across the country.

As a Black gay teenager in the post–World War II era, living day in and day out in a racist, heteronormative reality was challenging at best for McClintock. Although there is little archival evidence of his specific experiences as a gay teenager, in the 1950s and 1960s "American society... imposed a global policy of repression on homosexuality."[13] Therefore, the absence of McClintock's voice regarding his sexuality speaks volumes about this national repression. In the 1950s, the silencing of queer folk did not just occur through social shaming but became "an official object of government censure,"[14] resulting in a witch hunt of queer folks. Often, this resulted in the incarceration of gay Americans. McClintock departed from the trend of queer artists often became expatriates abroad to avoid the blatant bigotry of the United States, like James Baldwin who defected to France. Michael Trask's analysis of queer literary culture in the 1940s and 1950s identifies the subversive strategies of writers and finds the production of queer literature confirmed a worldwide community, threatening hegemonic powers, and social structures. Specifically,

> 1950s queer fiction partook of the period's impulse to see nonnormative sexuality as *symptomatic* of broader structural perversities. Hence James Baldwin writes *Giovanni's Room* as a study of the intersection of white supremacy, colonialism, and the repressed desire for the Other—Fanon's *Black Skin, White Masks* (1952) rewritten as a melodrama of the closet.[15]

Although Baldwin and McClintock dealt with heteronormative structures in the United States in differing ways, in their artistic endeavors, they upended white heteronormative standards through writing and directing, respectively.

Chicago has a rich history of gay life, where although it was unsafe to be out, queer communities found ways to communicate and socialize. For example, the code that "friends of Dorothy" (from *The Wizard of Oz*) meant someone was "in the life."[16] "For decades, gays in Chicago and across the world have used slang, clothing, jewelry, and mannerisms to signal their presence to each other, especially when it wasn't a safe matter to openly discuss."[17] Into the early 1950s, semi-annual drag balls were organized by Black clubs in Chicago, drawing hundreds of people to places such as the Coliseum Annex for Halloween and New Year's Eve. However, post-Prohibition law enforcement cracked down, and bars would be closed for same-gender dancing or if someone would "talk in a way that indicated they were gay."[18] In Gore Vidal's novel *The City and the Pillar* (1948) set in Virginia in the 1930s, the protagonist delineates between two categories of homosexuals: queens, who insisted on being flamboyant, and masculine, rigid men, who kept from being "known."[19] These two categories are limiting in terms of the scope of representation and assume that one always chooses how to present oneself. Nonetheless, this problematic theory reveals pressures that McClintock may have experienced as a Black gay man in Chicago.

FIGURE 1.2 Portrait of Young Ernie McClintock, age unknown.
Credit: From the private collection of Geno Brantley.

A Childhood Surrounded by Black Cultural Arts

As McClintock stated in an interview, in the 1950s, theatre was not necessarily part of his daily life as a youth, despite the rich history of Black Theatre in the midwestern city.[20] In his blunt manner he stated: "[M]ost Black kids had no relationship to any real theater. That was something that was just no part of the world we lived in."[21] Although McClintock was not exposed to theatre per se early on, his homelife was full of music and art. In a 1996 interview with Jamantha Williams Watson, McClintock recalled his family life that informed his artistic beginnings: "When I was growing up, in my home there was an attitude of cultural arts.... My father used to listen to the blues in his bedroom. My sister and mother played the piano."[22] He was drawn to live performance and frequented the Regal Theater as a child, where he was captivated by musicians and comics including Sarah Vaughan, Dinah Washington, Ella Fitzgerald, Moms Mabley, Butterbeans and Susie, Ella Johnson, and Cab Calloway.[23]

The Regal Theater is one of the most significant Black performing arts institutions in theatre history. The movie and stage show venue was built specifically to serve the Bronzeville African American community. This massive performing arts institution opened its doors in 1928, six years prior to the perhaps better-known Apollo in Harlem, New York. Both theatres connected the community to Black cultural forms. The Regal included the Savoy Ballroom and South Center department store. The theatre on 4718 South Parkway showcased an ornate lobby measuring 160 feet and had capacity for 1500 people.[24] According to Clovis E. Semmes, a comprehensive analysis of the Regal reveals a complicated relationship between white owners and Black artists; he uses the Regal Theater as a case study that examines "the collectivity of social forces that advance and constrain Black cultural and artistic production and structures of inequality that circumscribe African American life."[25] In other words, the segregation of Chicago during the life of the Regal (1928–1968) placed limitations on careers of Black performers, yet these performers continued to develop musical and artistic forms despite the constraints.

These performers' pursuit of art as a method of survival within the confines of discrimination and oppression can be traced back to the voyage over the Middle Passage. On the slave ships, enslaved people were forced to sing and dance to keep them healthy. Yet, as Douglas A. Jones Jr. articulates, "slaves turned the oppressive conditions of their netherworld performances into a *crucible of collective possibility*."[26] This collective possibility became a mode of survival. Hence, there is a "decidedly fraught relation that enslaved Africans and their descendants have had with cultural performance since the time of their earliest arrivals in the early seventeenth century."[27] Black cultural performance under oppression morphed into various forms, including plantation performances in the antebellum era and the reclamation of Blackface minstrelsy at the turn of the twentieth century.[28]

In the late 1940s and early 1950s, McClintock attended performances at the Regal Theater, which had established itself as the premiere Black performing arts venue. The Regal attracted diverse Black audiences, contributing "to the maintenance of an authentic Black culture because performers, Black or non-Black, had to meet the aesthetic demands and norms of Black audiences."[29] The audience culture of the Regal aligned with the idea of the Afrocentric practice of call and response. Call and response is a musical form originating in African American churches, where a soloist expresses a phrase and the collective ensemble responds.[30] Likewise, "At the Regal, Black audiences effectively reinforced Black aesthetic norms through their attendance and spending patterns and audience-based expressions of approval and disapproval."[31] McClintock would have been sitting in the audiences, absorbing both the performers on stage and the African American performance traditions and aesthetics that imbued performances and informed audiences' reactions.

As Semmes notes, the Regal was not without its problems in that white, corrupt producers were the major stakeholders of the Black cultural institution. Hence, in McClintock's formative years, he attended this prolific center of Black culture that was clouded by internal colonialism and cultural hegemony, and he also witnessed colonial practices on the streets of Chicago.[32] Internal colonialism, also known as domestic colonialism, "is when—though residents or citizens of the same country—one racial or ethnic group controls the vital institutions of another, and the groups are separated spatially."[33] The framework of cultural hegemony can be traced to philosopher Antonio Gramsci's *Prison Notebooks* (1926). Although Gramsci does not outright define cultural hegemony, he essentially stipulates that the ideology of the ruling class dominates a society's beliefs, interests, and standards. Historiographer Bruce McConachie identifies three patterns in the concept of domestic colonialism: a distinction between cultural hegemony and domination by force, an emphasis on language as a vehicle for cultural hegemony, and hegemonic culture always being contradictory and open to change.[34] McConachie distills these ideas by identifying how hegemonic culture is a dynamic force that "sets 'historical blocks' in conflict with one another."[35] These blocks are tethered to the ideology of the ruling class and influence the pulse of a culture asserting immoral and intellectual superiority.[36] Intellectual superiority can come in the form of language: for example, having a standard American English as the proper way to speak in American society leads to the denigration of dialects within pockets of culture with their own rhythms and speech patterns. However, as McConachie points out, there is space for activism and upending the dominant culture because the hegemony is inherently "dynamic and incomplete."[37] In the case of the Regal, white, corrupt stakeholders loomed over the institution, yet the musicians and artists who performed resisted the hegemonic forces, asserting African American cultural traditions and aesthetics.

Specifically, Chicago Paramount Pictures was the parent company of the Regal and paid off Chicago crime organizations to gain an advantage in the entertainment marketplace. As a result,

> The Regal benefited from connections to a monopolistic motion picture production, distribution, and exhibition conglomerate, to White organized crime, and to a system of racial oppression and segregation, which produced a captive Black market and which constrained business development.... Chicago's patronage-controlled city government maintained a working alliance with organized crime, which collectively advanced the interest of White ethnic groups, but which normally limited the political power and business activities of Black Americans.[38]

The Regal Theater occupied a paradoxical space in which the hegemonic systems oppressed and restricted Black expression from extending outside of the Blackbelt, and yet the ingenuity and innovation of Black performers and laborers inside made the Regal Theater a thriving Black cultural institution. The performers who graced the stage of the Regal influenced a young McClintock within the environment of a repressive society in which white hegemonic forces repressed Black political power and restricted business opportunities in his hometown.

McClintock Unearths His Theatrical Vocation, 1950s–1960s

From 1954 to 1956, McClintock attended Crane College (now Malcolm X College) and pursued an associate's degree in medical technology. He became an avid patron of theatre and live performance, eventually transitioning from audience member to performer. As an actor, "His introduction to the stage was entirely fortuitous and occurred while he was attending college, majoring in medical technology and working full-time."[39] His first role on stage was as Henry Gow in Noel Coward's *Fumed Oak* (1935) at Crane College, where he began to get noticed around campus as a talented actor. "'It felt good.... I was shy, believe it or not, and it was good for the ego, ya know?'"[40] To those who knew McClintock as a teacher and mentor, "shy" was not a term often associated with the opinionated director. However, his self-reflection suggests that the theatre provided him access to both his vocal and metaphorical voice.

During his time at Crane College, one of his coworkers gave McClintock a ticket to the national tour of Michael V. Gazzo's *A Hatful of Rain* (1955), where he saw Frank Silvera perform at the Selwyn Theatre—a life-changing moment. The original Broadway production starred Ben Gazzara, Shelley Winters, Anthony Franciosa, and Frank Silvera. Notably, Steve McQueen made his Broadway debut as a replacement for Gazzara in the role of Johnny Pope. The cast for the national tour included Vivian Blaine, Mark Richman, Harry Guardino, and Silvera (Figure 1.3). *A Hatful of Rain* graced the Selwyn stage for a short run between October 15 and November 3, 1956. McClintock was 19, working full-time, and discovering his newfound love for the stage. He attributed witnessing the production, and Silvera's performance in particular, as the moment he knew his life's work would be in the theatre.

McClintock was awestruck by the talent and theatricality embodied by the actors. He said he was "amazed at the intensity of realism on stage."[41] Gazzo's play follows a Korean War veteran, Johnny Pope, who sustains a leg injury and becomes addicted to morphine. The play charts Johnny's struggle with addiction and its impact on his Italian American parents, brother, and pregnant wife. This was a bold play for the 1950s, when conversations about and depictions of drug addiction in popular culture were rare. After all, the 1940s and 1950s was known as the golden age of Broadway, with smash hit shows like *Guys and Dolls* (1950) and *My Fair Lady* (1956), which sharply contrasted with *A Hatful of Rain*. In *Hatful*, Black actor Silvera played the father, John Pope Sr., alongside white actors who portrayed his sons, daughter-in-law, and wife. Initially blown

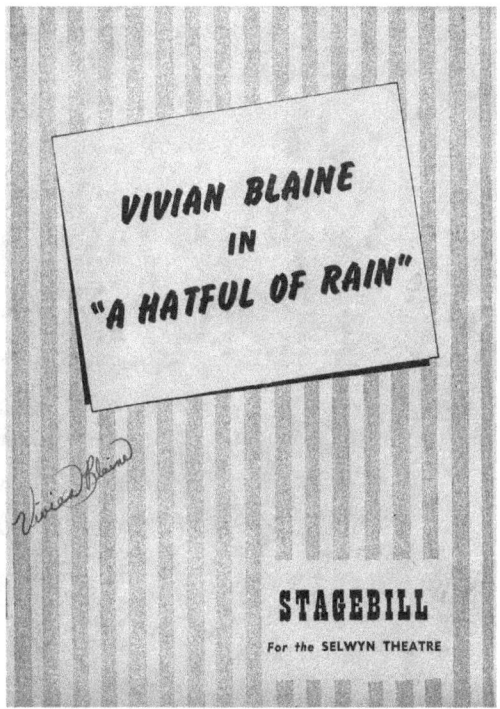

FIGURE 1.3 Signed Original Playbill of *A Hatful of Rain* at the Selwyn Theatre.
Credit: From the private collection of Elizabeth M. Cizmar.

away by the ensemble cast and their powerful performances, McClintock was further impressed and moved by the realization that Silvera was indeed Black:

> [McClintock's] astonishment deepened a few weeks later when he discovered that the actor who played the lead in this play about an Italian family was a black man. At that time, McClintock knew of no black stage actors. Fascinated, he bought a lot of tickets to other plays, took time off from work and gorged himself on plays for an entire week.[42]

Seeing a performer of the African Diaspora take up space and subvert casting norms made a profound impression on McClintock, as a young actor of color. Additionally, the play's content—which was taboo at best, and moved audiences—demonstrated the possibilities of including narratives often overlooked by the mainstream (Figure 1.4).

Silvera, a Jamaican-born Boston University graduate and award-winning actor, established himself as one of the most versatile actors of the 1940s, 1950s, and 1960s, despite the initial resistance of mainstream producers to cast a "light-skinned Negro."[43] He became known as "the man of a thousand faces" due to his versatility as an actor and played characters of many ethnicities, on stage and

FIGURE 1.4 Vivian Blaine, Steve McQueen, and Frank Silvera in *A Hatful of Rain*, 1955.

Credit: Billy Rose Theatre Collection, NYPL, New York City.

on screen. Garland Lee Thompson Jr. notes that in *Hatful,* almost nobody in the audience realized Silvera was Black: "Due to his looks or perhaps his surname of Silvera, Frank moved into the new elite inner circles of the leading American Theatre groups, where he became an active member of the famed Actors Studio of New York."[44] During Silvera's short time in Chicago, he made his way to the South Side to connect with his community. According to the *Chicago Tribune,* Silvera performed James Weldon Johnson's folk sermon "The Creation" and told a West Indian folk tale "each in the accent and idiom of the people they represented."[45] Silvera's effort to travel to the South Side and perform for people of African descent exhibits his wish to connect with his community.[46]

Forty years after McClintock witnessed Silvera's performance, he recalled, "It was a tremendous and provocative play for me. I never knew that you could put on stage something so real."[47] It motivated him to frequently attend performances and explore performance. That following week, he bought tickets to performances at venues across Chicago almost every night.[48] He was inspired to start taking acting classes at Crane College from 1954 to 1956, and then later at Roosevelt University from 1961 to 1962. McClintock's résumé suggests that after his time in Kansas—where he was simultaneously enrolled in the United States Armed Forces Institute and Kansas State University, taking courses in correspondence and personal administration—he returned to Chicago in 1961. From there, he took theatre classes at Roosevelt and then found his way to The Helen Espie Dramatic Arts Studio in Chicago in 1962. At Roosevelt, he landed a leading role in a class production. Fellow students began to recognize him as the leading actor on campus—classmates who had never spoken to him before they saw him on stage. His confidence grew until he thought, "[W]ell I could certainly have a little more of this type of treatment."[49] At this time in Chicago and across the country, safe spaces for young queer adults to work from a place of authenticity, and express themselves were lacking. Time and again, the theatre has been a safe haven for the misfits of society, a space where they can find camaraderie, explore identities, and develop self-confidence. As a gay, Black young adult, McClintock found his calling in the theatre. In Chicago, three years after seeing Silvera on stage and taking acting classes, McClintock appeared in three dozen shows in the Chicago area.[50]

On his actor's résumé, under college theatre experience, McClintock listed a mix of plays, from classical to contemporary, in which his roles ranged from small—such as the sailor in *A Taste of Honey* (1958) and the waiter and soldier in *Pantagleize* (1929)—to large—including Asagai in *A Raisin in the Sun* (1959) and Orestes in *Electra* (409 BC). Professionally, in Chicago, McClintock performed in *Enrico IV* (1922), directed by Gene Frankel at the Harper Theatre, as the second valet. When he moved to New York, McClintock landed small roles in notable productions with the New York Shakespeare Festival. Joseph Papp's "Mobile Theater," established in 1957, evolved into the New York Shakespeare Festival, ultimately becoming what's known today as the Public Theater.[51] In 2018, the Public revitalized the Mobile Theater to tour in Pennsylvania, Ohio, Michigan,

Wisconsin, and Minnesota. Renamed the Public Theater's Mobile Unit offers free performances across the country to the disenfranchised, including homeless and the incarcerated. Papp aimed to establish accessible theatre with progressive casting choices in a racially integrated company. The productions McClintock was involved in worked to connect with marginalized members of society, which presumably appealed to his growing aesthetic. After experiencing theatres and schools that were racially integrated, McClintock came to the conclusion that when he came to form his own company, it was necessary to establish an all-Black company, aligning with Black Power's separatist philosophy. McClintock was cast in two of Papp's productions: in *Henry V* (1599) as Michael Williams and in *The Taming of the Shrew* (1623) as Madcap. Notably, *Henry V* starred Robert Hooks, the first Black actor to star in a Public Theater production of Shakespeare. Hooks, a formidable figure in the Black Theater Movement, went on to form the Negro Ensemble Company, along with Douglas Turner Ward. McClintock and Hooks were contemporaries and both worked in a white-dominated theatre and mainstream plays before founding their own respective companies.

In a 1996 interview with Jamantha Williams Watson, McClintock mentions his "stint" in the US Army in 1960–1961. Although not much is documented in the archives beyond his résumé, his enrollment in the armed services aligns with the experiences of many others from the Black Arts Movement, such as renowned activist–poet Amiri Baraka (Air Force), revolutionary playwright Ed Bullins (US Navy), and celebrated producer–playwright–director Douglas Turner Ward (US Army). Between 1949 and 1973, the military employed one-third of the US population, with a significant number of volunteer enlistments as well as those drafted.[52] So by the time McClintock and his peers enlisted, it was rather common for young men to join the army to seek viable careers. In the post–World War II great migration from the South to the North, northern urban centers like Chicago failed to meet economic, social, and political aspirations.[53] In the words of historian Kimberly L. Phillips, Black men entered the army "as it was the only thing left to do."[54] In the army, at least, there was a promise of steady work, wages, job training, and educational opportunities.

Young African American men's enlistment and drafting into the military fueled frustrations, demonstrating that the government put men of color on the front lines abroad while enforcing the Jim Crow segregation laws established in 1865 during the Reconstruction era.[55] Notably, the 1950s and 1960s included the Korean War and the Vietnam War where many of these men were risking their lives for their country. In 1948, President Truman issued an executive order to desegregate the army due to rising protests and "the challenge that segregation posed to foreign policy."[56] For Truman, that challenge was fighting oppressive communist regimes while denying rights to Black folks in the United States, a theme that persisted during McClintock's time in the army (1960–1961). Although McClintock was not on the front lines of war, a theme in Black soldiers' experiences is the tension between the fact that they were enlisted to aid the US government's attempts to act as a moral compass for nations who violated human rights (as in the case of Nazi Germany and World War II), but after they returned home from war, Black veterans faced federally sanctioned segregation in public facilities, places of employment, schools, and voting taxations. The hypocrisy of being asked to fight and even die for a country built on the backs of enslaved Africans, and a government that sanctioned discrimination, increasingly came to the fore.

While stationed in Fort Riley, Kansas, McClintock learned how to use his ingenuity to achieve his goal of being a theatre artist. Initially, the Fort Riley Theatre Company did not consider him a potential company member: "They weren't too interested in me.... They didn't say it, but they hadn't had any black people in the theater company."[57] During production preparation, the company realized they had no company members skilled at makeup. McClintock offered his services, assuring them that he was adept at stage makeup (see Figure 1.5). He said, "I was lying through my teeth."[58] He committed to the process, checking out books from the library on stage makeup and practicing on his fellow soldiers. He later reflected, "Why these grown men allowed me to practice on them I don't know."[59] Through his perseverance and resourcefulness, McClintock was suddenly a makeup artist, and from there, he eventually became a performer with the company. Ingenuity and resourcefulness were quintessential McClintock qualities that sustained him over his 40-year career.

FIGURE 1.5 McClintock in Stage Makeup.
Credit: From the private collection of Geno Brantley.

Coming into His Own: Actor Training and the Rise of Radical Political Consciousness

From 1962 to 1964, prior to his move to New York, McClintock studied formal theatre training with Helen Espie, significantly influencing his acting technique. Espie, a Scottish immigrant, had created her own studio, The Helen Espie of Dramatic Arts Studio, located in Chicago's Fine Arts Building. Information on the school's history is not readily available, but Espie was known as a leading drama coach who worked with many actors from Second City comedy troupe,[60] including Bill Murray.[61] McClintock's student Thaddeus Daniels recalls that Espie taught McClintock how to read language by unpacking clues embedded in text.[62] Her focus on a performer breaking down a script word for word and understanding why a specific language is employed in dialogue influenced McClintock's Jazz Acting technique.

In her approach to text, Espie emphasized pronouns and absolutes. Her philosophy on pronouns was that each time an actor utters a pronoun, they need to know exactly how the character feels about that person, place, or thing. Once they identify how their character feels about that person, place, or thing, every time they articulate that pronoun on stage, they deliver the word with that intention. This can include feelings of jealousy, infatuation, adoration, hatred, vengefulness, and so forth. By identifying how one feels about that person, place, or thing, the vocal delivery yields expressiveness and specificity. Espie considered "never, ever, always, and don't" to be absolutes that should be considered as the guideposts of language.[63] Actors adding emphasis to these words yielded increased expressiveness in vocal delivery. If a character employs an absolute, they are asserting a strong point of view and the word should be expressed in an emphatic way, not simply glossed over on stage. For Daniels, McClintock's evolution of Espie's approach to absolutes evolved so he could connect his actors to the music and rhythm of a sentence. In addition to emphasis, McClintock's Jazz Acting technique considers things like the cadence of a sentence, the dialect of a character, the rhythm of speech, and the cultural idiom of a people. The lines of text are the melody, and the actor is the musician bringing their interpretation to those lines and that character. In an acting biography, McClintock wrote of himself for a brochure, he said he "gives much credit to Helen Espie with whom he studied acting and speech privately."[64] Espie did not necessarily identify the language as "melody," as McClintock did in Jazz Acting, but her thoughtful consideration of language laid the foundation for this staple component of McClintock's technique. McClintock took these concepts of unpacking and interpreting language based on the syntax and intention of a writer, and in the tradition of jazz, revised the understanding of language through an Afrocentric perspective.

While McClintock studied with Espie and performed in Chicago, the Black Power revolutionary spirit matured. The 1961 assassination of the first democratically elected prime minister of the Congo, Patrice Lumumba, exposed the hypocrisy and blatant disregard for bodies of African ancestry perpetuated by the US government. Lumumba was a significant leader in gaining Congolese sovereignty; the nation won independence from Belgium on June 30, 1960. The country was divided over how it should be governed—specifically, President Joseph Kasa-Vubu believed provinces should have more autonomy, whereas Lumumba advocated for a centralized government. Following Congo's independence, there was much upheaval, and the province of Katanga seceded from the country. Katangese leader, Moïse Tshombe, strongly opposed Lumumba's centralized politics. The country was unstable and Lumumba was a target for the rebels who rebuked centralized governmental structures. Lumumba then called upon the United States and United Nations to aid his efforts to suppress the rebel uprisings, which were backed by Belgian forces. The United States did not find it economically or politically beneficial to engage with this newly formed democratic state, so Lumumba's government accepted aid from the erstwhile USSR, even though Lumumba publicly refuted communist ideology.[65] During the height of the Cold War, US officials found an excuse to further distance themselves from Congo's civil unrest and plotted failed attempts to poison the Lumumba, which historians have suggested came from the desk of President Eisenhower. Kasa-Vubu dismissed the newly elected prime minister and placed him under house arrest. Lumumba escaped but was soon arrested, held in a military camp, and transferred to Katanga, along with his associates Joseph Okito and Maurice Mpolo. Notably, historian Madeleine G. Kalb recounts the CIA conducting a search in Congo to capture Lumumba and deliver him to the rebels.[66] When John F. Kennedy became president, he opposed such sanctions and intended to release Lumumba from prison. However, three days before Kennedy's inauguration, Lumumba was executed by firing squad by Katangese authorities, with evidence of Belgian involvement.

Prior to Lumumba's assassination, American Black writers primarily focused on the domestic sphere, with family dramas such as Richard Wright's adaptation of *Native Son* (1941) and Theodore Ward's *Big White Fog* (1937), yet reflected racial and class tensions across America. Scholar Harry Elam Jr. argues that in African American theatre of this time, the personal became political: "In the period from World War II to the new millennium, black playwrights have used the domestic setting as a microcosm of the social and cultural concerns impacting African American life."[67] However, perhaps due to the social and cultural exigencies of the times, family dramas were less prevalent in the 1960s and 1970s.[68] During the 1950s, many Black playwrights portrayed integrationist politics; for example, in Louis S. Peterson's *Take a Giant Step* (1959) the protagonist, Spencer Scott, is the only student of color in an integrated school and is suspended for correcting a teacher on the role of Black soldiers during the Civil War.[69] One watershed play is, of course, Lorraine Hansberry's *A Raisin in the Sun* (1959), which poignantly predicted the shift from the house to a reckoning with outside forces. Peniel Joseph contends that Hansberry "trumpeted the arrival of a cultural nationalism destined to be associated almost exclusively with Black Power militants."[70] Dramas celebrated the political awakening of the Black masses and critiqued the assumed apathy of the Black bourgeoisie. Amiri Baraka, poet and activist, led the charge against racism perpetuated by mass media and the commodification of art in his 1964 "A Poem for Willie Best." In this, he suggests that African American artists have been seen as merely "entertainers," reminiscent of Blackface minstrelsy. As part of the Black Arts community, McClintock addressed the collective struggle against cultural, political, and economic compromises in art through creating an institution as an act of self-determination.

Lumumba's assassination catapulted action-based initiatives and solidified the Black Power philosophy, the theoretical crux of McClintock's training program and productions. According to Peniel Joseph, the assassination of the Congolese leader transformed up-and-coming activists and Black nationalists into radicals. Theories, concepts, and ideologies culminated in action-based revolutionary initiatives, such as African Americans' reclamation of language to self-define and self-determine. For example, on February 15, 1961—two days after Katangan Secretary of State of Information Lucas Samalenge announced Lumumba's death[71]—nationalists stormed the United Nations in New York, and demonstrators included Dr. Maya Angelou.[72] When interviewed by reporters, the protestors of African descent proclaimed that they were no longer Negroes but Afro-Americans.[73] The failure of the United States to support Lumumba, and his subsequent murder, was a breaking point for Black Americans, who demanded social justice after centuries of dehumanization, daily discrimination from law enforcement, and stereotypes in popular culture. They worked to create a unified people across the African Diaspora. McClintock aligned himself with this reclamation when he named his school the *Afro-American* Studio for Acting and Speech in 1966, connecting him to his global community.

During this political turmoil at home and abroad, and coinciding with McClintock's resolve to open his own school, in 1961, he met Ronald Walker, who would become his life and creative partner. They met either in the army or in Chicago. Based on archival evidence, they moved from Chicago to New York sometime in 1964 or 1965. Although the Stonewall uprising in 1969 was a crucial moment for gay liberation, there were pockets of resistance across the country prior to this infamous rebellion. McClintock and Walker's relationship matured in the latter years of the homophile movement. According to the Library of Congress, the US homophile movement occurred post–World War II. This term "refers to the local, national and international social-political movement for gay and lesbian rights."[74] Prior to Stonewall, there were at least 60 homophile groups in the United States, including the Mattachine Society (est. 1950), Knights of the Clock (est. 1950), Daughters of Bilitis (est. 1955), and the Veterans Benevolent Association (est. 1945).[75] In 1963, the Eastern Regional Conference of Homophile Organizations (ECHO) was established to bring together local groups from New York, Philadelphia, and Washington, DC.

Although McClintock and Walker were not directly involved with these organizations as focus was on Black Theatre rather than gay liberation, it is important to note that many of the strategies employed by gay and lesbian activists were inspired by the civil rights movement and queer activists of color. For example, in their article "Different Fight, 'Same Goal': How the Black Freedom Movement Inspired Early Gay Activists," Jo Yurcaba references the 1960 Woolworth's sit-in in Greensboro, North Carolina, where Black college students protested racial segregation. Yurcaba argues that the Greensboro sit-in inspired three folks who identified as homosexual and nonconforming to refuse to leave Dewey's restaurant in Philadelphia. Yurcaba references Marc Stein's book *Rethinking the Gay and Lesbian Movement*, in which they write, "The sit-in at Dewey's is among a long list of examples that show a 'direct line' to the Black civil rights movement."[76] Additionally, activist figures like Bayard Rustin and Marsha P. Johnson have gained recognition as forerunners in gay liberation and queer activism. Yet, although McClintock and Walker were not directly involved in these organizations and did not protest at Stonewall, their radical inclusivity in theatrical spaces can be considered a form of social resistance.

Landing in New York: Training with Louis Gossett Jr.

McClintock realized the necessity of forming his own school and training actors after attending Louis Gossett's Gossett Academy of Dramatic Arts (GADA) from 1965 to 1966, which was an integrated conservatory in Lower Manhattan. McClintock received the Lorraine Hansberry Scholarship and began taking classes with an impressive faculty. Although he began as a student, training under Gossett, McClintock's intuition impressed the faculty to the point where the future Oscar winner asked the young actor to teach classes (Figure 1.5). McClintock taught alongside Gossett, acting legend James Earl Jones, and prolific Black historian Loften Mitchell. McClintock taught foundational acting courses Acting I: Technique and Character Development and An Introduction to Acting and Theatre (Figure 1.6). The introductory course provided an entry point for folks to take classes and learn about theatre without pursing a degree. They attended shows, took acting classes, and learned about theatre history. For McClintock, attending theatre was an integral part of students' education, and he incorporated performance attendance into his schools in both New York

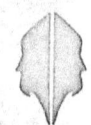 

GOSSETT ACADEMY OF DRAMATIC ARTS
11 EAST 17TH STREET • NEW YORK, N. Y. 10003 • 243-8325

June 1, 1966

To Whom It May Concern:

Ernie McClintock has been active as artistic director and instructor at the Gossett Academy of Dramatic Arts since its inception in February, 1966. He has been loyal and dedicated in all of his many projects at the school and was instrumental in setting up the entire scholastic program that was used here.

Ernie has directed three productions at the Academy all of which were of considerable artistic success. He has been active as an instructor with children and teenagers as well as adults.

An accomplished actor, Ernie appeared in a special production of THE ZOO STORY and his performance was truly outstanding.

I have complete confidence in Ernie McClintock's abilities and feel confident that he is qualified for any theatrical venture he might undertake.

Very truly yours

LOUIS GOSSETT
PRESIDENT

LG/MMR

FIGURE 1.6 Gossett Academy of Dramatic Arts (GADA) Course Offerings Pamphlet. *Credit*: From the private collection of Geno Brantley.

and Richmond, Virginia. As well as learning his craft as a teacher, the young artist began to direct, igniting a newfound passion:

> On weekends, McClintock began a performance group at Lou Gossett's school and found that he enjoyed directing a great deal more than acting. He became absorbed in directing—so absorbed that often he would

Afrocentric Roots in Chicago's Blackbelt (1937–1964) 45

quietly sneak into theatres where he would take mental notes. Sometimes he was actually thrown out.[77]

Hence, McClintock's unorthodox approach—to the point of trespassing in theatres to surround himself with as much theatre as possible and to learn from watching—seemed to be intrinsic to his personality and his drive. At GADA, he directed *African Collage, Epitaph to the Coagulated Trinity*, and *Two Rooms*,[78] for which he also held the title of artistic director.

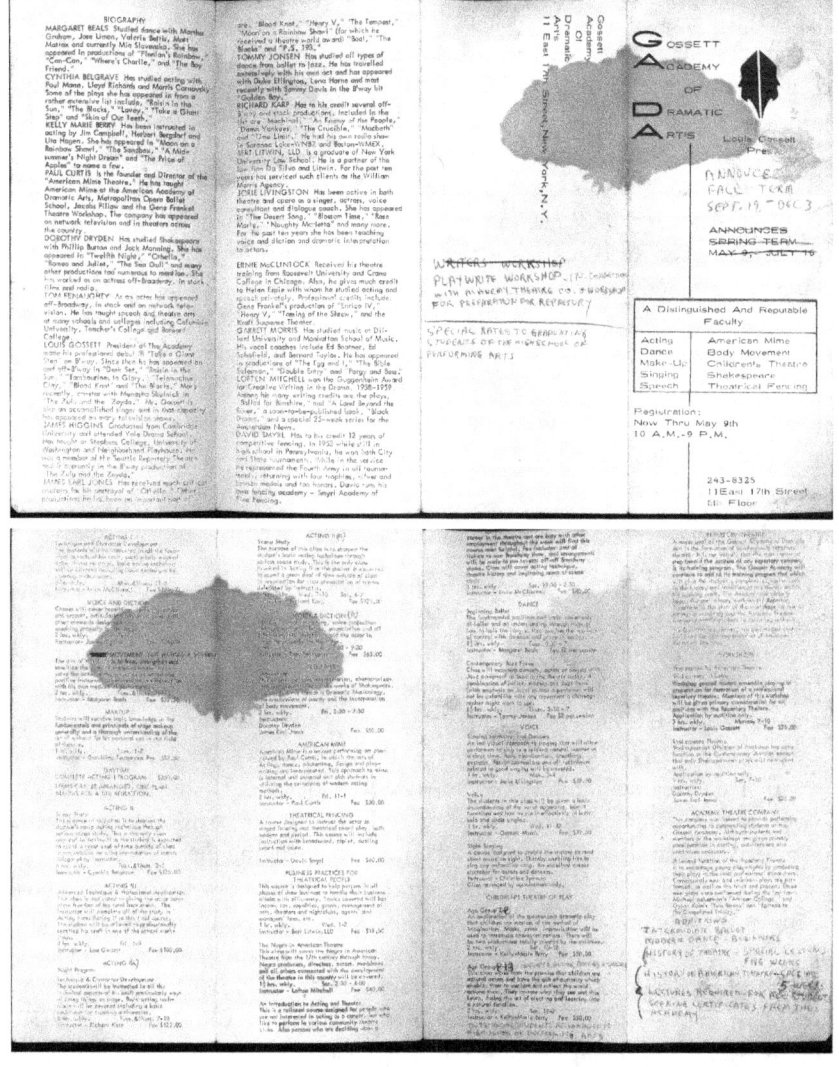

FIGURE 1.7 Letter of Recommendation from Louis Gossett Jr., June 1, 1966.
Source: From the private collection of Geno Brantley.

McClintock sought to create his own studio, and after six months of teaching at GADA, he moved to Harlem, where the Afro-American Studio for Acting and Speech began to take shape. Gossett wrote McClintock a favorable letter of recommendation (see Figure 1.7) for prospective future employers. Gossett wrote, "He has been loyal and dedicated in all of his many projects at the school and was instrumental in setting up the entire scholastic program."[79] In 1973, in an interview with PhD candidate Robert Wilson, when McClintock was asked about leaving GADA and starting his own school, he simply stated that he did not want to be in an integrated situation, but through the experience of working in an integrated school he had been "riddled by this burning desire to create a Black theatre school."[80] McClintock's pedagogical insistence on an all-Black school echoes Malcolm X's "The Ballot or the Bullet" speech, in which he prioritized Black unity over interracial alliances. McClintock revered Malcolm X and aligned with his philosophy so much that at his school and in his theatre companies throughout his career, he repeatedly produced a play about Malcolm X, N. R. Davidson's *El Hajj Malik*. From an acting standpoint, McClintock identified a need for Black self-expression rooted in Afrocentricity, a community of actors, and a professional Black Theatre school. He came to this artistic and educational awakening in 1965, the very same year that Malcolm X was assassinated. A turning point in the struggle for civil rights, the assassination was a pivotal moment for Black nationalists—which McClintock and Walker considered themselves to be—and Malcolm X's untimely death undoubtedly contributed to their own artistic awakening.

Conclusion

Certainly, one's upbringing and immediate surroundings influence who a person becomes and how they see the world. For McClintock, while the close-knit segregated Blackbelt exemplified racist zoning laws, it also provided a life full of and surrounded by Black cultural sensibilities and highlighted the importance of community. His childhood memories were tethered to music, art, and live performance, despite theatre not being at the center of his life at that stage. The experience of seeing performers who were his elders—such as Sarah Vaughan, Moms Mabley, and Dinah Washington—advancing their Afrocentric aesthetic on stage, connecting with a Black audience, and upending theatres under white ownership must have been powerful. Once McClintock saw theatre's potential to move an audience and learned about Frank Silvera, his desire to be a theatre artist was ignited. At a time when there was limited representation on television of people whose experiences mirrored his own, seeing these folks who were part of the African Diaspora ignited a calling in McClintock to create theatre by, for, and about Black people. He pursued education in formal schools and conservatories and performed across Chicago. In a sense, he was searching for something—a school, an Afrocentric approach that had not existed in his immediate reality. Certainly, Afrocentric acting techniques existed, but mainstream institutions did not prioritize diversifying their curricula.

When McClintock arrived in New York, he learned a great deal from Gossett and had his first introduction to directing and teaching. To pursue his own pedagogy and aesthetic, he moved to Harlem and created the very institution he was yearning for as a young artist. Alongside his contemporaries in the Black Theatre Movement, McClintock filled a gap in training to meet the needs of actors who looked like him. Over the next five years, McClintock, along with Ronald Walker and soon-to-be-friend Marc Primus, opened the Afro-American Studio for Acting and Speech, changing the lives of those who walked through the door.

Notes

1 Knupfer, "African-American Designers," 84.
2 Canaan, "Part of the Loaf," 167.
3 Canaan, "Part of the Loaf," 157.
4 Canaan, "Part of the Loaf," 162.
5 Haller, "Policy Gambling," 724.
6 Haller, "Policy Gambling," 724.
7 Chafe, *The Unfinished Journey*, 138–39.
8 Chafe, *The Unfinished Journey*, 106.
9 Elam, "African American Theatre," 375.
10 Chafe, *The Unfinished Journey*, 138.
11 Gorn, "Emmett Till."
12 "Emmett Till's Funeral."
13 Trask, "Gay and Lesbian Literary Culture in the 1950s," 157.
14 Trask, "Gay and Lesbian Literary Culture," 157.
15 Trask, "Gay and Lesbian Literary Culture," 157.
16 Wilson and Tribune Staff Writer, "Gay Life in Chicago."
17 Wilson and Tribune Staff Writer, "Gay Life in Chicago."
18 Wilson and Tribune Staff Writer, "Gay Life in Chicago."
19 Trask, "Gay and Lesbian Literary Culture," 158.
20 Melissa Barton's article on the Negro People's Theater in Chicago appropriated the notion of the "people's theatre" from a growing trend in the Depression era with a focus on the local "people's" culture. For more information, see Barton, "Speaking a Mutual Language."
21 Kamau, "All That Theater Jazz," 1.
22 Watson, "McClintock," 9.
23 Watson, "McClintock," 9.
24 Semmes, *The Regal Theater*, 3.
25 Semmes, *The Regal Theater*, 1.
26 Jones, "Slavery, Performance," 16, emphasis in original.
27 Jones, "Slavery, Performance," 15.
28 Blackface minstrelsy emerged in the nineteenth century; white men caricatured African American men in a corked blackface, solidifying and perpetuating stereotypes. Black performers Bert Williams and George Walker subverted the form and toured the American theatre circuit, eventually making it to Broadway. Williams and Walker reclaimed this painful theatrical device to challenge stereotypes and, through their success, paved the way for Black Americans on Broadway. For

more information on Black subversion in performance in the twentieth century, see Cizmar, "Charles S. Gilpin's *The Emperor*."
29 Semmes, *The Regal Theater*, 8.
30 Call and response has been acknowledged in various pockets of African American culture, including art and politics. For more information, see Burton and Gates, *Call and Response*.
31 Semmes, *The Regal Theater*, 8.
32 Semmes argues that domestic colonialism is a subcategory of cultural hegemony, which he defines as "the process by which the institutional and historical trajectory of one group calls into dissolution the independence, coherence, and viability of another," 11.
33 Semmes, *The Regal Theater*, 10.
34 McConachie, "Concept of Cultural Hegemony," 38–39.
35 McConachie, "Concept of Cultural Hegemony," 39.
36 McConachie, "Concept of Cultural Hegemony," 42.
37 McConachie, "Concept of Cultural Hegemony," 41.
38 Semmes, *The Regal Theater*, 10.
39 Kamau, "All That Theater Jazz," 1.
40 Watson, "McClintock," 9.
41 Kamau, "All That Theater Jazz," 1.
42 Kamau, "All That Theater Jazz," 1.
43 Thompson, "Frank Who?"
44 Thompson, "Frank Who?"
45 Ottley, "Negro Actor Frank Silver," 19.
46 There is no evidence that McClintock was present for this performance.
47 Watson, "McClintock," 9.
48 Watson, "McClintock," 9.
49 Kamau, "All That Theater Jazz," 1.
50 Ernie McClintock's obituary, from a program for a memorial service held in Richmond, Virginia. From the private collection of Geno Brantley.
51 "Mobile Unit."
52 Phillips, "All I Wanted," 43.
53 Phillips, "All I Wanted," 43.
54 Phillips, "All I Wanted," 43.
55 Ernie McClintock Resume. 2000. Accession 41088, Business Records Collection, The Library of Virginia, Richmond, Virginia. On his resume it states that he took "Miscellaneous Correspondence Courses" at the United States Armed Forces Institute from 1960 to 1961 in Kansas. In the archives there are two different résumés—one written in New York in the 1960s and the other written in Richmond in the 1990s.
56 Phillips, "All I Wanted," 47.
57 Kamau, "All That Theater Jazz," 1.
58 Kamau, "All That Theater Jazz," 1.
59 Kamau, "All That Theater Jazz," 1.
60 The Second City is an improvisational theatre troupe based in Chicago. They offer classes on improv, storytelling, and stand-up in Chicago Toronto, and Los Angeles. For more information: www.thesecondcity.com.
61 "Obituary of Helen Espie."
62 Thaddeus Daniels, interview by Elizabeth Cizmar.
63 Thaddeus Daniels, interview by Elizabeth Cizmar.
64 Gossett Academy of Dramatic Arts information pamphlet. From the Private Collection of Geno Brantley.
65 Joseph,*'Til the Midnight Hour*, 38.

66 Kalb, *The Congo Cables*, 63–67.
67 Elam, "Post-World War II African American Theatre," 375.
68 Elam, "Post-World War II African American Theatre," 381.
69 Elam, "Post-World War II African American Theatre," 378.
70 Joseph, *'Til the Midnight Hour*, 26.
71 Kalb, *The Congo Cables*, 225.
72 Serwer, "Maya Angelou."
73 Joseph, *'Til the Midnight Hour*, 40.
74 Library of Congress, "Before Stonewall."
75 Library of Congress, "Before Stonewall."
76 Yurcaba, "Different Fight."
77 Watson, "McClintock," 9.
78 On McClintock's résumé, neither the playwrights nor dates are listed for these plays. Gylan Kain's play *Epitaph To A Coagulated Trinity* was published in 1970, but McClintock left GADA in 1965. So it is possible he returned as a guest director, but the archival evidence is unclear. Ernie McClintock Resume. 2000. Accession 41088, Business Records Collection, The Library of Virginia, Richmond, Virginia.
79 Gossett Letter of Recommendation. From the Private Collection of Geno Brantley.
80 Ernie McClintock, interview by Robert Wilson.

Bibliography

Barton, Melissa. "Speaking a Mutual Language: The Negro People's Theatre in Chicago." *TDR: The Drama Review* 54, no. 3 (2010): 54–70.

Burton, Jennifer, and Henry Louis Gates, Jr. eds. *Call and Response: Key Debates in African American Studies*. New York: Norton, 2001.

Canaan, Gareth. "'Part of the Loaf': Economic Conditions of Chicago's African-American Working Class during the 1920s." *Journal of Social History* 35, no. 1 (2001): 147–74.

Chafe, William. *The Unfinished Journey*, 3rd ed. New York: Oxford University Press, 1995.

Cizmar, Elizabeth M. "Charles S. Gilpin's *The Emperor Jones*: Afrocentric Approaches and Subversion in Performance." *Theatre/Practice: The Online Journal of the Practice/Production Symposium of the Mid-America Theatre Conference* 11 (2022). https://www.theatrepractice.us/current.html.

Daniels, Thaddeus. Interview by Elizabeth Cizmar, August 15, 2015, Jersey City, NJ.

Elam, Harry, Jr. "Post-World War II African American Theatre." In *The Oxford Handbook of America Drama*, edited by Jeffrey H. Richards and Heather S. Nathans, 375–92. New York: Oxford University Press, 1998.

"Emmett Till's Funeral." American Experience, n.d., video clip, 01:43. Accessed April 5, 2022. https://www.pbs.org/wgbh/americanexperience/features/emmett-tills-funeral/.

Gorn, Elliott J. "Emmett Till and Civil Rights: Why We Remember His Name." *Time*, November 18, 2018. https://time.com/5440997/emmett-till-remembrance/.

Haller, Mark. "Policy Gambling, Entertainment, and the Emergence of Black Politics: Chicago from 1900 to 1940." *Journal of Social History* 24, no. 4 (1991): 719–39.

Jones, Douglas A., Jr. "Slavery, Performance, and the Design of African American Theatre." In *The Cambridge Companion to African American Theatre*, edited by Harvey Young, 15–33. Cambridge: Cambridge University Press, 2013.

Joseph, Peniel. *'Til the Midnight Hour: A Narrative History of Black Power in America*. New York: Henry Holt, 2006.

Kalb, Madeleine G. *The Congo Cables: The Cold War in Africa—From Eisenhower to Kennedy*. New York: Macmillan Publishing, 1982.

Kamau, Kwadwo Agymah. "All That Theater Jazz." *Style Weekly*, September 1, 1992, 1.

Knupfer, Anne Meis. "African-American Designers: The Chicago Experience Then and Now." *Design Issues* 15, no. 3 (2000): 84–91.

Library of Congress. "Before Stonewall: The Homophile Movement." LGBTQIA+ Studies: A Resource Guide. n.d. Accessed April 4, 2022. https://guides.loc.gov/lgbtq-studies/before-stonewall.

McClintock, Ernie. Interview by Robert Wilson, June 13, 1973, New York, NY. Countee-Cullen Harold Jackman Memorial Collection, Archives Research Center, Atlanta University Center.

McConachie, Bruce. "Using the Concept of Cultural Hegemony to Write Theatre History." In *Interpreting the Theatrical Past: Essays in the Historiography of Performance*, edited by Bruce McConachie and Thomas Postlewait, 37–58. Iowa City: University of Iowa Press, 1989.

"Mobile Unit." The Public Theater. n.d. Accessed April 7, 2022. https://publictheater.org/programs/mobile-unit/.

"Obituary of Helen Espie." *Chicago Tribune*, July 1, 1993. http://articles.chicagotribune.com/1993-07-01/news/9307010165_1_chicago-fine-arts-building-actors.

Ottley, Roi. "Negro Actor Frank Silver Delights South Side Audience," *Chicago Tribune*, November 11, 1956, 19.

Phillips, Kimberly L. "'All I Wanted Was a Steady Job:' The State of African American Workers." In *New Working Class Studies*, edited by John Russo and Sherry Lee Linkon, 42–53. Ithaca, NY: Cornell University Press, 2005.

Semmes, Clovis E. *The Regal Theater and Black Culture*. New York: Palgrave Macmillan, 2006.

Serwer, Adam. "Maya Angelou, Radical Activist." *MSNBC*, May 29, 2014. https://www.msnbc.com/msnbc/maya-angelou-radical-activist-msna338781.

Thompson, Garland Lee, Sr. "Frank Who? The Man of a Thousand Space." Frank Silvera Writers Workshop. Accessed February 1, 2021. https://thefsww.org/frank-who%3F.

Trask, Michael. "Gay and Lesbian Literary Culture in the 1950s." In *American Literature in Transition*, edited by Steven Belletto, 157–69. Cambridge: Cambridge University Press, 2017.

Watson, Jamantha Williams. "McClintock." *Black Masks* (August/September 1996): 9–10.

Wilson, Terry, and Tribune Staff Writer. "Gay Life in Chicago." *Chicago Tribune*, October 21, 1997. https://www.chicagotribune.com/news/ct-xpm-1997-10-21-9710210045-story.html.

Yurcaba, Jo. "Different Fight, 'Same Goal': How the Black Freedom Movement Inspired Early Gay Activists." *NBC News*, February 28, 2021. https://www.nbcnews.com/feature/nbcout/different-fight-same-goal-how-black-freedom-movement-inspired-early-n1259072.

2
SHAKING UP HARLEM (1965–1972)

In the winter of 1966, Ernie McClintock left his teaching position at the Gossett Academy of Dramatic Arts, and on March 28, 1966, the Afro-American Studio for Acting and Speech officially opened its doors in Harlem, the iconic neighborhood of Black culture and life. At the Gossett Academy, McClintock taught two courses, "An Introduction to Acting and Theatre" and "Acting I: Technique and Character Development," where he identified goals that later appeared at his own school: to establish an actor training institution for, by, and about Black artists. His impetus for opening the Afro-American Studio for Acting and Speech was not just due to the dearth of Afrocentric acting methods at a formal institutional level, but based on his observations of actors playing roles that were monolithic or misrepresentative of African American experiences. In an article on his technique, he gestures to these observations by stating that an actor is more than a "shell" aimlessly moving around the stage (Figure 2.1). In the studio's archives, McClintock does not chastise specific actors who missed the mark, presumably because he aimed to lift up his community. Rather, his observations are centered on pedagogical trends and output from the entertainment industry in terms of acting styles and characters written for Black folk. Walking up the stairs of the Afro-American Studio for Acting & Speech located on 15 West 126th Street, a new student would be greeted with the emblem of the Studio and a sign, "In this humble place, this very humble place, acting is taught" (Figures 2.2 and 2.3). The 126th Street location was the former home of the American Negro Theatre in the old Elks Lodge building, and so, the ancestors of previous generations had inhabited such a space.

McClintock posited that the majority of Black actors were not bringing their fullest selves to character creation and were imitating whiteness or producing superficial character portrayals. Thus, his school centered on a cultural

DOI: 10.4324/9781003187448-3

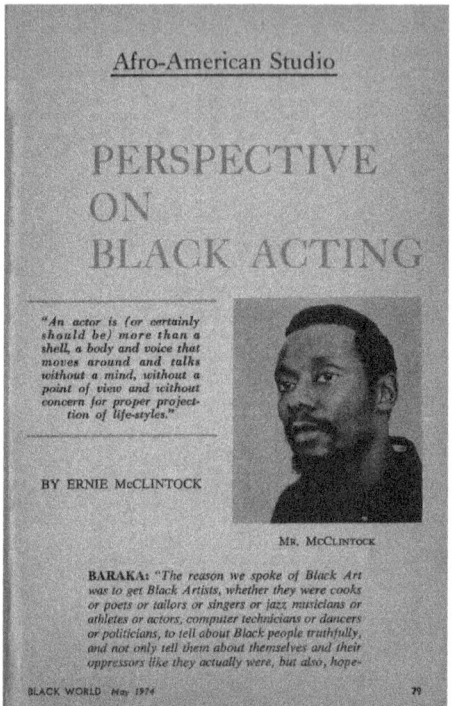

FIGURE 2.1 "Perspective on Black Acting," *Black World* May 1974.
Credit: Private collection of Elizabeth M. Cizmar.

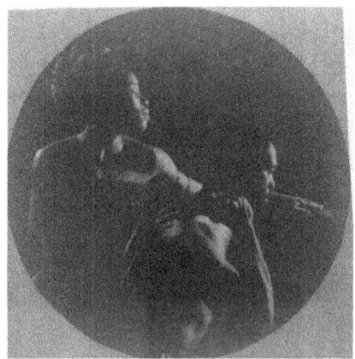

FIGURE 2.2 Logo of the Afro-American Studio for Acting and Speech. L to R: Joan Green, Carl Ajaye.
Credit: Private collection of Joan Green.

system outside of Stanislavski-based techniques, during an era when Lee Strasberg's Method was rising in popularity in mainstream training. Furthermore, McClintock understood the value of including multiple Black perspectives in a theatrical space. Due to his Black queer positionality, his worldview yielded a more inclusive aesthetic, and yet his conscious inclusivity paired with his sexual

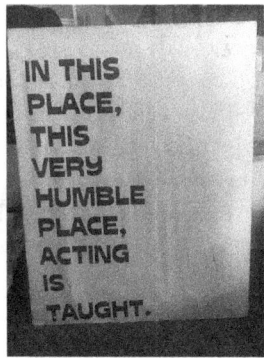

FIGURE 2.3 Sign Hung in the Afro-American Studio for Acting and Speech.
Credit: Private collection of Geno Brantley.

orientation are the very reasons he was excluded by many of his contemporaries and subsequently left out of theatre histories and practices.

This chapter explores the early days of the Afro-American Studio for Acting and Speech (1966–1972), highlighting how the development of the school and Jazz Acting reflected McClintock's core belief that self-expression and community building engenders an inclusive acting technique and performance aesthetic. As a gay Black man in the 1960s Harlem, McClintock and Ronald Walker, his life and creative partner, along with historian Marc Primus spearheaded a school centered on Black self-expression and storytelling. They felt an immense responsibility to their Black community and set high expectations for their students to commit to the school's mission, take off their proverbial armor, and trust their fellow ensemble members. For these actors, the technique taught them to connect to their individual and collective identities, which proved to be an effective and truthful approach in theatrical performance.

My research method for this chapter includes consulting secondary sources, diving into public and private archives, and interviewing McClintock's students to analyze the radical ways in which McClintock challenged the status quo in terms of identity through his teaching and productions. In the early 1960s, McClintock developed an acting technique initially referred to as "the theatre of common sense," renamed Jazz Acting in the early 1990s. The core principles of the technique remained steadfast, but his craft and pedagogy shifted according to the student demographic and sociopolitical factors. Jazz Acting is founded on the notion of a jazz ensemble, which roots a song in a melody yet invites moments of musical improvisation known as riffs. Jazz Acting teaches actors to find "melodies" in scripted and unscripted material to ground their performance. Melodies include the text itself, physical and vocal choices, script analysis, and observations of daily Black life. Once actors fully grasp these intellectual and physical aspects of character creation, they find riffs and play off one another in performance.

Here I apply an Afrocentric lens to the analysis and recovery of McClintock's legacy, focusing on self-expression and community healing. As defined by Molefi Kete Asante, Afrocentrism is a framework that is "a moral as well as an intellectual location that posits Africans as subjects rather than objects of human history."[1] McClintock's focus on Afrocentric actor training and unearthing the Black artist's authentic self also echoes Alain Locke's work from the Harlem Renaissance.[2] The synergy between McClintock and Locke's theories lies in their emphasis on the actor and their potential to propel social change: "A race of actors can revolutionize the drama quite as definitely and perhaps more vitally than a coterie of dramatists."[3] This chapter illuminates how McClintock's training responded to the shortcomings of Eurocentric training, which privileges white bodies and views Black bodies as objects. By creating the Afro-American Studio for Acting and Speech, his work features Black bodies and experiences. In this chapter, I analyze the fundamental elements of the technique and how he nurtured each individual's self-expression while healing their spirit.

For McClintock, fostering self-expression while engaging in community outreach yielded a diverse student population producing stories from various Black perspectives. It is important here to identify what inclusivity meant to McClintock, Primus, and Walker in the 1960s, which differs in some ways from contemporary notions and practices. McClintock included women's, Black Power, immigrant, and cis gay man narratives. From our contemporary vantage point, it is evident that he was not all-encompassing in thinking about nonbinary, disabled, and lesbian narratives.

In the context of the 1960s–1970s, in which the mainstream entertainment industries relegated Black identity to monolithic or stereotypical roles, McClintock's inclusive pedagogy promoted the multiplicity of Black identity in the theatre. Specifically, Breena Clarke, novelist and friend of the Studio pointed out that McClintock cast both light-skinned and dark-skinned women, which was not typical at other companies:

> ... it's a color issue. In the Negro Ensemble Company, dark skinned women weren't cast certainly not in leads... you can look at the history of productions and look at whose cast and make the leap and it's not a big leap. I'm not disparaging those women... But they were all of a certain color and that was the tacit agreement.[4]

As her partner, actor Helmar Cooper noted, the difference between McClintock's theatres and other institutions of the time was "the spirit of inclusion."[5] Despite his inclusive approach, particular sects of Black Power activists marginalized McClintock as an apolitical figure whose queer positionality and inclusivity might threaten aspects of their activism. As a result, the Afro-American Studio for Acting and Speech and his legacy have been left out of dominant history narratives.

When researching Ernie McClintock on the internet or in a library, there are few sources that emerge. The most extensive of these includes Mance Williams' *Black Theatre in the 1960s and 1970s* (1985), which is now out of print.

Williams provides a healthy overview of McClintock and acknowledges the Afro-American Studio for Acting and Speech as one of the prominent theatres in Harlem during the Black Theatre Movement. However, aside from these 3.5 pages, McClintock appears as a passing footnote or in a paragraph, at best. While figures like Amiri Baraka, Larry Neal, and Ed Bullins are critical to history, there are other figures like Ernie McClintock whose contributions are just as significant to the movement.

The chapter concludes with two prominent productions realizing jazz aesthetics in performance, *Where It's At* and *El Hajj Malik*, which brought the company notoriety and propelled McClintock into a place of prominence during the Black Arts Movement. These productions—one an unscripted street theatre performance and the other a biography of Malcolm X—illustrate the versatility of material of McClintock's company and the effectiveness of Jazz Acting as a performance technique. Both are political theatre, and *Where It's At* demonstrates how the technique allows actors to collectively create new material, connect directly to communities, and speak to the sociopolitical concerns of Black lives. McClintock's street theatre offered a variety of Black perspectives from his company members who were gay, straight, men, women, immigrants, Black Nationalists, and more. N. R. Davidson's play, *El Hajj Malik*, explores the life of Malcolm X from his adolescence to his assassination. The Afro-American Studio's production was political not just in performance but in the process of creation. For some, it might seem that a queer artist and an icon of Black masculinity and nationalism would be at odds. However, there is a strong synergy between McClintock and Malcolm X related to Jazz Acting, which directly correlates with Malcolm X's call for Black folks to self-determine outside white hegemony.

Filling a Gap

In the early 1960s, Ernie McClintock's belief that actor training catered to white bodies and white storytelling supports Shonni Enelow's notion that predominant acting techniques lack neutrality or objectivity.[6] McClintock pointed out that Stanislavski-based acting methods produced Black actors who were not being themselves or were imitating whiteness.[7] Establishing an Afrocentric technique challenged the status quo; McClintock's focus, however, was not necessarily impugning mainstream schools but filling a gap in actor training for people of color in the mid-twentieth century. Broadly speaking, the studio was created to provide actor training and mount productions that reflected Black culture and expressed Black perspectives during a volatile era in US history.

In addition to producing Black actors trained in Eurocentric methods, theatre departments at predominantly white institutions produced white narratives. In scene work, students were given roles written by white, male playwrights.[8] This "one size fits all" approach not only limits actors of color but fails to acknowledge the individuality of each student and often includes an overwhelming number of scenes by white playwrights, where student actors are cast in roles written for white bodies. In a 1969 interview with *Ebony* magazine, McClintock stated:

> Learning to act can be a great source of frustration for a talented Black person.... Few theatre schools possess training methods that will be of much value to his development... in white schools, you will be given scenes to perform that are based upon the white world—white characters dealing with white problems. Since scene work and character development is such an important part of training, Black actors need to work on scenes that involve Black characters dealing with Black problems.[9]

Furthermore, "imitating the imitation" in white-penned scenes implies that Black actors were not given tools for authentic self-expression. E. Patrick Johnson observes that the idea of authenticity suggests the existence of the inauthentic, a fake.[10] The inauthentic representation of Blackness can take the form of a stereotype, such as the coon, Black Brute, mammy, and lascivious mulatto, where "whites constructing blackness used to maintain white hegemony and in turn physical violence, poverty, institutional racism, and second-class citizenry for blacks."[11] The production and reproduction of stereotypes is a multilayered and complex social phenomenon whereby the oppressor becomes dominant and erases Black voices.[12] Mainstream schools trained actors to fulfill roles dictated by the entertainment industry—a business that upholds a white cisgender, heteronormative cultural system.

In the classroom and on stage, McClintock's teaching and productions are distinguished from his peer institutions in Harlem who produced plays from a singular genre of Black Theatre. For example, the New Lafayette Theatre (Robert Macbeth, artistic director and Ed Bullins, resident writer) produced plays that were socially conscious with a focus on Bullins' work that primarily centered on lives of urban Black folk. Barbara Ann Teer's National Black Theatre rejected all western ways of creating and producing theatre and developed what Teer referred to as "God-conscious art."[13] McClintock's students tackled a variety of writers and genres including womanist works, Black revolutionary plays, and Afro-Caribbean pieces. He showed how expanding inclusive programming for curriculum and production seasons requires more than just checking the proverbial diversity box. In 1971, McClintock explained his constant quest for versatile material: "I am always looking for more material... the most representative kinds of things for our students to work on, to give them a variety of material. We don't do one kind of Black material."[14] His dedication to exploring many facets of Blackness across the diaspora, including works by Ntozake Shange, Dereck Walcott, James Baldwin, Richard Wesley, and Amiri Baraka demonstrated how Blackness is not monolithic.

Gwendolen Hardwick, a studio pupil turned instructor, studied at New York University's prestigious Tisch School of the Arts after learning under McClintock's tutelage. She said that in her time at NYU, the teachers did not provide plays or scenes by Black authors. In sum, "they didn't know what to do with us."[15] For Tisch acting students' final culmination of their training, the school hired a white, Russian director to mount Anton Chekhov's *The Cherry Orchard* (1904). Along with three students of color, Hardwick refused to participate in a production constructed from a Eurocentric lens. She insisted that the school hire director Glenda Dickerson where Dickerson and the actors drew from different Greek tragedies, constructing a theatrical piece entitled *Atreus Aegyptus*. Glenda Dickerson was a playwright, director, theorist, and performer who was the second Black woman to direct on Broadway.[16] Along with Hardwick's commitment to activism prior to enrolling in the Afro-American Studio for Acting and Speech, her training with McClintock and Primus further nurtured her sense of self-determination. McClintock instilled agency in his students, which became intrinsically tethered to their artistic identity (Figure 2.4).

For McClintock, an Afrocentric school necessitated that Black actors connect with their history, culture, and writers who spoke to their experiences. He recognized Black actors' longing for self-healing and personal histories. Ultimately, he believed that if Black actors gained an education in their shared heritage, they would have a stronger sense of identity. For many African Americans, it is difficult to locate an extensive family tree because of the institution of slavery. The slave trade eviscerated cultures and tore humans from their families and homelands, making it difficult to trace one's lineage. Thus, an acting approach that asks students to engage in emotional recall, common in mainstream approaches, creates the possibility of reliving immediate and distant traumas that potentially reopen or exacerbate wounds. But there is an African American collective history, a connection to ancestry from the African

FIGURE 2.4 Candid Photo and Description, Marcus Hemphill, Glenda Dickerson, and Ernie McClintock following *Atreus Aegyptus* at NYU, December 1980.

Credit: Private collection of Geno Brantley.

continent and culture that adapted, survived, and thrived despite dehumanization from the slave trade and beyond. In McClintock's school, Black actors learning about their collective past aided them in healing from cultural trauma, connecting with their predecessors, and accessing their individual voices in the African continuum.

Foundations of the Technique: Healing and Self-Expression

In 1965, Ernie McClintock and Ronald Walker met Marc Primus, and a lifelong collaboration began. Three artists whom Primus describes as twice-marginalized (Black and gay) were the founding fathers of a school that healed young actors and taught students to bring their individual identities into a rehearsal environment consisting solely of Black artists. They met in the summer in New York, where McClintock was teaching at Gossett's academy but was yearning to open his own studio. After moving from San Francisco with his folkloric troupe, Primus's company began to turn a profit:

> [Ernie and Ronald] came over to my apartment and as soon as I knew they were on their way I took $100 and put it on the steps of the second landing in my apartment house so he would find the $100 so he could start his studio. He found it; he immediately knew that I put that money there... we rented him space on 133rd street in Harlem and that's how the first studio was founded.[17]

In March 1966, the Afro-American Studio for Acting & Speech officially opened in the epicenter of the Black Theatre Movement.

McClintock's queer identity in the 1960s Harlem created a pathway for acceptance of alternative points of view that are equally representative of the Black Arts Movement. As scholars E. Patrick Johnson and Marc Anthony Neal identify, the era of Black Power highlighted supposed contention between queer and Black identities. However, McClintock ruptures these notions not just by his presence in the Black Theatre Movement, but by his radical inclusivity. The spirit and practice of inclusion in the Afro-American Studio distinguishes this school from other companies in Harlem at the time. His inclusivity extended to his student population as well as the versatility of plays produced in the Advanced Workshop, which in 1973 became the professional arm of the studio, named the 127th Street Repertory Ensemble. Harlem, McClintock and Walker's newly adopted home, was socioeconomically depressed yet politically advanced where the couple connected directly with addicts, former sex workers, and criminalized people. Actors could sign up for courses even if they had no experience on stage. The structure of the program included rigorous study, discipline, and commitment to the craft. McClintock expected his students to take the vocation of theatre as seriously as he did.

ADVANCED THEATRE WORKSHOP is the major performing group at the Studio. Actors are selected for this workshop by the director.

Productions

1967-68
Clandestine on the Morning Line
Fortune and Men's Eyes
Moon on a Rainbow Shawl
Ododo
Amen Corner
Black Nativity

1969
Day of Absence
Dutchman
Take Care of Business
Roots
Clara's Ole Man
Where Its At

1970
Baptism
Where Its At "70"
Roots
Flowers for the Trashman
Clara's Ole Man
El Hajj Malik

1971
Baptism
Madheart
Black Dada Nihilismus
Shoes
Contribution
The Toilet
The Electronic Nigger
Voodoo Ceremony
El Hajj Malik

BOARD OF DIRECTORS

Ernie McClintock .... President
Ron Walker .... Vice-President
Pat Caldwell .... Secretary-Treasurer
Ray Davis · Aramentha Hamilton

STUDIO STAFF

Ernie McClintock .... Director
Marc Primus .... Associate Director
Ron Walker .... Technical Director
George Carter .... Special Projects
Francine Major .... Coordinator
Preston Davis .... Fund Raising
Bruce Wallace .... Asst. to the Director

"Stimulating the awareness of the Black experience and projecting it through Theatre."

AFRO-AMERICAN
STUDIO for
ACTING and SPEECH

**FALL
1972**

415 WEST 127th STREET
NEW YORK CITY 10027
866-5391-2-3

The Afro-American Studio is a member of the Black Theatre Alliance

---

The Afro-American Studio for Acting and Speech is dedicated to providing quality theatre training and productions within the Harlem Community. Over the past six years the studio has developed and refined a Black theatre curriculum.

The Basic Actor Training Program consists generally of 5 terms which are 10 weeks each. Instruction at the Studio is based on a technique which allows each student to use his own experience in portraying characters. Emphasis is placed on observations and use of various black life styles. In addition to receiving intensive training in theatrical techniques students become more aware of their identity through various sessions that deal with black culture and history.

This program made possible partially through grants and donations from the following:

Friends of the Afro-American Studio
New York State Council on the Arts
Rockefeller Brothers Fund
National Endowment for the Arts
Harlem Cultural Council
John Hay Whitney Foundation
Louise L. Ottinger Charitable Trust
Ann Pierson
Honor Moore

FALL TERM
Ten Week Study Program
September 11 thru November 18

SESSION ONE
Monday, 2-2:55pm
   MOVEMENT
Monday, 3-4:25pm
   BLACK THEATRE HISTORY
Monday, 5-5:55pm
   SPEECH
Thursday, 2-3:25pm
   STRETCHING OUT
Thursday, 3:30-6pm
   ACTING TECHNIQUE

SESSION TWO
Wednesday, 6-7:25pm
   STRETCHING OUT
Wednesday, 7:30-8:55pm
   BLACK THEATRE HISTORY
Wednesday, 9-10:00pm
   SPEECH
Saturday, 10am-12:25pm
   ACTING TECHNIQUE
Saturday, 12:30-1:25pm
   MOVEMENT

Total class fee $125.00 per term. For persons unable to pay the full amount at registration the following payment plan is offered:

$ 50.00 August 18
$ 50.00 September 16
$ 25.00 September 30

$125.00—Total payment must be made as specified above
Please note orientation and registration will be conducted on Friday, Aug. 18 at 7pm sharp.

Classes and Workshops

Acting Technique · Audition Preparatory · Black Aesthetic · Black Theatre History · Body Conditioning · Dance Workshop · Directors Training Program · Karate · Make-Up · Movement · Poetry Theatre · Production Workshop · Rehearsal and Performance · Scene Study · Speech · Stretching Out · Visual Communication · Vocal Technique · Vocal Workshop · Yoga ·

INSTRUCTORS

Woody Carter · Helmar Cooper · Guye Fortune · Jim Mallette · Ernie McClintock · Marc Primus · Milo Timmons · Ron Walker · Bruce Wallace ·

FIGURE 2.5 Brochure for the Afro-American Studio for Acting and Speech, fall 1971.
Credit: Private collection of Elizabeth M. Cizmar.

In a 1972 brochure for the Afro-American Studio (Figure 2.5), the offerings list courses in movement, theatre history, speech, and acting; however, the key difference between these classes at McClintock's studio versus Stanislavski's training is his Afrocentric underpinnings.[18] To approach characters in an acting class, one had to have a firm foundation in Black Theatre History and Stretching Out, a course designed for actors to achieve physical freedom. McClintock's acting technique also required students to be fully physically engaged, from their head to their toes, necessitating kinesthetic awareness of their bodies and stamina to sustain the rigorous demands. As Jazz Actor Jerome Preston Bates articulated "He really believed in not only actors speaking but encompassing the play, the character [lives] in your [body]...otherwise you just walk around stiff. He brought in choreographers and he really believed in movement and speech."[19] Hence, body conditioning, dance, karate, and yoga were folded into the training. Through this technique, the actors nurtured themselves and their greater community, and the studio became known as a "temple of healing."[20]

For McClintock, the healing occurred during training, so actors could portray characters through a Black perspective, connect the primarily Black audiences to a shared past, and unify in their present struggles. In 1972, he wrote the following mission statement:

> For the Black actor and audience, the theatre should culminate in a feeling of sharing of self in a spiritually uplifting and reflective, unique experience. The self-awareness and awareness of others should result in seeking more and greater such experiences, which in turn, will lead to conscious or unconscious positive actions.[21]

Part of this healing is a specific practice that contextualizes African-inspired values and the rehabilitation of dislocation and subjugation, beginning with the Middle Passage.[22] This framework reflects a collective historical memory of the trauma and the collective response of healing in a ritualized environment, the acting classroom.

In addition to being one of the founders, Primus was the instructor for Black Theatre History, guiding students' discovery of a shared Afrocentric history. He situates his pedagogical approach in what he refers to as a "democratic history."[23] The foundational texts he used to offset dominant narratives include Nathan Irvin Huggins's *Black Odyssey: The African-American Ordeal in Slavery* (1977) and Loften Mitchell's *Black Drama* (1967). He integrated his own exercise, known as historio-drama, where actors "performed roles of historical figures of that time period. It wasn't Patrick Henry, it was Patrick Henry's slave."[24] Notably, Primus's historio-drama predates Lin-Manuel Miranda's *Hamilton* (2015) in terms of actors of color portraying a range of historical figures. Unlike Miranda's reenvisioning of antebellum America, Primus included the perspectives of enslaved Africans.

Primus fondly recalled teaching at the studio, where students were eager to learn about African American history. By understanding the history of Black bodies crossing the Middle Passage and the tradition of Black performance on the American stage, students understood their role in the larger context of the Black Arts Movement and attained a clear sense of who they were as a culture and a people. Woody Carter, PhD, a student and later teacher at the studio, articulated:

> We had a role as part of the Black Power movement. We weren't on the front lines, but as Black people in Black Arts our role was to portray, clarify, explore, the Black experience for Black people so that they could have a better understand[ing] of themselves in relation to their place in time in terms of history and contemporary America. It was our responsibility through the theatre.[25]

These courses were essential to many of the students who had little or no education in their ancestral past and its profound connection to the present. Hence, with a curriculum based in African American history, the Afro-American Studio's pedagogy was a political act.

Primus began his courses with *Black Odyssey* because Huggins's account does not commence with enslavement in America but with Africans in their native lands.[26] Huggins highlights the capture and objectification of African bodies as not just an individual offense. Entire African villages were mutilated, whether or not the whole community was captured.[27] In the introduction, he states that the book "focuses on the emotional and spiritual essence of their experience; to evoke what I believe to have been the psychological and spiritual sense of order and place that was destroyed by the slave trade."[28] The enlightening point of view captures the reality that the tragedy of the Middle Passage included horrific brutality and violence toward the enslaved, and that the slave trade altered an entire framework of life—those left in Africa and those who faced the Middle Passage.[29]

Huggins's analysis of how African Americans translated their African roots in North America connects directly to a McClintock interview conducted by Rhett Jones in 1981 highlighting Blackness's relationship to whiteness. In the final chapter of his book, Huggins states, "The making of the Afro-American people was a process of blending the old with the new, changing the old into something that was new and that could survive a world in the making."[30] For example, Christianity became a spiritual base for many slaves even though they converted from their indigenous religions. They adapted their spiritual reality to Christianity by adding an African texture.[31] So there is a negotiation of the old and the new and, in the 1960s, an effort to define what Blackness is. McClintock took this notion even a step further by echoing James Baldwin, who said, "the artist has the responsibility not only to redefine himself in relation to his culture, but to redefine the culture which has created him."[32] Before one can redefine a culture, one must understand the oppression and the history of that culture. Huggins traces the journey of Africans to the New World, where people were dehumanized and tortured, yet somehow their cultural spirit survived. Those in the African diaspora created a community that traced back to their African roots. In Black Theatre History, the students were able to learn about their history and identify their pride and power in the diaspora.

Shifting to the practical realm of training, a class known as Stretching Out laid the groundwork for accessing self-expression in rehearsal and performance. Before engaging with text and character, beginner actors had to become comfortable in their bodies and trust their peers. To establish a safe environment, the class provided a space outside the white hegemonic everyday world to be spiritually and mentally free. Similar to other techniques, McClintock believed that "relaxation, both physically and mentally is key" to approaching character[33]; this was not just a solitary exercise, as opposed to other Eurocentric studios like the Actors Studio.[34] In the Afro-American Studio, McClintock emphasized trusting oneself and the ensemble to foster a dynamic where individuals could riff in performance (Figure 2.6).

The actors engaged in whimsical exercises to loosen up, such as embodying an animal and doing trust falls. One controversial exercise included students taking off all their clothes with the intention of being uninhibited physically and mentally. Although many students agree that this exercise was a bit excessive, the idea was that if one can be free and open physically, when it comes time to encounter a role outside their comfort zone, they will have the freedom and confidence to execute the character. These exercises resulted in actors who were fully embodied and took risks: "An Afro-American Studio actor was recognized as being more open than other actors in New York. You could see that as soon as they hit the stage."[35] There is a certain palpable electricity when an

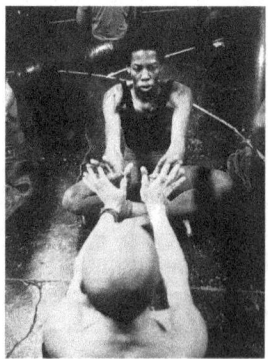

FIGURE 2.6 Physical Warm-Up Exercises at the Afro-American Studio for Acting and Speech.

Credit: Private collection of Geno Brantley.

actor who studied under McClintock makes their entrance on a stage—they are fully in their bodies and completely focused on the present moment.[36] As Helmar Cooper describes "The technique was really to be alive on stage. To live every minute. Don't wait for your cue. People live every minute. That's what...I remember most clearly. Everyone minute you are on stage, be alive."[37] To achieve such vitality and in the moment responses to fellow ensemble members, the foundational aspects of the technique were crucial. When Greta Walker, journalist from the *New Yorker* magazine audited Stretching Out, she witnessed "one student at a time rolled over a prone line of other students lying side by side [and] brought forth a chorus of giggles and groans."[38] The students engaged in tension and release exercises, isolating parts of their body, and as the session progressed and the teacher and pupils became more relaxed "the final exercises involved a great deal of spontaneity,"[39] reminiscent of a jazz ensemble.

While Black Theatre History bridged the ancestral past to the present moment and Stretching Out aimed to open the actor up and trust the ensemble, the basic acting technique class trained students to apply self-expression in scene work. Self-expression is not an ethereal concept but a rigorous framework linked to Malcolm X's charge for African Americans to self-determine. McClintock believed that the actor's independent character creation was a pivotal component in the artistic process:

> The most important part of the creative process is that the creative artist has his creative input, which goes beyond just interpreting what someone else wants. That's part of it, but it's only part. The other part is what the actor wants, being true. A lot of actors find themselves restricted by having to work in situations with directors who are interested in only their point of view being presented.[40]

McClintock required actors to enter the rehearsal hall armed with ideas, physical choices, and an intimate knowledge of their character. Self-expression pushes against the idea that an actor is simply a puppet for a director to manipulate. However, this is not to suggest that the director does not unify the ensemble with vision and guidance. In an acting lecture in 1972, McClintock clearly stated: "[the] director is always the final voice—you cannot alter anything he has not approved. In rehearsals, it's a different story—you can try as many things as you want up to a point."[41] In his view, it was the actor's responsibility to bring a play to a director, who would shape it and make adjustments, and the actor must learn how to make compromises. Hence, McClintock's idea of self-expression implies that the actor was just as much an author of the character as the playwright. The director's job was to curate those artistic choices. The actor's job was to show up for rehearsals, on time, with specific ideas of how to bring the character to life—making the intellectual analysis fully physicalized and vocalized.

Character Creation: Analysis, Center of Gravity, Rhythm, and Community Observations

McClintock's technique developed over the course of his teaching, but there are three fundamental components that ground actors in cultivating self-expression: character analysis, the character's center and rhythm, and community observations. With these tools, actors accessed parts of their identity while using their imagination to create characters. These choices, which were committed to memory and exhaustively rehearsed, became the gateway to riffing in performance—the pinnacle of Jazz Acting.

McClintock's character analysis perhaps resembles Eurocentric approaches, but the distinction is that Jazz Acting is tied to self-determination, whereby Black actors assert their artistic autonomy. McClintock outlined six questions for actors to answer in their preparation work: Who am I? Who am I talking to? Where am I? What are the environmental circumstances? What does the character want and why? What would I be doing if I were the character in this situation?[42] This analysis entails the actor beginning with the script and ascertaining all the information they can from the playwright's text. McClintock insisted that the actor must "understand who that character is better than anyone including the writer, the director."[43] The actor deduces the character's identity from the script and draws on their imagination to fill in the gaps, such as educational background, family makeup, religious beliefs, etc. In this analysis, it is crucial for the actor to answer, "What is the most important thing [the character] does that is not in the time of the play?"[44] In class, McClintock would ask a variety of questions related to the character analysis, and the onus was on the actors to come up with the answers. "I don't know" was an unacceptable response that usually resulted in being dismissed from class. An actor exercising self-expression must be adequately prepared to understand the character's life and make discoveries in rehearsal.

In McClintock's training, physical expression was just as important as figuring out the internal motivations and objectives for a character. Moreover, he taught actors to bombard the audience with information, which included physicality. Just as in everyday human interactions,

> You are known by what you do, not by what you say. None of us allows ourselves to believe totally in those words that are spoken to us; if so, we are foolish. More often, indeed, we judge people by their actions.[45]

In scripted plays, actors are restricted by language and obligated to deliver the playwright's words. Jazz Acting's focus on physicality provided an opportunity to communicate with the audience via the character's center of being and rhythm.

The center is "the place from whence the character lives."[46] This can be a part of the body's shape, but it can also suggest how an actor uniquely interacts with their own space. McClintock often used John Wayne's swagger as an example of the character's center. Wayne's swagger is so distinct that his center might be his arms or upper torso, but is not necessarily limited to one part of the body.[47] In an interview, when asked about her role as the apparition in *Dream on Monkey Mountain*, Bolanyle Edwards postured her body as if the apparition's center emanated from her chest. She said, "I was ethereal and spooky and weird. I loved that role. I walked on the catwalk all dressed in white and float back and forth."[48] By creating a detailed physical and internal life of the character, actors fully explore relationships in the script, which allows for improvised moments.

In addition to the character's center, the actor chooses an exact speed and tempo of body and voice. McClintock wrote, "For most Black people, music is the most significant part of their existence. Music is so much a part of the Black experience that it cannot be deleted in a Black theatrical production."[49] This includes the physical speed and tempo of the body and the character's vocal cadence, speed, and rhythm, all inspired by the script and manifested by the actor's imagination. Afrocentricity posits rhythm as the core of African American transcendence to the spiritual realm.[50] Rhythm is discovered through the act of speaking, which echoes orality in storytelling: "Language itself compounds the problems of the unknown, for it is being made as the speaker speaks."[51] This conceptual framework provides space for the actors to release themselves from the restrictions of Eurocentricity, access self-expression, and ultimately riff.

In the late 1960s, many actors in mainstream schools were asked to engage with emotional recall, which asks them to relive past traumatic experiences to achieve emotional intensity. At the Afro-American Studio, McClintock considered such methods to be gimmicks or tricks. He argued that if you are thinking, for example, about a dead family member, you aren't staying true to the character and are focusing on a result. He said, "Don't ever work for a result—crying is a result. We cannot work for the emotion. The emotions will come as a result of all the other things."[52] By working for a result, many actors are taught or think that they need to feel that emotion to successfully execute the role. Moreover, if acting teachers ask their students to become the character by focusing on their personal suffering, they exploit students' trauma as a means of submerging themselves in the character's emotional mindset. McClintock did not teach his students to "become the character"; rather, his approach holistically taught actors to make choices from their own physicality/experiences and apply it to character creation or, as he articulated, "Us as the character."[53]

McClintock encouraged his students to observe Harlemites and draw physical particulars from their surroundings. He used the term "observations," which I have recast as "community observations," to delineate this approach. Other techniques include character observations, and McClintock wanted his actors to become keen observers of Black life in their communities. This approach was based on observing many people and collecting idiosyncrasies to augment the creation of a character, even if an activity seemed antithetical to the character. Specifically, an actor is tasked with studying a person and selecting habits and repeated gestures to perform in front of the class. Some examples include biting one's nails (suggesting anxiety) or crossing one's arms across their body (suggesting insecurity). By using these physical elements to create character, actors are not required to become anxious or insecure by thinking about personal situations that engender a particular response.

The level of specificity of community observations further offsets the pitfall of a generalized idea of who a person is or a stereotype. For example, if an actor is cast as a character of a lower socioeconomic class in the urban North, he may unintentionally portray a generalized "ghetto" dialect with an aggressive demeanor, perpetuating a stereotype akin to the Black Brute. Traced back to D. W. Griffith's *Birth of a Nation*, "The black brute was a barbaric black out to raise havoc."[54] This stereotype represents Black rage laden with subhuman and feral qualities. The Black Brute has remained in our cultural consciousness, as seen in the 1970s blaxploitation films. Black Arts Movement playwrights, such as Ed Bullins in *Goin' a Buffalo* and Richard Wesley in *The Mighty Gents*, explore the depth, humanity, and rhythm of life in specific communities. Community observations can be an antidote to stereotypes and may augment character creation with specificity and authenticity.

Where It's At: Community Healing and Self-Expression

With the pedagogical belief that actor training should supply a tactile method in rehearsal and performance, in 1969, McClintock created the Advanced Theatre Workshop, a precursor to the 127th Street Repertory Ensemble (est. 1973). Advanced Theatre Workshop programming included collectively-authored work I refer to as McClintock's street theatre genre. One production, *Where It's At*, garnered attention from mainstream newspapers, namely the *New York Times*, and Black publications, such as the *New Amsterdam News*. In what one might call early versions of devised theatre, the actors created work by responding to the politics of the 1960s under the theme of dissecting Blackness in America. Each actor-writer's ontological experience and voice was welcome in creating and performing these pieces. By examining *Where It's At* as a case study of McClintock's brand of street theatre, this analysis illustrates how actors applied self-expression to collectively-authored pieces aimed at expanding community healing across the New York boroughs.

The content of McClintock's street theatre featured the individual actor's response to their lived reality in which the audience was incorporated into the presentation. A diverse group of actors with distinct experiences and nuanced identities brought their own self-expressions to creating theatrical content. A 1969 flyer for *Where It's At* (Figure 2.7) says: "We guarantee a unique evening as we offer you a kaleidoscope of ourselves reacting to our environment in own

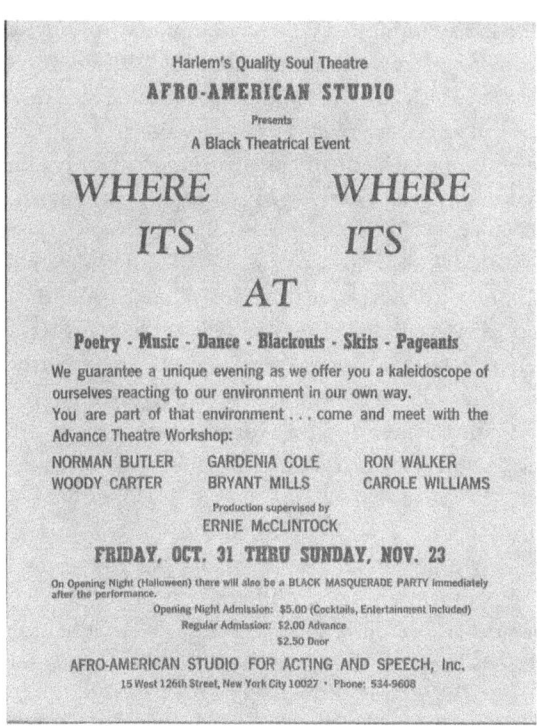

FIGURE 2.7 *Where It's At* flyer.
Credit: Errol Hill Collection, Dartmouth College.

way. You are part of that environment."[55] With the image of a kaleidoscope, the street theatre hearkens back to Paul Carter Harrison's description of the kaleidoscopic character in the African diaspora,[56] which McClintock embraced in cultivating Black actors from various backgrounds. Although each person's expression and/or experience varies, McClintock's students were all grappling with the fight for equality in the 1960s. In a 1970 interview with Doris Freedman on the public radio show "Artists in the City," McClintock references the civil unrest in the country, then exacerbated by Richard Nixon's presidency. Nixon's election resulted in many theatres closing because of slashed federal funding for the arts. The US economy stagnated, and the nation's continued involvement in the Vietnam War propelled citizens to protest for peace.[57] McClintock encouraged his students in productions like *Where It's At* to express their opinions about America through their art.

According to Primus, McClintock produced *Where It's At* "over and over, again,"[58] and each time the final product was infused with different topical subjects important to the unique makeup of each cast. These shows involved a variety of performance styles, including dance, poetry, and music. The only criteria for the material was that it must emanate from the experience of living in their current conditions in the Harlem community. In a photo album buried in the archives, there are two newspaper articles: "'Where It's At-70' Touring 4 Boros" and "'Where It's At' with Jones Play" publicizing the event and previewing the performances. In addition to an image of actor Cindy Burroughs holding a "Patrice Lumumba Killed" protest sign,[59] there is a drawing of other protest signs reading: "Free Huey," "Malcolm X Assassinated," and "Bobby Seale Bound-Gagged in Court" (Figure 2.8).[60] By drawing attention to the assassination of Patrice Lumumba (see Chapter 1) and Malcolm X and the trials of Newton and Seale, the actors at the Afro-American Studio were part of a larger conversation inviting dialogue with fellow New Yorkers.

Where It's At affected audiences because each piece addressed issues that resonated with actors and audiences alike. The actors arrived at each performance location with a truck that transformed into a stage. In a 1970 article about the rising popularity of street performance, McClintock's street troupe was featured:

> The stage was unfolded and set up near... the end of the block. It was a three-level platform with a cloth backdrop in the tricolor stripes of the black liberation movement. The generator was parked at the other end of the block... to keep the deep growl of its motors from intruding on the performances.[61]

By about 9:45 p.m., the performance began, and the show "gave impressions of life in the city in dramatic sketches poetry, pantomime and song."[62] The Afro-American Street Theatre, as it was dubbed by the *New York Times*, toured the neighborhoods of Harlem, the Bronx, Brooklyn, Queens, Staten Island, and Manhattan.[63] In the radio interview, Doris Freedman asked McClintock if his street theatre was something new. He responded,

> I don't know if what I feel about it is new. I feel that certainly the kind of thing we are doing now comes out the immediate experiences of the majority of the people we play before in the street.[64]

He tells a story about a run when the cast was setting up the stage and singing folk songs, and locals began joining in the song, which became a communal performance itself.

McClintock brought his troupe to the streets in unconventional pieces that recognized the sharp contrast between an enclosed theatre and outdoor space. Scholar Mance Williams's account of the Black Theatre Movement noted how McClintock's early work cultivated the actor's craft in this context: "the actor must maintain the artistic standards of the production while responding

FIGURE 2.8 Newspaper Clippings About *Where It's At*.
Credit: Private collection of Geno Brantley.

to the reactions of the audience."[65] The outcome was an immediate identification with strangers in unexpected circumstances and locations, such as the Bushwick section of Brooklyn, where spectators came out of their homes, set up chairs in front of the stage, listened on stoops, or watched through their windows.[66] Audience reactions differed from neighborhood to neighborhood, and in this case, the primarily Latinx crowd did not enthusiastically respond to themes related to Black pride and the Black community's struggle with drug addiction. But there were efforts to strip away the pretension often associated with theatre in the context of an exclusive space with a proscenium arch. Ultimately, McClintock's traveling street theatre performances took the form of a mobile community center, resounding with the studio's goals to heal, self-determine, and connect with diverse communities. Additionally, *Where It's At* was not the only piece of poetry theatre. McClintock established a women's poetry theatre directed by Helmar Cooper where novelist and partner of Cooper, Breena Clarke, reflects that it "was an early model for the…choreopoem and probably Ntozake Shange would agree."[67] The concept of the street poetry theatre, therefore, provided opportunities to expand inclusion and authorship to Black women in the Studio.

El Hajj Malik: Jazz Acting in Performance

In all of McClintock's productions, there is symbiotic play between the individual's self-expression and the ensemble's collective voice, whether one analyzes collectively-authored work or scripted work, such as N. R. Davidson's *El Hajj Malik: The Dramatic Life and Death of Malcolm X*. This play was presented by the Afro-American Studio's Advanced Workshop and opened on September 11, 1970. McClintock considered the play a "contemporary Black Classic,"[68] and throughout his career, he revived it in New York and Richmond. A gay secular director producing a play about a religious Muslim icon of traditional Black masculinity may seem contradictory, but McClintock's refusal to conform to heteronormativity and cower in the face of oppression echoes Malcolm X's unwavering commitment to Black liberation. Primus articulated:

> I think that Malcolm X was and still is our prince. Malcolm X is still our lord. He was my lord and Ernie's lord too. We both admired him in spite of the fact that he was a Muslim and we didn't believe in religion. He was close to our hearts. He always was and we tried to follow him and be as honest as he was and he was our model. If Ernie were alive today he would sit here and tell you that Malcolm X is the only prince that we have ever had.[69]

Primus's reverence and certainty of McClintock's belief emphasizes the historical significance of Malcolm X's life story. Primus, Walker, and McClintock aligned with Malcolm X's ideology—as opposed to Dr. Martin Luther King Jr.'s initial peace-driven strategy. The gravitation toward Malcolm X and his ideological stance relates to Jazz Acting in terms of self-determination and personal agency without regard for white incumbent frameworks in civic and artistic engagement. McClintock and Malcolm X took proactive approaches, although one was secular and the other religious. Even though they differ in terms of sexual orientations, faith, and means (political versus cultural), their philosophy derived from their need to uplift their communities and their refusal to negotiate with racist institutions.

For McClintock, inclusivity was political in that this progressive framework also incorporated the works of Black Nationalists, a group Primus contends they were part of, as well as street theatre, plays by women, and queer perspectives. Although his actor training and productions were revolutionary acts in Harlem, factions of the community labeled McClintock as apolitical. A. Peter Bailey observed this circulating opinion:

> Director McClintock and the Studio have been accused of not being political enough despite the fact that their productions are by and about Black people. They aren't necessarily revolutionary productions and non-revolutionary productions, although both tendencies in the Black theatre movement need to be encouraged and supported and both need to develop theatrical forms which will appeal to the Black masses.[70]

Discrimination became more aggressive against a company led by three gay Black men, which perhaps rubbed against the belief systems among sects of the Black Arts Movement. A company member who wishes to remain anonymous recalls some members of a neighboring Black Theatre who would attend the shows, shout gay slurs at the actors, and then abruptly leave mid-performance. Although this anecdote is important in understanding the discrimination the Afro-American Studio for Acting and Speech faced, it does not categorize holistically the sentiments of heterosexual Black folks. Specifically, Breena Clarke and Helmar Cooper recall how McClintock and Walker would always look out for their son, Najeeb Harb. She asserts, "There are Ernies and Rons that help raise their children – you could not find better examples of male behavior than Ronald Walker and Ernie McClintock."[71] However, there is a friction that existed within the Black Arts Movement with regard to masculinity and sexuality.

E. Patrick Johnson and Marc Anthony Neal locate this friction of queer and Black in the context of McClintock's lifetime. Neal argues that the Black Power era was "when hyperblack, hypermasculine, hypersexual male icons seemed logical retorts to ongoing ideological threats centered on notions of American masculinity."[72] As a prominent figure of the Black Arts Movement and an unapologetic gay Black man, McClintock disrupted and even threatened hypermasculine ideology. After all, being inclusive of Black perspectives, also includes those that considered themselves Black Power advocates. In other words, as Cooper asserts,

> We thought everyone had value. I consider the Studio political in that it was humanist. That is what Ernie wanted. We didn't picket, we tried to make sure everyone could feel welcome. You didn't have to do be this, that or the other – just come.[73]

Considering Neal's scholarship, McClintock's advocating for the principles of the Black Power movement through productions like *El Hajj Malik* while simultaneously promoting a variety of Black perspectives were not mutually exclusive.

The production is significant in that the play lends itself to emphasizing Malcolm X's call for self-determination but also maintains a clear collective identity throughout, in which McClintock took the notion of inclusivity a step further. Davidson's text explicitly insists on an ensemble production in which eight men all play Malcolm X and two women played the female roles, including that of Malcolm's wife, Betty Shabazz. *New York Times* critic Clive Barnes posed the question of how a theatrical event even considers representing Malcolm X: "[McClintock] solved this basic theatrical question beautifully. They make everyone Malcolm X"[74] (Figure 2.9). In this staging, the women played the female roles in addition to portraying Malcolm X, a powerful statement about the presence of women in the struggle for civil rights. In terms of character creation, Bolanyle Edwards recalls that the transition an actor makes from character to character is made through a shift in the rhythm of the body, physicality, and speech. "A moment before the character change I would close my eyes and see the other character and begin making/hearing speech, vocal changes, and body changes in my mind."[75] McClintock's direction was grounded in his acting technique: he brought the ensemble to life every time he produced *El Hajj Malik*, and every performance accessed physicality, rhythm, and speech to riff on Davidson's melody. On opening night, the production astonished Black and white critics and piqued the curiosity of audiences across racial lines.

McClintock identified *El Hajj Malik* as an ideal script for fully realizing the ensemble aesthetic in performances resulting in what Barnes called "an intellectually and emotionally provocative production."[76] The music, dance, and physical expression from the individual actors telling the story of Malcolm X undulated between the individual's perspective, a liberation from social expectations, and a proud celebration of people who had suffered similarly but knew their self-worth. Primus reminisced,

> Ernie made it into a kind of musical thing, N. R. Davidson wrote it, but Ernie created it. I've never seen another *El Hajj* that was like Ernie's. He

FIGURE 2.9 Production Candid, *El Hajj Malik*. Center: Helmar Cooper, Down R: Joan Green.
Credit: Private collection of Geno Brantley.

was no usual person now. The other experiences I had in theatre was nothing like with Ernie McClintock. Because Ernie McClintock theatre was about the development of a person as opposed to an actor creating just a character.[77]

As Primus suggests, McClintock's artistic vision extended beyond a director's concept of political theatre to an art form riffing between and with individual experiences, overlapping with the ties that bind multiple Black experiences.

Although the immediate community in Harlem found *El Hajj Malik* to be a transformative experience, well-known reviewer Gottfried Martin of *Women's Wear Daily* critiqued the production more harshly. He saw the Afro-American Studio's 1971 production at the Martinique Theatre and wrote,

> This production has now been moved into the white community... It had been staged in the style of production companies, a group creation using dance movement, incantation, and ensemble improvisation. McClintock has done this on an elementary level, and especially through the first act, it is slow and aimless, as much the directors fault as the author's.[78]

He notes that the musical dance scenes in a café were irrelevant, but those who either acted in or witnessed *El Hajj Malik* remember these moments as true jazz riffs, building community between performer and spectator.

Reviews are subjective, but the criteria for judging this play from the standpoint of a white western gaze is problematic. McClintock addressed the challenges of such reviews in an article in the *Black Theatre Alliance* magazine in 1979 titled "Published Criticism and its Positive Effect on Black Theatre."[79] In the article, he argues that criticism serves a major function in the theatre in that (1) it offers historical value, recording an event, and offers a record for future generations; (2) the critique is either positive or interesting enough to motivate theatre-goers to support the theatre; and (3) there is aesthetic value of measuring the quality of the production.[80] He writes,

> Black Theatre is about Black people, performed, written and produced by Black people, intended for the consumption of Blacks in order to educate, agitate, stimulate and/or provoke them into a greater understanding of themselves and their situation in the hope of motivating them to attain and assist others in attaining a better life.[81]

FIGURE 2.10 Display ad 31, *New York Times*, December 3, 1971.
Credit: Proquest Historical Papers: The New Time with Index.

Although Martin's review acknowledges the need to tell Malcolm X's story, he fails to situate his critique in this definition or even acknowledge that Afrocentric theatre is aesthetically different from white theatre. Furthermore, as Clive Barnes notes, the explosive shape of the play in McClintock's production is typical of Black theatre practice but may seem alien to white audiences.[82] Aside from the Black/white divide in the reception of *El Hajj Malik*, theatre communities uptown and downtown were talking about the Afro-American Studio, and audiences flocked to performances to experience this atypical, electric, and participatory play (Figure 2.10).

Conclusion: Time to Move to 127th Street

When the Afro-American Studio for Acting and Speech opened in 1966, McClintock's intention was to establish actor training drawing on Black culture and experiences with a dual focus on self-expression and a cohesive ensemble aesthetic. The technique and studio were geographically and philosophically outside the mainstream Stanislavski-based methods prevalent in lower Manhattan. Developing an Afrocentric technique resulted in a subversion of Eurocentric techniques, a political act challenging the status quo. The principles in what became known as Jazz Acting included healing and self-expression, values that stuck with McClintock throughout his career. Through academic courses and practical classes, his training struck a balance between finding common ground among those of African descent and fostering the individual artistic voices of each ensemble member.

Within the gestalt of the Black Power movement, McClintock, Walker, and Primus founded the Afro-American Studio in a major Black cultural hub, alongside other companies of the Black Theatre Movement. However, the studio was an anomaly in that although it promoted the principles of Black Power, self-determination, and community building, the three leading figures were openly gay-identified. But at the essence of self-determination and community building are the principles of individual self-expression and inclusivity of a multitude of Black perspectives. The Afro-American Studio reflected and embodied these principles on a daily basis, which afforded the company longevity beyond the historical time period of the Black Arts Movement, into the twenty-first century.

When considering the versatility of productions such as *Where It's At* and *El Hajj Malik*, the Afro-American Studio further distinguished itself from its peers. Evidenced by interviews, archival research, and performance analysis,[83] McClintock successfully realized an acting technique that yielded a profound experience for actors and audience members alike. Through his actor training and the high caliber of productions in the Advanced Theatre Workshop, the theatre community started to take notice in and out of Harlem, and the studio became a household name in New York. Phones started ringing and requests were made for touring productions across the country. Despite discrimination, McClintock and Walker persevered. McClintock continued to grow his company, and in the fall of 1972, the studio moved to 127th Street.

The following chapter traces the evolution of McClintock's Advanced Theatre Workshop, which became the 127th Street Repertory Ensemble. McClintock maintained inclusivity in his casting choices and season planning, in which he implemented and subverted the English repertory model by revising it,[84] like a jazz riff, and infusing self-determination and community building. In the 1970s, he recognized a need to unify Black plays and playwrights and challenge the white western canon. Through a repertory model, McClintock developed what he called the Contemporary Black Classics to initiate conversations about which plays should be canonized in Black Theatre History, aiming to establish a repertoire of Black plays for present and future generations.

Notes

1 Asante, *Afrocentric Idea Revised*, xii.
2 Alain Locke and W. E. B. Du Bois debated over whether Black art should be rooted in self-expression or propaganda. Du Bois asserts that art is critical to political progress and contends that all art is and should be propaganda; "Criteria of Negro Art." Locke rejected a primary focus on protest because it necessarily situates Black artists in an inferior position. He articulated, "[Propaganda] perpetuates the position of group inferiority even in crying out against it"; Locke, "Art or Propaganda?," 334.
3 Locke, "The Negro and the American Theatre," 263.
4 Clarke, interview.
5 Cooper, interview.
6 Enelow, *Method Acting and Its Discontents*, 5.
7 Glover, "White Imitations Dropped," 1.
8 In their genesis, Stanislavski-based techniques (i.e. the Method and Practical Aesthetics) were fulfilling the needs of naturalistic narratives of playwrights such as Clifford Odets, Arthur Miller, and David Mamet. Hence, as Enelow argues, these techniques are truly tied to white heteronormative narratives.
9 Bailey, "Black Theatre Takes Revolutionary Works."
10 Johnson, *Appropriating Blackness*, 3.
11 Johnson, *Appropriating Blackness*, 4.
12 Despite these grotesque images still circulating in historical and contemporary performances, there are actors who subvert these stereotypes in performance and bring nuance through their acting craft (i.e., Viola Davis in *The Help*). For a full study of the historical and theoretical development of Black stereotypes, refer to Bogle, *Tom, Coons, Mulattoes, Mammies, and Bucks*.
13 For more information on the various theatre companies and their missions during the Black Arts Movement, refer to Mance Williams' *Black Theatre in the 1960s and 1970s: A Historical-Critical Analysis of the Movement*.
14 "Ernie McClintock: Doris Freedman Interviews."
15 Hardwick, interview.
16 Long, "The Black Feminist Theatre of Glenda Dickerson."
17 Primus interview.
18 In contemporary actor training, each course often feels like a separate entity in which, for example, lessons in the Alexander Technique feel contrary to Method-based

acting classes. The Alexander Technique is a movement-based awareness approach for an actor to maintain overall bodily health, with a particular focus on the spine. Method-based courses in a first-year curriculum at the Actors Studio encourage actors to go inward to personal experiences following whatever physical impulses emerge, without thinking about the body.

19 Bates, interview.
20 Primus interview.
21 McClintock, "Perspective on Black Acting," 80.
22 Eyerman, *Cultural Trauma*, 6.
23 Primus uses the term "democratic history" as an alternative framework to traditional histories such as Larry Schweikart and Michael Allen's *A Patriot's History of the United States* (2004). Primus interview. Ultimately, he contends that his pedagogy aligns with activist-scholar Howard Zinn. Zinn was a self-described democratic socialist and an ally in the civil rights movement as well as an antiwar advocate.
24 Primus interview.
25 Carter interview.
26 Carter interview.
27 Huggins, *Black Odyssey*, 3.
28 Huggins, *Black Odyssey*, 3.
29 Huggins, *Black Odyssey*, 25–26.
30 Huggins, *Black Odyssey*, 203.
31 Huggins, *Black Odyssey*, 70.
32 Jones, "The Black Performing Arts," 7.
33 McClintock, "Perspective on Black Acting," 83.
34 From my training at the Actors Studio Drama School as a white actor, I learned that a main tenet in all acting, voice, and movement classes is "relaxation is a fundamental skill of the Stanislavski actor." In this training, the emphasis is on the Stanislavski actor, which McClintock's system avoids. For the Method-trained actor, each student in "Basic Technique" in the first six weeks spends hours on the floor achieving maximum relaxation in isolation, with eyes closed. When the actor feels tension in the body or is distracted, they are meant to give a "full sound" or a guttural moan. A distraction most often meant hearing another student phonate a full sound, and so there is a chain effect. Through this full sound, the actor releases tension and returns to breath work, which eventually moves on to sense memory work.
35 Primus interview.
36 This observation is based on seeing McClintock's students in contemporary performance, for example, Richard Wesley's *Autumn* (2015) at the Billie Holiday Theatre in 2016, directed by Walter Dallas. Jazz Actors Jerome Preston Bates and Dorian Missick performed with Pauletta Washington, Terria Joseph, Brent Langdon, Count Stovall, and Lekethia Dalcoe.
37 Cooper, interview.
38 Walker, "If You Must Act, Act Now."
39 Walker, "If You Must Act, Act Now."
40 McClintock interview by Wilson.
41 Ernie McClintock, "Acting Technique Lecture," February 1972.
42 Al Suavae Mitchell, "Character Analysis," lecture notes, August 2015.
43 Ernie McClintock, "Acting Technique Lecture," February 1972.
44 Ernie McClintock, "Acting Technique Lecture," February 1972.
45 McClintock, "Perspective on Black Acting," 81.
46 Mitchell interview.
47 Mitchell interview.
48 Edwards interview.
49 McClintock, "Perspective on Black Acting," 84.

50 Asante, *Afrocentric Idea Revised*, 49.
51 Asante, *Afrocentric Idea Revised*, 46.
52 Ernie McClintock, "Acting Technique Lecture," February 1972.
53 Recording, February 2, 1972.
54 Bogle, *Tom, Coons, Mulattoes, Mammies, and Bucks*, 13.
55 "Black Theatre Companies."
56 Harrison, "Praise/Word," 7.
57 Chafe, *The Unfinished Journey*, 391.
58 Primus interview.
59 The first sign regarding Patrice Lumumba refers to the Congo leader's assassination, written about in the introduction.
60 The first sign refers to Huey P. Newton, who cofounded the Black Panther Party in 1966. The "Free Huey!" campaign was a nationwide movement to protest Newton's 1967 arrest and 1968 conviction for the alleged murder of police officer John Frey. The reference to Bobby Seale refers to Seale's 1970 trial, in which he was part of the original Chicago Eight charged with conspiracy and inciting a riot at the 1968 Democratic National Convention. The judge ordered him to be bound and gagged after Seale vocally protested in court.
61 McClandish, "1250 Performances Are Given Here During Season," 41.
62 McClandish, "1250 Performances Are Given Here During Season," 41.
63 Williams, *Black Theatre in the 1960s and 1970s*, 48.
64 "Ernie McClintock: Doris Freedman Interviews."
65 Williams, *Black Theatre in the 1960s and 1970s*, 47.
66 McClandish, "1250 Performances."
67 Clarke, Interview.
68 In 1978, McClintock defined the contemporary Black Classics as

> plays written by Black writers with a pre-dominance of Black characters that contain elements of significant concern to a large number of Blacks. They also have a high standard of literary excellence (as defined by Blacks) and deal with subject matter of historical consequences that their absence would leave a substantial gap in Black history. For a full analysis, refer to Chapter 3. Bailey, "Rapping with Ernie McClintock," 1.

69 Primus interview.
70 Bailey, "New York: Afro-American Studio for Acting and Speech."
71 Clarke, interview.
72 Neal, *Looking for Leroy*, 143.
73 Cooper, interview.
74 Barnes, review of *El Hajj Malik*.
75 Edwards interview.
76 Display ad 31, *New York Times*, December 1, 1971.
77 Primus interview.
78 Gottfried, review of *El Hajj Malik*.
79 McClintock, "Published Criticism," 2.
80 McClintock, "Published Criticism."
81 McClintock, "Published Criticism."
82 Barnes, review of *El Hajj Malik*.
83 Evidence includes accounts from the actors at the Afro-American Studio, written requests from colleges/universities for the company to tour the production, and reviews.
84 The traditional repertory theatre typically suggests that a company has a resident group of actors who perform a collection of plays in tandem throughout the season.

Bibliography

Acting Technique Lecture. Afro-American Studio for Acting and Speech, February 2, 1972. Private collection of Geno Brantley.

Asante, Molefi Kete. *The Afrocentric Idea Revised*, 2nd ed. Philadelphia: Temple University Press, 1998.

Bailey, A. Peter. "Black Theatre Takes Revolutionary Works to Community." *Ebony*, August 1969, 127–30.

Bailey, A. Peter. "New York: Afro-American Studio for Acting and Speech." *Black Theatre*, n.d., 5.

Bailey, A. Peter. "Rapping with Ernie McClintock." *Black Theatre Alliance Newsletter*, February 1978, 1–2.

Barnes, Clive. Review of *El Hajj Malik*, written by N. R. Davidson, directed by Ernie McClintock, Martinique Theatre, New York. *New York Times*, November 30, 1971, 57.

Bates, Jerome Preston. Interview by Elizabeth M. Cizmar, August 31, 2015, Brooklyn, NY.

"Black Theatre Companies: Afro-American Theatre (Ernie McClintock), 1970–1983." Papers of Errol G. Hill, Rauner Special Collections Library, Dartmouth College.

Bogle, Donald. *Toms, Coons, Mulattoes, Mammies, and Bucks: An Interpretive History of Blacks in American Films*, 4th ed. New York: Continuum, 2001.

Carter, Woody. Interview by Elizabeth Cizmar, September 29, 2015, Skype.

Chafe, William. *The Unfinished Journey*, 3rd ed. Edited by Nancy Lane. New York: Oxford University Press, 1995.

Clarke, Breena. Interview by Elizabeth M. Cizmar, May 29, 2016, Jersey City, NJ.

Cooper, Helmar. Interview by Elizabeth M. Cizmar, May 29, 2016, Jersey City, NJ.

Davidson, Jr., N. R. "El Hajj Malik." In *New Plays from the Black Theatre*, edited by Ed Bullins, 202–46. New York: Bantam Books, 1972.

Du Bois, W. E. B. "Criteria of Negro Art." In *Call and Response: Key Debates in African American Studies*, edited by Henry Louis Gates Jr. and Jennifer Burton, 328–33. New York: Norton, 2001.

Edwards, Bolanyle. Interview by Elizabeth M. Cizmar, August 25, 2015, Atlanta, GA.

Enelow, Shonni. *Method Acting and Its Discontents: On American Psycho-Drama*. Evanston, IL: Northwestern University Press, 2015.

"Ernie McClintock: Doris Freedman Interviews Founder and Director of the Afro-American Studio for Acting & Speech." *New York Public Radio*, August 30, 1970. http://www.wnyc.org/story/ernie-mcclintock/.

Eyerman, Ron. *Cultural Trauma: Slavery and the Formation of African American Identity*. New York: Cambridge University Press, 2003.

Glover, William. "White Imitations Dropped by Acting School in Harlem." *Times-Picayune*, December 24, 1972, 1.

Gottfried, Martin. Review of *El Hajj Malik*, written by N. R. Davidson, directed by Ernie McClintock, Martinique Theatre, New York. *Women's Wear Daily*, December 1, 1971, 20.

Harrison, Paul Carter. "Praise/Word." In *Black Theatre: Ritual Performance in the African Diaspora*, edited by Paul Carter Harrison, Victor Leo Walker II, and Gus Edwards, 1–12. Philadelphia: Temple University Press, 2002.

Huggins, Nathan Irvin. *Black Odyssey*. New York: Vintage Books, 1977.

Johnson, E. Patrick. *Appropriating Blackness: Performance and the Politics of Authenticity.* Durham, NC: Duke University Press, 2003.
Jones, Rhett. "The Black Performing Arts in New York City." *Afro-Americans in New York Life and History (1977–1989)* 5, no. 1 (1981), 7–12.
Locke, Alain. "Art or Propaganda?" In *Call and Response: Key Debates in African American Studies*, edited by Henry Louis Gates Jr. and Jennifer Burton, 333–35. New York: Norton, 2001.
Locke, Alain. "The Negro and the American Theatre." In *The Black Aesthetic*, edited by Addison Gayle Jr., 260–63. Garden City, NJ: Doubleday, 1971.
Long, Khalid Yaya. "The Black Feminist Theatre of Glenda Dickerson." In *The Routledge Companion to African American Theatre and Performance*, edited by Kathy A. Perkins, Sandra L. Richards, Renée Alexander Craft, and Thomas F. DeFrantz, 180–85. New York: Routledge, 2018.
Loui, Lola. Interview by Elizabeth Cizmar, September 2, 2015, Bronx, NY.
McCandish, Philips. "1250 Performances Are Given Here during Season." *New York Times*, August 27, 1970, 41.
McClintock, Ernie. "Acting Technique Lecture, the Afro American Studio for Acting & Speech." From the Private Collection of Geno Brantley, February 2, 1972. Magnetic Reel.
McClintock, Ernie. Interview by Robert Wilson, June 13, 1973. Countee-Cullen Harold Jackman Memorial Collection, Archives Research Center, Atlanta University Center.
McClintock, Ernie. "Perspective on Black Acting." *Black World* (May 1974), 79–85.
McClintock, Ernie. "Published Criticism and its Positive Effect on Black Theatre." *Black Theatre Alliance Newsletter* 4, no. 3 (March 1979), 2.
Mitchell, Al. Interview by Elizabeth Cizmar, August 24, 2015, Atlanta, GA.
Neal, Mark Anthony. *Looking for Leroy: Illegible Black Masculinities.* New York: New York University Press, 2013.
Primus, Marc. Interview by Elizabeth Cizmar, August 25, 2015, Atlanta, GA.
Robinson, Vivian. "The First Ten Years of AUDELCO." *Black American Literature Forum* 17, no. 2 (1983), 79–81.
Schweikhart, Larry and Michael Allen. *A Patriot's History of the United States: From Columbus's Great Discovery to the War on Terror.* New York: Sentinel, 2004.
Walker, Greta. "If You Must Act, Act Now." *New York Magazine*, September 1971, 63–66.
Williams, Mance. *Black Theatre in the 1960s and 1970s: A Historical-Critical Analysis of the Movement.* Portsmouth, NH: Greenwood Press, 1985.

3
CANONIZING THE CONTEMPORARY BLACK CLASSICS (1973–1981)

With the success of N. R. Davidson's *El Hajj Malik* in 1971, enticing downtown audiences to make the pilgrimage to Harlem to witness McClintock's electrifying performance aesthetic, the Afro-American Studio for Acting and Speech became known as a major player in the Black Theatre Movement. Ernie McClintock considered these full-scale productions to be part of the Advanced Theatre Workshop of the Studio. Since 1967, the Advanced Theatre Workshop had yielded 30 major productions, and, in 1973, McClintock and his partner, Ronald Walker, opened the 127th Street Repertory Ensemble, the professional theatre wing of the acting school, located at 415 West 127th Street in Harlem, New York (Figure 3.1). The complex was not a theatre in the conventional sense but a community center offering a variety of entertainments and resources for local artists. In 1972, the *Tri-State Defender* reported on the opening of the complex where the 127th Street Repertory Ensemble performed: "The two-story former brewery which will house the Afro-American Studio Theatre Center provides the various instructors and students of the theatrical, poetry, dance, and musical groups with two floors of space and over 20,000 sq. ft. of working area."[1] In addition to an art gallery with sculptures and paintings by Harlem artists, the space included two theatres, with a seating capacity of 250 and 100, respectively, and enough space to organize scene workshops and professional development seminars. McClintock and Walker held an open house in the artists gallery on September 10, 1972, introducing the space to the Harlem community. On September 18, 1972, the inaugural production opened with a Baraka Festival featuring the playwright's controversial 1969 Black revolutionary one-acts: *Madheart, Experimental Death Unit 1,* and *Great Goodness of Life (A Coon Show).*[2] After a successful run of the Baraka Festival, McClintock and Walker officially instituted the 127th Street Repertory Ensemble with two

82 Canonizing the Contemporary Black Classics (1973–1981)

FIGURE 3.1 Company Members from the 127th Street Repertory Ensemble.
Credit: Private Collection of Geno Brantley.

primary goals: form a Black repertory company and establish a common canon of Black drama. McClintock made deliberate choices about a given season, reviving particular works from, for example, Amiri Baraka and N. R. Davidson. Through the lens of jazz aesthetics, these productions aimed to initiate conversations about which playwrights should be canonized in theatre history. From 1973 to 1981, McClintock began establishing the Contemporary Black Classics by producing revivals, thereby creating a repertoire of Black plays for present and future Black theatre communities.

As discussed at length in Chapter 2, *El Hajj Malik* was an important play in the Afro-American Studio's repertoire not just because its success but because McClintock considered Davidson's play a Contemporary Black Classic. McClintock defined the Contemporary Black Classics as

> plays written by Black writers with a pre-dominance of Black characters that contain elements of significant concern to a large number of Blacks. They also have a high standard of literary excellence (as defined by Blacks) and deal with subject matter of such historical consequence that their absence would leave a substantial gap in Black history.[3]

After reading McClintock's article "Published Criticism and its Positive Effect on Black Theatre," referenced in Chapter 2, I deduce that Afrocentric-trained critics and experienced theatre artists are qualified to assess those standards. In the article, published in 1979 in the *Black Theatre Alliance* magazine, McClintock details the credentials critics evaluating Black theatre need and proposes an initiative to recruit such individuals. Specifically, McClintock suggests drama critics evaluating Black theatre should be socially and politically conscious, educated in Black history, and tapped into current events. They should have an excellent education in all areas of theatrical production and command of the English language.[4] McClintock's assessment of Black theatre criticism echoes Amiri Baraka's 1968 critique of white theatre artists and critics:

> The liberal white man's objection to the theatre of revolution (if he is "hip" enough) will be on aesthetic grounds. Most white Western artists do not need to be "political," since usually, whether they know it or not, they are in complete sympathy with the most repressive social forces of the world today.[5]

Through the Black Theatre Alliance, McClintock proposed recruiting ten candidates who would enroll in a Black Theatre aesthetic development workshop, creating a faction of critics who would then publish their reviews and increase audiences. His objectives for this initiative included ensuring a future for the Black Theatre Movement and raising the standards of productions by any means necessary,[6] echoing Malcolm X's revolutionary call.

In programming the 127th Street Repertory Ensemble, McClintock devoted 50 percent of the season to producing Contemporary Black Classics. The other half of the season consisted of a combination of family entertainment plays, topical plays, historical plays, street theatre, and Afrocentric plays by authors outside the United States. Careful programming included primarily Black writers with a few exceptions, such as plays from South African playwright Athol Fugard, that "deal primarily with Blacks."[7] This chapter focuses on McClintock's notion of the Contemporary Black Classics and the considerable contribution this made to the Black Arts Movement. Based on exhaustive research on the 127th Street Repertory Ensemble productions as well as McClintock's pedagogy, I propose that during this time period (1972–1981), a production could become a Contemporary Black Classic if it chronicled historical events from an Afrocentric perspective, thereby revising a dominant historical narrative and subverting traditional white western storytelling.

Significantly, the Contemporary Black Classics were not meant to be a stipulated list of plays and the criteria of a Contemporary Black Classic could change based on the cultural and political context. McClintock said, "Some may argue over whether or not the plays the Studio has chosen are master works, but the theatre is the place to have this discussion."[8] Beyond McClintock's definition, there is little archival evidence prescribing the requirements. Therefore, it was a fluid concept and McClintock encouraged the Black theatre community to engage in debate about contenders, establish criteria, and evaluate the concept of the Black Aesthetic formulated by Larry Neal in 1968. Broadly speaking, the Black Aesthetic aimed to reevaluate white western aesthetics and the social function of art according to an African American cultural tradition.[9] Significantly, Black feminist thinkers such as poet Nikki Giovanni opposed Amiri Baraka's theatre of assault, arguing that it promoted a hypermasculine rhetoric. By providing space for these important debates, McClintock ensured that canonizing the Contemporary Black Classics was an inclusive process. McClintock provided a space and a formalized strategy for the collective community to begin thinking about, identifying, and debating the distinct qualities that reflected Afrocentric theatre.

Although McClintock's efforts to conceptualize the Contemporary Black Classics echoed the Black Theatre Movement's efforts to unify and ensure the continuation of Black theatre for generations to come, his contemporaries did not adopt this aspect of programming, creating their own missions and approaches to producing socially conscious theatre. It is also true, as mentioned in Chapter 2, that some factions of the movement did not actively support McClintock and his company because of his gay identity. Individuals with these heteronormative views may not have embraced or participated in the Contemporary Black Classics because it was created by a gay man. But with revivals such as *El Hajj Malik*, which garnered the attention of critics and audiences alike, the Contemporary Black Classics became more visible in the Movement. In interviews with his former students, it was clear that his vast knowledge and understanding of Black literary traditions and Black Theatre was integral to their education, beyond acting classes. McClintock always prioritized training actors in all facets of Black Theatre, rather than aiming for commercial success.

During the 1970s, members of the Black Theatre Movement aimed to unify and celebrate each other's work through organizations such as the Black Theatre Alliance (BTA) and the Audience Development Committee, Inc. (AUDELCO). McClintock was the first vice president of the BTA to pool funding with his peers to appeal to local government and garner more financial and practical resources for Black Theatre. It was also during this time that the annual AUDELCO awards[10] were established to celebrate excellence in Black Theatre, with McClintock hosting the first ceremony in 1973. From 1973 to 1981, McClintock worked alongside other leaders in the BTA and AUDLECO to rally the Black theatre community. Through a close analysis of both his curation of the Contemporary Black Classics and the content of these works, I argue that McClintock was foundational to the Black Arts Movement and African American Theatre History. The two plays I explore, Amiri Baraka's *Slave Ship: A Historical Pageant* (1967) and James de Jongh's *Do Lord Remember Me* (1978), were exemplary Contemporary Black Classics, fully realized through Jazz Acting. In line with McClintock's criteria, they channel African roots, chronicle Black history, and reclaim American history through Jazz Acting. However, despite McClintock's importance to the Movement, I also illustrate how discrimination against McClintock prevented collective involvement from his fellow artists in the Black Arts Movement. This analysis of the Contemporary Black Classics makes an important contribution to African American theatrical traditions in terms of performance, theory, and historical significance.

Situating the Black Aesthetic

Understanding the Contemporary Black Classics in the 1970s involves unpacking how McClintock situated high literary standards within the framework of the Black Aesthetic. Based on my analysis of the plays, performances, and engagement with Black theatre scholars, I assert that "high standards of literary excellence" included a reciprocal relationship between written text and oral tradition, a musicality and rhythm of speech that is distinct to the constituency the play is representing, and, finally, a narrative that either gives voice to a silenced community, and/or revises the western narrative of a person or experience.[11] In examining the symbiotic relationship between the written word, historical context, and live performance, I draw on the scholarship of Henry Louis Gates, Jr., Kathy Perkins, Sandra L. Richards, and Michael L. Pinkney in African American literary theory and performance analysis. Additionally, in contending that the Contemporary Black Classics revise the western narrative of a person or experience, my work is in conversation with scholarship that has critiqued literary and performance canons that recreate hegemonic notions of economics, gender, and nationalism, including John Guillory, Barbara Harris Smith, and Elaine Showalter.[12]

The Black Aesthetic is a controversial topic in that positing the existence of a singular Black Aesthetic can perpetuate the idea that Black identity is monolithic. Aside from its racial and cultural specificity, Black Aesthetic thought has historically been dominated by heterosexual men. Black cultural theorist Larry Neal and playwright Amiri Baraka were at the forefront of establishing the Black Aesthetic as part of the political aims of Black art in the 1960s and 1970s. The Black Aesthetic of the 1960s is part of the African Continuum, and Baraka draws on the philosophy of W. E. B. Du Bois and is inspired politically by the Black Nationalist Movement. Larry Neal's article "The Black Arts Movement" speaks of aesthetics and political action as it relates to all areas of artistic expression—visual art, poetry, literature, music, etc.—whereas Baraka specified the Aesthetic in theatrical terms in his essay "The Black Revolutionary Theatre" (1965). Prominent Black women such as Barbara Smith and Nikki Giovanni opposed the hypermasculine rhetoric touted by some of those leaders.[13] Early in the movement, important figures like Amiri Baraka and Ron

Karenga subscribed to a militaristic approach in not just artistic content but in the day-to-day operations. Specifically, Karenga encouraged collective, unified Black art arguing: "Individualism is a luxury we cannot afford...and is, in effect, non-existent."[14] At this time, part of Karenga's vision to strengthen Black communities was "the reconstructing and revolutionizing of the black family in which men were men and women were women, in surprisingly conservative ways."[15] Notably, Karenga later retracted his claim that women should be a compliment to men, recognizing that he was influenced by sexism in American culture at large. Nonetheless, in the early 1970s, the movement was heteronormative and male-focused. In her essay "Black Poems, Poseurs, and Power" (1969), Nikki Giovanni argues that militarism and art are inherently opposed and that the focus on militarism encourages competition among Black artists, which not only effectively excludes and/or silences Black women but also does little to promote Black liberation for all.[16] She argued that the Movement should be inclusive of both men and women.

In "Black Cultural Nationalism" (1968), Karenga declares that Black art should be "revolutionary. In brief, be functional, collective and committing."[17] To be "functional," the art had to expose the enemy while uplifting Black people and supporting the revolution. "Collective" suggested that art must emanate from the people and be returned in a form more vibrant than it was in real life. "Committing" referred to the unwavering commitment of both the artist and the observer to the revolution and the struggle. McClintock's pedagogy alludes to these three qualities of the Black Aesthetic, which are repeated by scholars such as Larry Neal in "The Black Arts Movement" (1968). McClintock's technique, which fosters individual creative agency in his actors, also answers Neal's call for Black Arts and the Black Power philosophy to "relate broadly to the Afro-American's desire for self-determination and nationhood."[18] Neal notes that both notions are nationalistic in that self-determination relates to the relationship between art and politics, whereas nationhood is concerned with the art of politics. This rhetoric resonates with the late 1960s radical call to eviscerate white institutions and assert a Black male presence, echoing hypermasculine militarism.

McClintock's work supports the Black Aesthetic in terms of "writers re-evaluating Western aesthetics, the traditional role of the writer, and the social function of art."[19] As explained in the Introduction, writers in the white western tradition of storytelling typically follow Aristotle's prescription for linear narratives with a clear beginning, middle, and end. Afrocentric plays do not always subscribe to western criteria, instead implementing circular structures. The social function of the art suggests that Black art is meant to destroy white cultural norms, speak to the spiritual and cultural needs of Black people, and initiate activism in Black communities.[20] Notably, within McClintock's reevaluation of art, he privileges the actor's role in creating scripted and unscripted theatrical events. Although McClintock employed the term Black Aesthetic, based on interviews and analysis of his technique and productions, I contend that he views the Black Aesthetic as an evolving concept as opposed to a fixed definition. Thus, conversations around the criteria of the Contemporary Black Classics and disagreement about what plays might be considered for this category would contribute to the development of evaluating the Black Aesthetic.

In a 1973 interview published in *The Paper*, journalist Vicky Hunter noted that McClintock's focus on the Black Classics was a significant departure from the programming of other Black theatres. McClintock understood that the 127th Street Repertory Ensemble was not just a place of entertainment but also an educational institution. Therefore, self-determination and community building did not just exist within the walls of the Afro-American Studio for Acting and Speech. His pedagogy extended into his season planning at the 127th Street Repertory Ensemble. He remarked,

> Any day of the week you can pick up a newspaper and find a Shakespearean play being done somewhere in the city. But it's not the same for Black plays... Who determined that *Hamlet* or *The Cherry Orchard* was a classic?[21]

McClintock is situating the Contemporary Black Classics as a theatrical intervention as well as a critique of western histories and storytelling.[22] Perhaps even more importantly for his students and future generations, he wanted to contribute to a Black cultural system in Harlem, decidedly separate from white mainstream commercial theatre.

Community Efforts to Unify

The 1970s saw ample opportunities for Black unification in which this discussion of the Contemporary Black Classics would offer another pedagogical opportunity to ensure longevity for the Movement. As part of this gestalt, two organizations were formed in the early 1970s: the BTA and AUDELCO. McClintock was a presence in these organizations, demonstrating his leadership in the Black Arts Movement. Although there were differing opinions and aims among theatre companies in Harlem, Black leaders in these institutions, including Hazel Bryant, Ernie McClintock, Roger Furman, Barbara Ann Teer, Vinette Carroll, Joseph Walker, and Woody King Jr., wished to unify and collaborate Black theatrical institutions.

When playwrights Delano Stewart, Hazel Bryant, and Roger Furman formed the Black Theatre Alliance in 1971, McClintock took on the role of vice president. Until it went defunct in 1984, the BTA garnered resources for Black theatres and provided a sense of self-reliance. The BTA was particularly crucial to sustaining theatres in the early 1970s when the Nixon Administration's economic policy slashed funding for the arts.[23] In 1973, NYU PhD candidate

Robert Wilson, under the mentorship of James Hatch and Richard Schechner, interviewed McClintock for his dissertation on the Black Theatre Alliance. When Wilson asked why the BTA was necessary, McClintock replied:

> Two and half years ago [Black] people began to understand that Black theatre was indeed a Movement and was not something that was about the individual artist, but about a whole art form and that we were all in the same boat...We needed to collectively take advantage of some of the opportunities...that was not there for us as individuals. You see, it's much easier for someone to give to 16 theatres, to a collective, than it is to an individual theatre.[24]

McClintock acknowledges the practical aspect of coming together as a Black theatre community, but he also recognizes that this Movement includes overlaps within Afrocentric storytelling. In his estimation, in order for the Movement to live in perpetuity, theatres had to collaborate effectively, which meant putting aside their artistic and/or personal differences. Although the Black Theatre Alliance disbanded in 1984, it successfully unified theatres and found commonality in promoting and developing Black theatre.

Black theatres, and McClintock's specifically, became accustomed to operating on a shoestring budget and understood that Black theatres were different from and therefore should not mimic white mainstream theatrical enterprises. McClintock trained his actors for the reality of the entertainment industry, in which new theatres and schools built with million-dollar budgets were of the commercial ilk. He said:

> For Black students there must be an understanding, in the training situation, that the real Black theatre experience is different... I hope to install the reality of the Black theatre experience as opposed to the glamour and the romanticism of the commercial theatre. [Black students] should certainly have the best but they must learn to develop whatever resources they do have.[25]

McClintock's pedagogy aligns with the Black Arts Movement philosophy of creating art separate from white, mainstream models on Broadway and Off Broadway, including developing a repertoire of Afrocentric plays. His commentary also echoes the Black Power Movement's separatist approach, which called out the capitalist system for imposing unjust economic constraints on people of color in the United States.

Engaging in conversations about the Contemporary Black Classics is part of the Black Theatre Alliance's efforts to create a formalized organization promoting Afrocentric theatres. As explored by journalist and author A. Peter Bailey in "A Look at the Contemporary Black Theatre Movement" in 1983,

BTA-affiliated theatres depended on local government and private endowments such as the Rockefeller and Ford foundations for funding. Bailey argues that the lack of formal funding was the result of the press treating community-based Black theatres like "fly-by-night sideshows rather than as the cultural forces that they are."[26] If companies could receive positive press and establish a canon of Contemporary Black Classics, then the Movement could persist and evolve based on Black cultural codes and standards:

> By coming together we are legitimizing ourselves rather than looking to THEM to legitimize us, these theatres are an important viable part of the Black community, they are representative of Black culture and belong in our communities and are as important as anything else. That's what we are saying by coming together.[27]

This is why establishing the Contemporary Black Classics, a repertoire of recognizable Black drama, was such a large part of McClintock's belief system and season planning.

Two years after the BTA was formed, Vivian Robinson established the Audience Development Committee, Inc., an organization that held an awards ceremony honoring excellence in Black theatre Off and Off-Off Broadway. The AUDELCO awards continue to produce an annual awards show in Harlem. As co-organizer of the inaugural event, McClintock hosted the first ceremony in 1973 at the Afro-American Studio Theatre Center. In front of an audience of 200, Robinson stated that "a tradition of honoring and applauding our own must begin" and "recognition of your contributions is long overdue."[28] McClintock and Walker received a First Annual Recognition AUDELCO in 1973. In 1976, they took home the Board of Director's Award for Continued and Sustained Effort in Production. In total, McClintock won seven AUDLECOs, and his actors, designers, and collaborators, including Gregory Wallace, Al Suavae Mitchell, Helmar Cooper, and Jerome Preston Bates, have won numerous awards. The AUDELCOs were part of this overarching effort to establish honors and traditions in the public eye. Certainly, African American theatrical traditions and an oeuvre of dramatic literature existed prior to the 1970s, from plantation performance to the premiere of Lorraine Hansberry's *A Raisin in the Sun* in 1959, but through the Contemporary Black Classics, the 127th Street Repertory Ensemble aimed to institutionalize their theatrical traditions, uplift Black communities, and honor the work of artists as part of this cultural-political entity.

Framing the Contemporary Black Classics

In a 1973 interview, Vicky Hunter distinguishes the 127th Street Repertory Ensemble from peer institutions based on this notion of reviving plays and developing a genre from this repertoire of historical and contemporary plays. Hunter states, "Ernie McClintock, the founder of the Afro-American Studio, in his decision to breathe new life into the Black Classics, has departed from what most Black theatre groups are doing."[29] For McClintock, the distinction between the Black Classics and the Contemporary Black Classics is that the former were written by playwrights prior to the start of the Black Arts Movement circa 1965, while the latter were penned from 1965 onward. He considered plays such as *A Raisin in the Sun* (1959), James Baldwin's *The Amen Corner* (1954), and Langston Hughes' *Black Nativity* (1961) Black Classics and continued to produce these plays over the course of his 40-year career in New York and Richmond. Notably, they all emanate from queer writers, one of whom is a woman, highlighting the diversity of voices within Black drama. These and other writers of the Black Classics who were well-known throughout the wider theatre community laid the foundation for the Black playwrights of the 1960s and 1970s.

The two plays explored in this chapter, Amiri Baraka's *Slave Ship* and James de Jongh's *Do Lord Remember Me*, reflect the priorities of the Black Arts Movement in terms of reclaiming African roots, Black history, and Afrocentric culture. It was necessary to continually revive these plays to put them in the larger canon. McClintock believed these plays should be as familiar to theatre goers as Arthur Miller's *Death of a Salesman* (1949) or Tennessee Williams's *The Glass Menagerie* (1944). He observed that his contemporaries mainly produced new plays but did not spend time reviving Classics or any that they might consider Classics.[30] Moreover, he emphasized that the revival of a Contemporary Black Classic should be established to self-reflect on and evolve the genre. As Jazz Actor Dr. Indira Etwaroo articulated, "Similar to jazz, before one graduates to riffing, one must be disciplined and well-versed in the codification and canonization within the form."[31] A critical aspect of the form in *Slave Ship* and *Do Lord Remember Me* is that they are ensemble-centric pieces, a cornerstone in McClintock's acting theory and production value. Whether reviving a play or performing the same role night after night, actors were never to repeat the same performance, a sharp contrast to mainstream practices. For example, in the majority of productions on Broadway, stage managers are required to write meticulous staging/choreography notes and actors are contractually obligated to set blocking.[32] In McClintock's theatre, the commitment to the ensemble dynamic required a constant state of discovery in the jazz tradition.

Slave Ship and *Do Lord Remember Me* explore America's colonization and capture of African people through a portrayal of the residual effects of the Middle Passage in the contemporary world. These plays connect directly to Primus's integration of Huggins's historical framework in *Black Odyssey* taught in Black history courses, as discussed in Chapter 2. In framing his book for the reader, Huggins identifies his historical and literary lens:

> Focusing on [the slaves] ordeal of oppression and enslavement, I have wanted to touch wherever possible the emotional and spiritual essence of

their experience. That has brought me to choose a style, often evocative and impressionistic, which departs from the conventional descriptive and analytical exposition of standard histories. Through that choice, I have wanted to bring the reader closer to the minds and hearts of a people who had to endure and make choices under conditions and circumstances which are outside our experience to know.[33]

Huggins's impressionistic style and homage to the tenacity of the ancestors is a critical intervention in American history. In literary theory, the impressionistic style focuses on the individual's perception of events, which are categorized as subjective and emotional rather than objective and intellectual. Hence, according to western standards, impressionistic experiences are generally understood as ahistorical. Huggins uses the term "impressionistic" to point to the fact that African Americans' experiences of American history are considered subjective, whereas the dominant white narrative is accepted as objective. Baraka's and de Jongh's plays provide a similar historical record rooted in Afrocentricity, acknowledging the painful past while honoring the survival of their people.

Both plays are set in the Antebellum South and through an evocative, impressionistic style, give voice to former slaves' lived experiences in order to reclaim the ancestral bodies that have been distorted and/or erased by traditional history. I borrow the term "reclaim" from Harvey Young, who defines reclaim as "to take something back. It is to possess something in the present while knowing that it only has recently been back in your possession. It is to know the past in the present as you work toward the future."[34] Therefore, McClintock's continual revival of these productions and effort over three decades to establish them as Contemporary Black Classics demonstrates his reclamation of American history through Afrocentric storytelling. McClintock continued to evoke ancestral bodies, inspired by the text and executed in performance, to commemorate the resilience of those that made the Middle Passage. *Slave Ship* and *Do Lord Remember Me* advance the Jazz Acting technique in theory and practice by engaging actors in the Contemporary Black Classics, which are rooted in Black history and initiate social change through historical and performative intervention.

Slave Ship

Across college campuses and in regional theatres, Amiri Baraka is most well-known for his Obie award-winning play *The Dutchman* (1964) rather than *Slave Ship: A Historical Pageant* (1969). A. Peter Bailey observes that the former was written by LeRoi Jones before he adopted his Black revolutionary name, Amiri Baraka, in the late 1960s.[35] Furthermore, Bailey asserts that *Slave Ship* is geared toward Black audiences whereas *The Dutchman* is aimed at mixed audiences. Ronald Milner, a prominent Black Arts Movement writer, describes *Slave Ship* as "a whole, fantastic, dynamic rhythmical drama of the slavery thing done in one flowing motion that never stops. It's the best play written yet on the whole panorama of slavery."[36] From the opening moments of the Historical Pageant, rhythmic and haunting sounds including heavy chains, drums, banjo music from a plantation, ship noises, and the sound of whips inundate an audience sitting in darkness. The stage directions then describe smells of the sea, defecation, urine, and incense, along with cries and moans. This vulgar sensorial portrayal of a slave ship yields a rhythmical drama, as Milner states, constant throughout the play. In Bailey's assessment, mainstream critics glossed over *Slave Ship* because it centered solely on Black experience, the enslaved Africans' voyage across the Atlantic.

Similar to how poet Haki R. Madhubuti (born Don L. Lee) famously said, "We must destroy Faulkner, dick, jane, and other perpetrators of evil."[37] *Slave Ship* aims to destroy white hegemony. In Baraka's famous 1965 treatise "The Revolutionary Theatre," he wrote that all revolutionary theatre must accuse and attack: "It is a political theatre, a weapon to help in the slaughter of these dimwitted fat-bellied white guys who somehow believe that the rest of the world is here for them to slobber on."[38] In *Slave Ship*, the white characters are Voices of White Men, Captain, Sailor, and Plantation Owner-Eternal Oppressor. Throughout the play, the white characters are torturing, mocking, and dehumanizing Black bodies. With a few exceptions, the white characters are only disembodied voices, often laughing while inflicting torture. The play includes battle scenes between whites and Blacks with the Black characters physically attacking the white oppressors after making the Middle Passage. For example, when Man 3 is in chains with "the constant crazy laugher of the sailors," he proclaims, "I kill you devils. I break these chains. I tear your face off. Crush your throat. Devils. Devils."[39] The absence of actual white bodies on stage and the Black character's threats of "I kill you" rather than "I will kill you" represent a direct assault on white hegemony.

However, another important aspect of the play is the tenacity of the enslaved, or as Baraka articulated, "[The Revolutionary Theatre] should be a theatre of World Spirit. Where the spirit can be shown to be the most competent one in the world. Force. Spirit. Feeling."[40] The play includes moments of strength of spirit with Yoruban dance and the pulse of African drums. Baraka further nuances the relationship between the characters and the Christian church with spiritual songs, which have historically been part of the spiritual nourishment of Black communities. Simultaneously, the play critiques white Christianity and assimilationists through the character of the Preacher. The Preacher essentially acquiesces to the white oppressor when he finally says, "We Kneegrows are ready to integrate."[41] The Preacher therefore becomes an instrument of white hegemony, essentially a critique of assimilationist strategies in the 1960s. The penultimate moment of the play includes a white voice proclaiming they cannot kill white Jesus God, then, as the lights fade and the drums and voices of the slave ship emerge, the white voice pleads for his life, lets out an earth-shattering scream, and dies. The lights come up and the characters dance, celebrating their survival and the destruction of the white thing, inviting the audience to join the party. As the playwright details, "somebody throw the preacher's head into the center of the floor, that is, after the dancing starts for real."[42]

In his book *Schoolbook Nation* (2003), Joseph Moreau argues that economic factors led to the erasure of an accurate history of slavery. McClintock's notion of the Contemporary Black Classics functions as a direct historical intervention. Moreau consulted more than a 100 history books from the Civil War to the early 2000s, and his analysis reveals how various interest groups influenced textbooks for middle schools and high schools. He begins his chapter on "Race and the limits of Community" with references to Andrew C. McLaughlin's *History of the American Nation* (1919), which describes the colonial south and a devotion to liberty despite class differences. However, as Moreau points out, non-whites, from slaves to Native Americans, are barely visible in this history.[43] The traditional narrative intentionally avoided the controversial issue of how capitalism was built on the backs of slaves and continues to perpetuate the consequences of economic class disparities. The truth regarding social inequality and economic exploitation clashed with the national myth of democracy and boundless economic opportunity.[44] As a Contemporary Black Classic, Baraka's play is reflective of Black Nationalism[45] and challenges America's distorted view of slavery by giving voice to ancestral bodies.

As two prominent figures of the Black Arts Movement, Baraka and McClintock share a foundational belief in Black Power and view theatre as an instrument of social justice, yet they diverge in terms of their approaches to the creation of art and development of the actor. McClintock focused on developing training techniques for Black actors. When he was asked if Baraka had influenced his theatre he said,

> Not really, no....The Afro-American Studio is an educational theatre school. We are not primarily a theatre, [we are] a community theatre. That is an important distinction. This means that when I started the studio I was concerned first with the development of Black actors.[46]

Marc Primus, who worked with Baraka prior to meeting McClintock, noted Baraka's hesitant support of the Afro-American Studio's productions of his work:

> I think Baraka came to see *Baptism* but not quite clear. He supported us doing his work but he didn't seem to be an admirer of the work. He understood the gayness underneath [the company]. He knew that he had to balance it with the pseudo-machismo, I think. So he wasn't openly supportive of the theatre.[47]

Although Baraka's assertions of Black hypermasculinity created friction, McClintock's primary goal was self-determining a theatrical space for Black actors.

In the revolutionary one-acts, Baraka employs homophobic slurs to reference white men asserting hypermasculine rhetoric. The dilemma of identity, stereotypes of aggression, and emasculation of a Black gay male connects to a collective past of humiliation and denigration on the slave block. In other words, homophobia was projected to affirm the masculinity and strength of the Black man to fight the straight, white men in power. One might ask why an out-gay director would produce such problematic plays. According to Woody Carter, who directed Baraka's *Great Goodness of Life* under McClintock's mentorship, the 127th Street Repertory Ensemble did not glorify violence or encourage hate speech. Rather, the mission was to produce complex and truthful plays about Black people, "the good, the bad, and the ugly."[48] Actor Helmar Cooper situated McClintock's relationship with Baraka's oeuvre as both artistic and political:

> Ernie was seduced constantly by the magic of language. Maybe you say something I don't like but look how magnificently you are saying it. Look at the words, how powerful that statement is. Maybe that power is something I can use. Maybe that power is not the way to go. So let me do this play and make it clear, for example, the character hates women. Let's see what the audience thinks.[49]

Undoubtedly, Baraka's poetic and visceral language embodied on stage empowered and challenged McClintock's actors and audiences, and presumably the director himself.

For the actors, McClintock's Jazz Acting provided the tools to bring *Slave Ship* to life in a safe way, yielding a powerful performance. As explored in Chapter 2, McClintock's institution was known as a temple of healing, fostering self-expression and trust within the ensemble, rather than relying on drumming up past traumas to produce emotion. *Slave Ship* confronts dominant political and cultural institutions' denial of reconciliation by prescribing and distributing images, smells, and sounds, including drums, screams of the tortured, rocking of the ship, moaning, and sounds of the wind and ocean. In an Afrocentric impressionistic style framework, *Slave Ship* begins in darkness with a cacophony of torture, leaving the audience no choice but to confront this conveniently neglected part of American history. The characters travel through time, experiencing oppression and dehumanization from everyone from plantation owners to religious leaders, continually struggling to break free from shackles, negotiate stereotypes, and wrestle with demands to align with the oppressor through integration.

McClintock's technique approaches this cultural trauma not through emotional recall but with a physical and rhythmic method. In rehearsals, McClintock started with a warm up exercise that involved relaxing while seated in a chair, connecting to breath with eyes closed. The actors turned their heads to the left for four counts and then to the right for four counts about half a dozen times. After the relaxation, the actors kept their eyes closed and he cued them to make the sounds of the wind, then the water. He instructed, "Sound out how you feel."[50] Then, in rhythmic chanting, the men sounded out "ah" and then the women followed suit. This recorded rehearsal demonstrates the director's ability to create a haunting and terrifying mood simply with breath and sound. The introduction to the play itself and the ominous tone encapsulates Huggins's description of the Middle Passage:

> Like the thunder following the lightning, a spark of life would pass through them all. But here, in this darkness, rocking, the voice could awaken only the most feeble echo, and nothing would come back on the ears save the hiss and roar of the sea, the whine and whir of the wind, the moans and whimperings of desolation.[51]

McClintock guided his actors much like a conductor directs an orchestra. The rehearsal of sounds concluded with McClintock uttering "Quiet, quiet." As the ensemble eventually faded out, he instructed, "Breathe."[52] The director's delicate approach to intense and raw material provided Black actors a safe way to approach work rooted in the pain of slavery and the triumph of the spirit.

Music was an essential part of honoring the pain and spirit prescribed by Baraka and executed by McClintock. In all of McClintock's productions, music and dance engaged in dialogue with one another. Ronald Walker, the technical director, crafted the score for the productions at a meticulous and measured pace, which clashed with the director's demanding pace and exacting method. Balancing these two seemingly opposite approaches provided the actors insight into the collaborative process between the designers, actors, and director during rehearsal.[53] In *Slave Ship*, the author details that African drums and percussive sounds sustain throughout the play and specifies the integration of the following songs: "African Sorrow Song," "Lord, Jesus, Deliver Me," and "When We Gonna Rise." These songs and spirituals, alongside wails and groans and the wind and sea, tell the story of slavery from the perspective of the enslaved. The details of bodily functions, the rancid smells, the sounds of chains, the corpses thrown off the ships, the cries of children, and the laughter of the white slave owner all capture the dehumanization of the Middle Passage and the beginning of slavery.

McClintock considered *Slave Ship* part of the Contemporary Black Classics because it used vignettes to create a circular structure, tracing the history of slavery, a pivotal origin in the African continuum, through to the 1960s and 1970s. Structurally, the wails and moans of the slaves, the shackles, the cries, the wind, the sickness, the songs, and the rhythms persist throughout the play, evoking the ancestral bodies at the bottom of the Atlantic Ocean. A fundamental component of the Contemporary Black Classics featured in *Slave Ship* are stage directions that allow the performer and director to interpret and improvise these vignettes, echoing call and response.

Baraka's play reflects an impressionistic style by offering a subjective interpretation of the Slave trade by the enslaved in a harrowing, circular narrative. Technique-wise, the melody of the play includes recognizable images such as a Blackface minstrel; however, the stage directions do not offer a firm description of this stereotyped character, instead giving the actor agency to create his own jazz riff and portray the Negro through his own interpretation with the potential to assault the hegemony by reclaiming history:

> Lights up on a shuffling "Negro." Lights off...drums of ancient warriors come up...hero-warriors. Lights blink back on, show shuffling man, hat in his hand, scratching his head. Lights off. Black dancing in the dark...Show Slave, raggedy ass, raggedy hat in hand, shuffling toward the audience shuffling, scratching his head and butt. Shaking his head up and *down agreeing with massa, agreeing, and agreeing, while the whips snap.*[54]

Using the term "Negro" reflects the language of a historical moment. In post-Antebellum America "Negro" became common parlance and eventually replaced the term "colored." In the late 1960s, Malcolm X and James Baldwin refuted "Negro" as a term traced back to slavery, relegating African Americans to second-class citizenship. In Baraka's description of the character shuffling toward and interacting with the audience, the playwright leaves room for the actor to comment on whatever historical moment the play is being performed. The character shuffling, projecting a lack of intelligence, performing for the slave master traces back to the dehumanization of the captures in Africa and the suffering on the slave ships. Baraka includes the banging of the African drums to remind the audience, like a resounding echo, that the past is very much part of the present. Furthermore, despite horrific oppression and collective memory, the spirit of the African homelands persists. Baraka's play rewrites history in terms of the memory of the Middle Passage and the spiritual strength of those from African descent.

Slave Ship aligns well with the criteria for a Contemporary Black Classic, playing with both written western text and Afrocentric oral tradition, connecting to the ancestors through musicality and rhythm, giving voice to slaves, and revising the traditional history of Antebellum and post-Antebellum America through the eyes of Black men. Certainly, Baraka was a controversial playwright whose language marginalized and/or excluded Black women's and queer folks' voices. However, under McClintock's framework, as a Contemporary Black Classic, it invites the Black theatre community to debate the viability of the piece and discuss whether it should indeed be considered part of the canon or if it reflects a historical moment. Furthermore, the relationship between Baraka's revolutionary oeuvre and McClintock's theatre reveals a complexity regarding hypermasculinity and queer sexuality in the 1960s Black Arts Movement. McClintock's affinity for Baraka's plays complicates the traditional understanding of the Black Arts Movement as exclusionary of queer voices and challenges the myopic view of Baraka as solely perpetuating homophobia and misogyny.

Do Lord Remember Me

Whereas Amiri Baraka's *Slave Ship* is grounded in provocative images, sounds, and smells to assault white hegemony, *Do Lord Remember Me*, written in 1978, is based on recorded interviews of former slaves in the 1930s. As a Contemporary Black Classic, McClintock's productions of *Do Lord Remember Me* in Harlem and Richmond gave agency to former slaves by adding their narratives to the larger African continuum. The play, and McClintock's approach in general, harkens to Harvey Young's notion of Critical Memory, where the director identified similarities among the characters and acknowledged experiential overlap while not presuming that all Black bodies have the same memories.[55] The playwright's writing process and the adaptation of these slave narratives recorded in the 1930s further engage in Critical Memory. Refining the script over six years with staged readings and workshop productions, the play became an overlap of the narratives in a circular non-western structure. James de Jongh pieces together the disparate stories from the enslaved in Virginia, linked through this "peculiar institution."[56] As a Contemporary Black Classic, *Do Lord Remember Me* upsets the traditional western narrative and through Jazz Acting reclaims former slave narratives, providing opportunities for self-determination and community building.

Although the play's text is primarily word-for-word documented accounts, de Jongh did eschew a representational style akin to a documentary, which echoes McClintock's insistence on theatricality in lieu of commonly practiced naturalism. de Jongh morphed the narratives to embody theatricality with a particular emphasis on music, which connects to Jazz Acting's implementation of music and rhythm as foundational. de Jongh notes in the stage directions:

> Afro-American musical forms are important elements in *Do Lord Remember Me*, but the play should not be misconstrued to be a musical. The songs should be performed as expressions of the musical legacy of slavery, arising spontaneously from the action of memory and sung, without any formal accompaniment, to hand clapping, foot stomping and improvised harmonies.[57]

Two of the stylistic forms that are important elements of the play are spirituals and work songs. These musical forms originated in the Antebellum South, both are religious, and both hide coded messages for slave escape routes and contend with multiple levels of promise and catharsis.[58] Scholars such as jazz musician and theorist Dr. Barry Long trace the foundations of jazz to spirituals and work songs.[59] According to the Library of Congress, "Spirituals are typically sung in a call and response form, with a leader improvising a line of text and a chorus of singers providing a solid refrain in unison. The vocal style abounded in freeform slides, turns, and rhythms."[60] The stage directions instruct the actors to allow the music to arise spontaneously without formal accompaniment. This directive reflects how the work songs would have been "punctuated with space for labor—the swinging of the hammer, the chain, and so forth."[61]

McClintock's implementation of music and rhythm in character development relates to de Jongh's structure in theory and practice. McClintock describes the integration of music as part of the lived experience of Black actors, reminiscent of spirituals and work songs:

> We hear music in our heads constantly. We walk to it, we work by it, we hum it, we sing it. What we sing, hum, hear in our head, pat our feet to, repeat and speak out lyrics from, depends on who we are, what our situation is, and what we want....A Black actor must think about his characters and influence them with their music. Patting feet, snatches of tunes, shaking shoulders while sitting, dancing to get across the room rather than walking, slapping thighs, snapping fingers, clapping hands, instantaneous body vibrations...like when you get the spirit...all are important manifestations of the Black experience.[62]

Musicality in *Do Lord Remember Me* is distinct from the mainstream musical because spiritual and work songs are meant to occur like an improvisational conversation with the dialogue, divergent from the traditional white musical form following strict verse and chorus.

In both structure and content, the Slave character represents collective memory that evokes the stories of the slave narratives through the struggle to remember. The struggle to remember relates to William Blight's theory of Structural Amnesia, which asserts that the authority structure of America is sustained and evidenced by Jim Crow laws, acquiescence to lynchings, acceptance of "coon songs," and the exploitation of Blackface minstrelsy.[63] A Stanislavsky-based technique would not serve this impressionistic character, and a Method-trained actor, for example, would most likely resist the playwright's assertion that an actor can embody spirituality. de Jongh explained that the Slave character came into being in the way that a group of individuals telling stories around a fire can make a character emerge out of the flames.[64] In this way, the character, the "dark-skinned" Slave, emerges as the storyteller, a virtual character.

de Jongh's description of the hero with a dark-skinned complexion is significant because directly challenges the dominant white master narrative, which associates dark-skinned complexions with stereotypes of Africans as aggressive savages. A stereotype that has evolved over the years into that of the dark-skinned thug.[65] George Yancy offers a present day account of colorism when he notes:

> My darkness is a signifier of negative values grounded within a racist social and historical matrix that predates my existential emergence. The meaning of my blackness is not intrinsic to my natural pigment, but has become a value-laden "given," an object presumed untouched and un-mediated by various contingent discursive practices, history, time, and context.[66]

Therefore, through the Slave, de Jongh addresses this experience by creating a dark-skinned man who has been subjected to dehumanization but throughout the play self-heals and asserts self-determination.

The Slave's odyssey begins on the auction block, almost completely nude in McClintock's productions, the actor then becomes Nat Turner, and ends the play as Albert Jones, a Civil War solider from the northern army. The bold choice to employ nudity was not a gratuitous decision but offered a symbolic "being and becoming"[67] of the Slave character. The significance of the bare body is that it begins brutalized on the slave block, then criminalized as Nat Turner, and concludes in the hero's uniform. The Slave's journey highlights a dark-skinned African American portraying strength, pride, and liberation as opposed to the white oppressor's dehumanization of the slave and projection on the criminalized body. The Slave revises and reclaims the distorted image of Turner created, in the past, by Thomas R. Gray and in the present, by author William Styron.[68] In Styron's 1967 book *The Confessions of Nat Turner*, the author paints Turner as a sexual deviant through scenes in which the protagonist and his rival, Will, fantasize about sexually assaulting white women. This portrait of Turner reflects the Black Brute stereotype, perpetuating myths about Black men as rapists. In de Jongh's reclamation, Nat Turner enacts the bloody deeds on stage, narrated by the slaves, is hanged on stage for his crimes, and is ultimately transformed into Albert Jones, who is "proudly taking leave of his family to enlist."[69] The bare body objectified on the slave block morphs into a criminalized body and then, finally, into a symbol of strength and pride as the Slave effectively enacts his own liberation.

An important aspect of *Do Lord Remember Me* in terms of the development of the Jazz Acting technique is the potentially traumatic experience of reenacting the demoralization of African Americans stripped nude on the slave block. Even when an actor properly uses Method training, the act of embodying a tortured human life for those who inherited the legacy of slavery would be challenging, at best.[70] Actor dl Hopkins, who played the Slave in the 1995 revival in Richmond, recalls that costuming was always the last thing on everyone's mind. Before the opening of the play, McClintock told Hopkins that Ronald Walker, the "sweetest man you ever met," would help with the garment.[71] In Walker's unassuming tone he said, "Come out of your pants and underwear. It's like a loincloth. Don't worry about it. It's going to be all right. We are gonna tie the knot in such a way that when it's pulled, everything comes off."[72] Hopkins chuckles when he tells this story because he admits that young women attended the performances, and he would do some pushups in preparation. Ed Broaddus, who played the auctioneer, brought him on stage: "Ed brings me out, and my look of scared—I was scared. They bid on me. It wasn't going the way [the auctioneer] wanted. So he pulled the string."[73] The genuine fear for Hopkins in that moment was related to his embarrassment in front of women and the whirlwind of costuming that Walker and McClintock cleverly integrated.

The core of the anecdote contributes to current conversations of Black Acting Theory by revealing an important directorial strategy for traumatic and painful material.[74] From a character analysis perspective, actors trained under McClintock were instructed to write their biographies in the third person because "Ernie was keen on keeping it a character."[75] Although actors distanced themselves from their biographies, in performance, the young actors did not put on age make-up or wigs. McClintock demanded, "no make up, he didn't believe in hiding the visage," and "what you do in rehearsal, you do in performance."[76] In other words, the rehearsal process was atypical; usually productions introduce props, costumes, and set pieces during tech week. In J. W. Robinson Horne's review, he described the production as provocative and comic, with oral narratives that "ran the gamut from tales of slave horror to slave humor."[77] By approaching this painful story through the lens of Jazz Acting, actors came to understand the Afrocentric writing style of de Jongh and invest in these characters, promoting self-determination and community healing.

Discrimination in the 1970s

The very notion of creating a contemplative space for the Contemporary Black Classics in the 1970s as part of the overall efforts to unify Black theatres and ensure the continuation of the Black Theatre Movement for future generations is a critical piece of history. But McClintock's aesthetic aimed to be inclusive, and his deliberate programming included the Contemporary Black Classics alongside other genres such as Black Classics, topical plays, and collectively-authored street plays. McClintock also practiced inclusivity in terms of the make-up of the student population and company members. Within the context of the 1960s and 1970s, where Black bodies were incarcerated, murdered, and stereotyped, McClintock's Afro-American Studio and 127th Street Repertory Ensemble gave a voice to Black actors who had been ostracized from their communities, including sex workers, former drug dealers, and dark-skinned actors considered to be outside the perceived norms of light-skinned beauty. Establishing an inclusive company disrupts neat and tidy definitions of the Black Arts Movement leaders and participants. Having a Black queer artist as a member of the Black Theatre Movement further shakes up and perhaps even threatens hypermasculine heteronormative rhetoric. The Afro-American Studio was known as a premiere acting school in Harlem in the 1970s and his productions impressed audiences, but rumors about the company that circulated in New York have kept his contributions on the periphery of the Black Arts Movement history.

In the late 1970s, when Levy Lee Simon arrived in New York City and started acting classes at the Apollo Theatre, actor Bruce Jenkins suggested Simon audition for the 127th Street Repertory Ensemble. Simon asked around the Harlem neighborhood to get a sense of who Ernie McClintock was and what his company produced. The response was both admiration for McClintock's work, yet blatant homophobia. Simon writes:

> Basically, I got the same response from just about everyone; raised eyebrows and "Ernie? Oh, well they do good work but Ernie and his company are a bunch of freaks." Apparently Ernie was gay and rumor had it that in order to get into the company you had to perform some type of sexual act. It was rumored that the company had regular orgies and sex parties...For some reason, intuitively, I felt that the rumors might have been exaggerated...More than anything, I wanted to be in a company that did good provocative theatre and unanimously people conceded that.[78]

These rumors were unfairly fueled by McClintock's controversial staging choices, such as the nudity in *Do Lord Remember Me*, and have never been substantiated in the archives or in the interviews I conducted with McClintock's students. Nonetheless, marginalization of gay men in the 1970s was certainly not unique to Harlem or the Black community and was part of the greater inequity rampant in society. Simon goes on to describe how McClintock and his company members walked down the street with a particular kind of "confidence, like they were special, free and easy," yet they there was also something "madly defiant" about them.[79] His use of the word "free" harkens back to the acting technique used in the initial phases of development through the course known as "Stretching Out." This fundamental course, discussed in Chapter 2, encouraged actors to free themselves from self-consciousness, achieve ultimate expression, and learn how to access individualized self-expression.

Those that studied with McClintock and performed in the 127th Street Repertory Ensemble were known in Harlem as some of the best trained actors of the time and the most well-versed in the variety of genres within Black theatre. Simon observed,

> Black theatre goers in the know quietly conceded that the best theatre work in New York by a Black Company was performed by Ernie McClintock's 127th Street Repertory Ensemble, a bunch of rowdy, crazy misfits that just didn't give a damn.[80]

Through the technique learned in the acting classroom and rehearsal studio, the actors became uninhibited and unapologetically themselves. Because of the technique and McClintock's innovative directorial style, actors were able to tackle the work of Amiri Baraka and James de Jongh and help McClintock achieve his goal of establishing a common theatrical canon for the entire Black theatre community.

Conclusion

Understanding Ernie McClintock's notion of the Contemporary Black Classics as a fluid conversation highlights the pedagogue's desire to include multiple voices in establishing such a canon, as opposed to asserting his opinion alone. In the contemporary moment, teachers and directors should incorporate plays such as *Slave Ship* and *Do Lord Remember Me* to broaden the scope of theatre education in both theory and practice. By engaging with the Contemporary Black Classics, artists and scholars can begin to dismantle and decolonize the skewed notion of what has traditionally been considered a "classic" in western education, an education from which African American plays are largely absent. Hence, reviving the Contemporary Black Classics does more than create a list of plays with particular cultural criteria. Rather, it aligns with African American literary and performance traditions while contributing a crucial piece of scholarship that critiques the white western traditional narrative. Broadly speaking, McClintock's conceptualization of the Contemporary Black Classics speaks to the current debates and conversations around decolonizing theatre history happening at conferences, including the Association for Theatre in Higher Education and the American Society for Theatre Research. The notion of Contemporary Black Classics enriches and expands teleological, chronological, and causal critiques of the canon found in scholarship offered by John Guillory, Barbara Harris Smith, and Elaine Showalter. In addition to considering the economic, nationalist, and male-centered limitations of the canon, the Contemporary Black Classics are an effective model for reconsidering static categories, and inviting debate, different perspectives, and flexibility.

McClintock's Contemporary Black Classics also connects with scholarship that has illuminated erased histories, African American literary theory, and dramatic philosophy. In Henry Louis Gates Jr.'s work, which analyzes Black literary theory from African Folklore to a modern-day powerful vernacular tradition, does not explicitly criticize the western canon. However, by unearthing the very existence of culturally rooted poetry, literature, and plays, Gates' work implicitly challenges assumptions about (white) American literary traditions. McClintock's efforts to initiate conversations about canonizing the Contemporary Black Classics also aligns with the work of Kathy Perkins and Sandra L. Richards who wrote an article in 2010 about Black women playwrights. They astutely remark that "no one has yet taken the task of narrating their history."[81]

Perkins and Richards argue that white drama criticism has a shallow understanding of Black culture, demonstrating that McClintock's role in the BTA in creating workshops to train critics and thinkers in the Black theatre tradition is still necessary in the twenty-first century. McClintock's work as a pedagogue and his artistic pursuits in producing the Contemporary Black Classics echoes artist-scholar Mikell Pinkney's assertion that the dominant narrative regarding the work created by African American artists "within the scope of their own perspectives and experiences has been either an imitation of European forms and structures...oddly abstracted and imitative African ritualistic stylings... based on not much more than emotional and melodramatic rants or simplistic comedic-musical entertainments."[82] The very existence of the Contemporary Black Classics establishes an ever-evolving oeuvre of Afrocentric works that chronicle historical events and figures according to Black culture and history, rewriting a dominant historical narrative, subverting white storytelling, and challenging stereotypes within those stories.

McClintock continued to revive these plays throughout the 1990s in Richmond, where he introduced many generations to these works, demonstrating the necessity of reaching a wider audience and student population. It is clear that the absence of African American theatre history in theatre education privileges white classical works by household names such as Shakespeare and Chekhov, and that the preeminence of these white playwrights not only fixes a false notion of literary excellence but also excludes playwrights who meet these high standards while reflecting the traditions of the African diaspora. As McClintock suggests, without the Contemporary Black Classics, there would be a substantial gap in history regarding slavery and the tenacity of a culture in the face of oppression, and the contributions of an entire demographic of contemporary America would continue to be relegated to second-tier status.

Chapter 4 will trace McClintock and his company into the 1980s where the onset of the AIDS epidemic began to plague the United States and gay men were further ostracized. He continued to produce the Contemporary Black Classics, but he also began to integrate queer narratives into his repertoire. This provided space for alternative images and stories of gay men as well as productions centering Black women, helping to empower and uplift the community. His establishment of a true repertory theatre, which continued to impress critics and audiences alike, began to take shape in his 1982 season of Peter Shaffer's *Equus*, Ntozake Shange's *Spell No. 7*, and Errol John's *Dream on Monkey Mountain*. These three plays, representing queer sexuality, womanism, and Afro-Caribbean identity, performed in one season, demonstrate how McClintock became even more exacting in his season selection. The following chapter will unpack these three productions under the framework of a repertory ensemble and explore how the 1982 season propelled the 127th Street Repertory Ensemble into even more prominence, sweeping the AUDELCO awards and, with *Equus* in particular, astonishing audiences with complex and reverent images of Black queer sexuality.

Notes

1. "New Afro-American Studio Theatre Centre to Open," 14.
2. Baraka's revolutionary one-acts also include *A Black Mass*. Baraka, *Four Black Revolutionary Plays: Experimental Death Unit 1, A Black Mass, Madheart, Great Goodness of Life*.
3. Bailey, "Rapping with Ernie McClintock," 1.
4. McClintock, "Published Criticism and Its Positive Effect on Black Theatre," 2.
5. Baraka, "The Revolutionary Theatre," 3.
6. McClintock, "Published Criticism and Its Positive Effect on Black Theatre," 2.
7. Bailey, "Rapping with Ernie McClintock," 1.
8. Hunter, "Afro-American Studio: Spotlight on The Black Classic," 4.
9. Neal, "The Black Arts Movement," 29.
10. In 1973, Vivian Robinson founded the Audience Development Committee, Inc., holding annual awards for excellence in theatre to stimulate support and enthusiasm for Black theatre productions and artists. For more information visit https://www.audelco.org/.
11. See Gates, *The Signifying Monkey*.
12. Guillory poses the canon as "cultural capital," which has less to do with social hierarchies, and more to do with elitism and access to such works. *Cultural Capital: The Problem of the Literary Canon* persuasively argues that the notion of aesthetics in Eurocentric terms emerged in the eighteenth century to resolve the disconnect between production and consumption by claiming it harmonized artistic elements, while in reality it used commodified art to feed capitalism. Barbara Harris Smith's *American Drama: The Bastard Art* has been critiqued for privileging text over performance, her work calls attention to the effort to create a national identity, which is white, straight, and male.

    Showalter's groundbreaking opus, *A Literature of Their Own*, identifies an oeuvre of literature that chronicles women writers' struggle to form a sense of identity within a male-dominated world via three stages: the Feminine, the Feminist, and the Female. Her work focuses on primarily white women and she has been critiqued for her lack of postcolonial thought.
13. Notably, there is scholarship around Black women's significant role in the Black Arts Movement, both on and off the stage. Refer to LaDonna Forsgren's *Sistahs in the Struggle* and *In Search of Our Warrior Mothers*, which focus on Black women's contributions to the Black Arts Movement, and Gayle Addison Jr.'s *The Black Aesthetic*, a collection of essays with varying opinions on the Black Aesthetic.
14. Karenga, "Black Nationalism," 35.
15. Smethurst, *The Black Arts Movement*, 87. Smethurst's argument nuances the role of misogyny and homophobia in the Black Arts Movement:

    > In short, a paternalistic, often homophobic, masculinism was a powerful strain within the Black Arts and Black Power movements as it was in many ideologies and social lives of post-World War II bohemians and countercultures. However, it was not the only strain.

    He posits that to define these movements solely as misogynistic with overt machismo is inaccurate and oversimplifying. Doing so limits the multitude of voices within the Black Arts Movement, such as Ernie McClintock.
16. Giovanni, "Black Poems, Poseurs, and Power," 711–15.
17. Karenga, "Black Nationalism," in *The Black Aesthetic*, 33. In this essay, Karenga draws on the work of Leopold Senghor, Senegalese poet, and political and cultural theorist. Senghor is a major figure in developing the concept of Négritude, a literary theory established by francophone intellectuals during the 1930s with the goal of raising Black consciousness in the diaspora.

18 Neal, "The Black Arts Movement," 29.
19 Neal, "The Black Arts Movement," 29.
20 Neal, "The Black Arts Movement."
21 Hunter, "Afro-American Studio," 4.
22 For more on scholarly critiques and analyses of traditional history and historiography, refer to William Chafe's *The Unfinished History* and John Ernst's *Liberation Historiography*. Refer to *SOS—Calling All Black People* (edited by John H. Bracey Jr., Sonia Sanchez, and James Smethurst) for a comprehensive overview of Theory/Criticism, Statements of Purpose, Poetry, Drama, and Fiction/Narrative.
23 Evan Vassar, "Nixon, The Supreme Court and Busing."
24 Ernie McClintock, interview by Robert Wilson.
25 Hunter, "Afro-American Studio," 4.
26 Bailey, "A Look at the Contemporary Black Theatre Movement," 21.
27 McClintock interview by Wilson.
28 Robinson, "The First Ten Years of AUDELCO," 80.
29 Hunter, "Afro-American Studio," 4.
30 Hunter, "Afro-American Studio," 4.
31 Etwaroo, interview.
32 Sara Bradley is a Broadway and Off-Broadway Stage Manager in New York. Her recent Broadway projects include *The Book of Mormon* (2011–2020), *Junk* (2017), and *The Heidi Chronicles* (2015). Sara Bradley, interview by Elizabeth M. Cizmar, September 12, 2016, email.
33 Huggins, *Black Odyssey*, lxxii.
34 Young, *Embodying Black Experience*, 135.
35 Bailey, "A Look at the Contemporary Black Theatre Movement," 19. Similar to many African Americans during the 1960s and 1970s, Baraka changed his name in an effort to shed the name passed down from plantation owners and reclaim Africanity.
36 Bailey, "A Look at the Contemporary Black Theatre Movement," 19.
37 Neal, "The Black Arts Movement," 29.
38 Baraka, "The Revolutionary Theatre," 2.
39 Baraka, *Slave Ship*, 137.
40 Baraka, "The Revolutionary Theatre," 2.
41 Baraka, *Slave Ship*, 134.
42 Baraka, *Slave Ship*, 145.
43 Moreau, *Schoolbook Nation*, 137–38.
44 Moreau, *Schoolbook Nation*.
45 Black nationalism was a movement established in the early nineteenth century, led by Paul Cuffee and Martin Delaney who argued that equality in the US would never be achieved and so they promoted migration back to the continent. At the turn of the nineteenth century, Booker T. Washington identified as a Black nationalist but focused on racial unity and economic self-sufficiency, maintaining a separatist philosophy. Post-World War I, Marcus Garvey inherited Black nationalist philosophy and, like Cuffee and Delane, called for African Americans to return to Africa. The Nation of Islam, founded in 1931 by the honorable Elijah Mohammed, adopted the Black nationalist ideology with a strict practice of racial separatism, declaring whites were responsible for the demise of humanity, and creating community programming and rehabilitation for their people. The most visible figure is Malcolm X, an icon for Black activists. The institutions of the Black Theatre Movement derived from a Black nationalist agenda to create theatre for, by, about, and near Black lives. For a comprehensive history of Black nationalism, see Wilson Jeremiah Moses, ed., *Classical Black Nationalism: From the American Revolution to Marcus Garvey* and William L. VanDeburg, ed., *Modern Black Nationalism: From Marcus Garvey to Louis Farrakhan*.
46 McClintock interview by Wilson.

47 Primus, interview.
48 Carter, interview.
49 Cooper, interview.
50 Warm-Up Exercise.
51 Huggins, "Black Odyssey," 52.
52 Warm-up Exercise.
53 Etwaroo, interview.
54 Baraka, *Slave Ship*, 137.
55 Young, *Embodying Black Experience*, 18.
56 The slaves interviewed in the 1930s referred to slavery as a peculiar institution. de Jongh, *Do Lord Remember Me*, 4.
57 de Jongh, *Do Lord Remember Me*, 6.
58 Long email correspondence.
59 Long email correspondence.
60 Refer to the Library of Congress digital archives for a complete history of religions folksongs, key figures like abolitionist Frederick Douglass and composer Henry T. Burleigh. "African American Spirituals," Library of Congress.
61 Long, email correspondence.
62 McClintock, "Perspective on Black Acting," 84.
63 Blight, *History and Memory in African American Culture*, 63.
64 De Jongh, interview.
65 Bogle, *Toms, Coons, Mulattoes, Mammies, and Bucks*.
66 Yancy, *Black Bodies, White Gazes*, 3.
67 Young, *Embodying Black Experience*, 18–19.
68 Styron, *The Confessions of Nat Turner*.
69 de Jongh, *Do Lord Remember Me*, 46–47.
70 White Ndounou, "Encountering Black Culture in Acting Classrooms and Beyond."
71 Hopkins, interview.
72 Hopkins, interview.
73 Hopkins, interview.
74 Monica White Ndounou, Sharon Bridgforth, Omi Osun Jones, Lisa L. Moore, Sharrell D. Luckett, and Tia M. Shaffer are scholars who address these issues in their scholarship.
75 Hopkins, interview.
76 Hopkins, interview.
77 Horne, "Jazz actors' "Do Lord..." laudable."
78 Simon, *Odyssey Towards the Light*.
79 Simon, *Odyssey Towards the Light*.
80 Simon, *Odyssey Towards the Light*.
81 Perkins and Richards, "Black Women Playwrights in American Theatre," 541.
82 Pinkney, "Shades of Blue," 2.

Bibliography

"African American Spirituals." *Library of Congress*. Accessed February 17, 2017. https://www.loc.gov/item/ihas.200197495/

Bailey, A. Peter. "A Look at the Contemporary Black Theatre Movement." *Black American Literature Forum* 17, no. 1 (Spring 1983): 19–21.

Bailey, A. Peter. "Rapping with Ernie McClintock." *Black Theatre Alliance Newsletter* (February 1978), 1–2.

Baraka, Amiri. *Four Black Revolutionary Plays: Experimental Death Unit 1, A Black Mass, Madheart, Great Goodness of Life*. London: Marion Boyers, 2009.

Baraka, Amiri. "The Revolutionary Theatre." *Liberator*, July 1965, 1–3.
Baraka, Amiri. "Slave Ship." In *The Motion of History and Other Plays*, 132–50. New York: William Morrow and Company, Inc, 1978.
Blight, David. "W. E. B. Du Bois and the Struggle for American Historical Memory." In *History and Memory in African-American Culture*, edited by Geneviève Fabre and Robert O'Meally, 45–71. New York: Oxford University Press, 1994.
Bogle, Donald. *Toms, Coons, Mulattoes, Mammies, and Bucks: An Interpretive History of Blacks in American Films*, 4th ed. New York: Continuum, 2001.
Bracey, Jr., John H., Sonia Sanchez, and James Smethurst, eds. *SOS—Calling All Black People: A Black Arts Movement Reader*. Amherst: University of Massachusetts Press, 2014.
Bradley, Sara. Interview by Elizabeth M. Cizmar, September 12, 2016, email.
Carter, Woody. Interview by Elizabeth M. Cizmar, September 29, 2015, Skype.
Chafe, William, *The Unfinished Journey*, 3rd ed. Edited by Nancy Lane. New York: Oxford University Press, 1995.
Cooper, Helmar. Interview by Elizabeth M. Cizmar, May 29, 2016, Jersey City, NJ.
de Jongh, James. *Do Lord Remember Me*. New York: Samuel French, 1977.
Ernest, John. *Liberation Historiography: African American Writers and the Challenge of History, 1794–1861*. Chapel Hill: University of North Carolina Press, 2004.
Etwaroo, Indira. Interview by Elizabeth M. Cizmar, February 15, 2017, Brooklyn, NY.
Gates, Henry Louis, Jr. *The Signifying Monkey: A Theory of African American Literary Criticism*. Oxford: Oxford University Press, 1988.
Giovanni, Nikki. "Black Poems, Poseurs, and Power." In *Call and Response: Key Debates*, edited by Henry Louis Gates Jr. and Jennifer Burton, 711–15. New York: Norton, 2001.
Guillory, John. *Cultural Capital: The Problem of Literary Canon Formation*. Chicago: University of Chicago Press, 1995.
Harris Smith, Susan. *American Drama: The Bastard Art*. Cambridge: Cambridge University Press, 2006.
Hopkins, dl. Interview by Elizabeth M. Cizmar, September 9, 2015, Richmond, VA.
Huggins, Nathan Irvin. *Black Odyssey*. New York: Vintage Books, 1977.
Hunter, Vicky. "Afro-American Studio: Spotlight on the Black Classic." *The Paper*, March 14, 1973, 4.
Jones, Omi Osun Joni L., Lisa L. Moore, and Sharon Bridgforth, eds. *Experiments in Jazz Aesthetics: Art, Activism, Academia, and the Austin Project*. Austin: University of Texas Press, 2010.
Karenga, Ron. "Black Nationalism." In *The Black Aesthetic*, edited by Gayle Addison Jr., 32–38. Garden City, NY: Doubleday & Company, 1971.
Long Barry. Interview by Elizabeth M. Cizmar, February 17, 2017, email.
McClintock, Ernie. Interview by Robert Wilson, June 13, 1973. Countee-Cullen Harold Jackman Memorial Collection, Archives Research Center, Atlanta University Center.
McClintock, Ernie. "Perspective on Black Acting." *Black World*, May 1974, 79–85.
McClintock, Ernie. "Published Criticism and its Positive Effect on Black Theatre."*Black Theatre Alliance Newsletter* 4, no. 3 (March 1979), 2.
Moreau, Joseph. *Schoolbook Nation: Conflicts over American History Textbooks from the Civil War to the Present*. Ann Arbor: University of Michigan Press, 2004.
Neal, Larry. "The Black Arts Movement." *Drama Review* 4, no. 12 (Summer 1968): 28–39. https://doi.org/10.2307/1144377.

"New Afro-American studio Theatre Centre to open." *The Tri-State Defender*, September 2, 1972, 14.

Perkins, Kathy and Sandra L. Richards. "Black Women Playwrights in American Theatre." *Theatre Journal* 62, no. 4 (2010): 541–45.

Pinkney, Mikell. "SHADES OF BLUE: A Season of Resurrected Writers and Reclaimed Music—the Blues." *Continuum: The Journal of African Diaspora Drama, Theatre and Performance* 2, no. 2 (2016): 1–11.

Primus, Marc. Interview by Elizabeth M. Cizmar, August 25, 2015, Atlanta, GA.

Robison Horne, J. W. "Jazz Actors 'Do Lord...' laudable." *The Richmond Afro-American and the Richmond Planet*, January 4, 1995, A14.

Robinson, Vivian. "The First Ten Years of AUDELCO." *Black American Literature Forum* 17, no. 2 (1983): 79–81.

Showalter, Elaine. *A Literature of Their Own: British Women Novelists from Brontë to Lessing*. London: Virago, 1982.

Simon, Levy Lee. "The Ernie McClintock and Nathan George Experience." In *Odyssey Towards the Light: A Memoir*. Unpublished manuscript, accessed from author December 7, 2015, Microsoft Word file.

Smethurst, James Edward. *Black Arts Movement: Literary Nationalism in the 1960s and 1970s*. John Hope Franklin Series in African American History and Culture. Chapel Hill: University of North Carolina Press, 2005.

Styron, William. *The Confessions of Nat Turner*. New York: Vintage Books, 1993.

VanDeburg, William L., ed., *Modern Black Nationalism: From Marcus Garvey to Louis Farrakhan*. New York: New York University Press, 1997.

Vassar, Evan. "Nixon, the Supreme Court, and Busing." *Nixon Foundation*, April 2, 2015. https://www.nixonfoundation.org/2015/04/nixon-the-supreme-court-and-busing.

Warm-up Exercise. 127th Street Repertory Ensemble, January 23, 1975. Private Collection of Geno Brantley.

White Ndounou, Monica. "Encountering Black Culture in Acting Classrooms and Beyond." *Theatre Topics*, 19, no. 1 (March 2009): 95–102.

White Ndounou, Monica. "Introduction." Lecture, Tufts University, Medford, MA. September 6, 2012.

Wilson, Jeremiah Moses, ed., *Classical Black Nationalism: From the American Revolution to Marcus Garvey*. New York: New York University Press, 1995.

Yancy, George. *Black Bodies, White Gazes*. Lanham, MD: Rowman & Littlefield Publishers, 2008.

Young, Harvey. *Embodying Black Experience: Stillness, Critical Memory and the Black Body*, 4th ed. Ann Arbor: University of Michigan Press, 2013.

4
QUARING THE BLACK THEATRE MOVEMENT (1981–1986)

Even though the concept of the Contemporary Black Classics developed by Ernie McClintock in the 1970s did not gain popularity within the Black Theatre Movement at large, the 127th Street Repertory Ensemble became known as a formidable company producing provocative, socially conscious, groundbreaking theatre in the early 1980s. While McClintock continued to teach actors in a classroom setting, he also considered the rehearsal hall training ground for actors who auditioned to be part of the professional company. Levy Lee Simon, Jerome Preston Bates, Morgan Freeman, Gregory Wallace, and Bruce Jenkins are just a few of the actors who were invited to the company in the late 1970s and early 1980s. Stand-out actors from the Afro-American Studio who had trained with McClintock, including Bolanyle Edwards and Joan Green, would also transition to the professional company. Although the 127th Street Repertory Ensemble was established in 1973, it was during the 1982 season that the company found its shape and identity with three plays in rep: Derek Walcott's *Dream on Monkey Mountain* (1970), Ntozake Shange's *Spell #7* (1979), and Peter Schaffer's *Equus* (1973). With these plays, McClintock found innovative ways to promote tenets of Black Power, such as self-determination, by subverting the traditional English repertory model. He also further developed jazz aesthetics, moving beyond the acting technique employed by the students and applying it to the production of seasons. In this way, McClintock's jazz aesthetic promoted Afrocentrism and inclusion in season planning, a strategy that yielded praise from critics and audiences alike. This successful uniting of three plays representing three distinct Black perspectives through the lens of jazz aesthetics made the 1982 season a pivotal year in McClintock's career.

Archival research, play analysis, and interviews with actors from the 127th Street Repertory company reveal that McClintock's exacting play selection

DOI: 10.4324/9781003187448-5

and directorial approach in the early 1980s were strategies employed to pursue a more inclusive theatrical enterprise, which accomplished his innovation of a repertory model. At the 127th Street Repertory Ensemble the concept of inclusion extended to Black revolutionaries, womanists, queer folks, and Afro-Caribbean identities. Although this is not an exhaustive account of the "kaleidoscope of Black identities"[1] throughout the diaspora, McClintock's approach set an important example for his actors and for future generations of theatre artists. He also pushed this inclusivity to consider queer narratives, which were largely absent during this historical moment. Through jazz aesthetics, McClintock provided space for storytelling outside a white heteronormative framework. This chapter highlights the significance of McClintock's legacy as it relates to his strategies as an artistic director and the efficacy of Jazz Acting as it is applied to plays with divergent styles.

I further assert that McClintock's Black repertory theatre used jazz aesthetics to revise and subvert the English repertory model. Developed in the early twentieth century, a repertory theatre is "one that stages its plays in rotation, building over a period of a year or more a store of productions that are offered to the public on a regularly changing basis."[2] A company will typically perform a different play each night, supplemented by premieres of new plays. Although this system has become popular in summer festivals, the American theatre has been relatively unsuccessful in producing a repertory theatre.[3] Overall, repertory theatres in Europe and the United States did not typically produce plays by Black playwrights. McClintock appropriated this model, revised it, and established a Black repertory theatre, the 127th Street Repertory Ensemble.

Although McClintock never explicitly stated that it was a subversion of a white form, the inclusion of queer, womanist, and Afro-Caribbean voices in the 1982 season ensured the plays were not only outside the white western theatre tradition, but also distinguished them from other companies within the Black Theatre Movement. This was perhaps most notable with *Equus*, a British play that McClintock revised to center on American Black queer sexuality. Although Walcott's prolific dream play and Shange's homage to Black city life were produced by other companies, it was rare to have all these voices represented under one roof and in one season, tying together themes of dreams, desperation, and desire (Figure 4.1). In publicity materials, McClintock stated:

> We present theatre that is INTRIGUING, STIMULATING, PROVOCATIVE, RELEVANT, and TRUTHFUL. The same as most black theatres. But, our way of presenting is the big difference. We give you BEAUTY, STYLE, DARING, SURPRISES, CONTROVERSY, SENSUALITY along with high artistic standards. In other words, our theatre is IMMEDIATE, TODAY, VOTAL, VIVID, AND VIRILE. We respectfully challenge you to three (3) daring adult evenings of dreams, desperation, and desire.[4]

FIGURE 4.1 127th Street Repertory Ensemble's 1982 Season Poster.
Credit: Poster courtesy of the Errol Hill Collection, Dartmouth College.

The season in its totality is significant, connecting these divergent plays as urgent and provocative. As explored in Chapter 3, the very existence of McClintock's presence within the movement, in the Black Theatre Alliance and Audience Development Committee, Inc., disproves the myth that Black militancy dominated socially conscious theatre. As a theatre artist, his queer positionality created space for the inclusivity of Black female actors and Black gay actors. However, it was not just the welcoming of a multiplicity of identities but the expansion of his theatre season in the repertory model that had the crowds flocking to the theatre and earned the ensemble an unprecedented 19 AUDLECO nominations (Figure 4.2).

By looking at the historical context of the early 1980s and unpacking the Black repertory model, this chapter will demonstrate how McClintock

```
                    AFRO-AMERICAN STUDIO'S
                127TH STREET REPERTORY ENSEMBLE
                     Ernie McClintock, Dir.

         Individually Exceptional - Collectively Phenomenal

             MAYBE NOW WE'LL BE ABLE TO CONVINCE YOU

         19 AUDELCO BLACK THEATRE EXCELLENCE AWARD NOMINATIONS FOR
                               1982

     AN UNPRECEDENTED HAPPENING IN THE 10 YEAR HISTORY OF THE AUDELCO AWARDS

     DRAMATIC PRODUCTION OF THE YEAR- DREAM ON MONKEY MOUNTAIN
     DRAMATIC PRODUCTION OF THE YEAR- SPELL #7
     DRAMATIC PRODUCTION OF THE YEAR- EQUUS

     DIRECTOR, DRAMATIC PRODUCTION    -Ernie McClintock- SPELL# 7
     DIRECTOR, DRAMATIC PRODUCTION    -Ernie McClintock- EQUUS

     Lead Actor, DRAMATIC PRODUCTION -Gregory Wallace- EQUUS

     Supporting Actor, DRAMATIC PRODUCTION - Bruce Jenkins- DREAM ON MONKEY
                                                                    MOUNTAIN
     Supporting Actor, DRAMATIC PRODUCTION - Gregory Wallace-EQUUS
     Supporting Actor, DRAMATIC PRODUCTION - Jerome Preston Bates- EQUUS

     Supporting Actress, DRAMATIC PRODUCTION-Ceal Coleman- SPELL #7
     Supporting Actress, DRAMATIC PRODUCTION-Lola Louis  - EQUUS

     CHOREOGRAPHY - Bernard Lunnon - DREAM ON MONKEY MOUNTAIN
     CHOREOGRAPHY - Lydia Abarca   - SPELL #7
     CHOREOGRAPHY - Jerome Preston Bates - EQUUS

     SET DESIGN - Ron Walker- DREAM ON MONKEY MOUNTAIN
     SET DESIGN - Ron Walker- SPELL #7

     LIGHTING DESIGN - Ron Walker/Geno Brantley- DREAM ON MONKEY MOUNTAIN
     LIGHTING DESIGN - Ron Walker/Geno Brantley- SPELL #7
     LIGHTING DESIGN - Geno Brantley/Ron Walker- EQUUS

                        For TOURING Information
                         Call (212) 289 5900
              or write - 127th Street Repertory Ensemble
                         415 W. 127th Street
                            P.O. Box 979
                            N.Y.C. 10027
```

FIGURE 4.2 127th Street Repertory Ensemble's 1982 AUDELCO Award Nominations.

Credit: Advertisement Courtesy of the Errol Hill Collection, Dartmouth College.

continued to evolve his company and acting technique in the rehearsal hall despite changes in the political ecosystem that adversely affected Black theatre. It explores how McClintock's understanding of intersectionality made space for the inclusion of multiple identities in the 127th Street Repertory Ensemble, paradoxically making him a visionary while also alienating him from larger discussions of the Black Arts Movement. Finally, through E. Patrick Johnson's quare theoretical lens, I use the development of the Black repertory model in the 1982 season, which featured *Dream on Monkey Mountain*, *Spell #7*, and *Equus*, to demonstrate how, in practice, his inclusivity expanded the possibilities of Black theatre and welcomed marginalized voices.

A Quare Framework

E. Patrick Johnson's quare framework provides a productive lens to unpack McClintock's repertory structure and 1982 season. As Johnson articulates in "'Quare' Studies, or (almost) everything I know about queer studies I learned from my grandmother," while the genesis of queer theory queried selfhood, agency, and experience, "it is often unable to accommodate the issues faced by gays and lesbians of color who come from 'raced' communities."[5] Johnson's theory interrogates identity claims that exclude rather than include, citing the exclusion of homosexual identities in Black nationalism's claims of "Black authenticity."[6] The typical image of a Black nationalist is a hypermasculine militant who claims Black authenticity. As such, Johnson suggests that "Black authenticity has increasingly become linked to masculinity in its most patriarchal signification."[7] Although McClintock was politically aligned with the principles of Black nationalism, he was categorically excluded due to his sexual orientation. Johnson identifies the emergence of queer theory and the limits therein:

> Queer theory emerged from post-structuralist critical theory to include voices beyond the gay or lesbian identifications. As Judith Butler notes, "queer" is a constructed linguistic practice: Queer derives its force precisely through the repeated invocation by which it has become linked to accusation, pathologization, insult. This is an invocation by which a social bond among homophobic communities is formed through time. The interpellation echoes past interpellations, and binds the speakers, as if they spoke in unison across time."[8]

In his historical moment, McClintock did not employ the term queer, which echoes Butler's argument regarding the limitations of reclaiming a term that was initially used to shame those outside the heteronormative and gender binary. She contends, "To recast queer agency in this chain of historicity is thus to avow a set of constraints on the past and the future that mark at once the *limits* of agency and its most *enabling conditions*."⁹ Along with many queer theorists, by establishing strict definitions and constraints on queerness, scholars run the risk of homogenizing queerness, contradicting the very notion of the theory itself. Beyond the limitations of concretizing queerness, Johnson suggests that although Butler's theory helps us understand the social construction of gender,

> what is the utility of queer theory on the front lines, in the trenches, on the street, or any place where the racialized and sexualized body is beaten, starved, terminated from employment—indeed, when the body is a site of trauma?¹⁰

Thus, quare studies offer space for inclusivity, bringing the perspectives of BIPOC and gender non-confirming individuals into these conversations and studies.

Quaring the Black Theatre Movement provides a useful framework to focus on that inclusion because, by definition, both these terms, queer and Black Power, as binaries limit intersectionality. In Johnson's work, the genesis of "quare" emanates from his southern grandmother's nuanced conception and application of the term. Although Johnson identifies quare as a culturally specific positionality, I propose it is applicable as a framework when thinking about the level of nuance McClintock brought to the Black Theatre Movement in the politically and culturally specific context of early 1980s Harlem. And although these case studies from the 1982 season include two productions that do not reflect queer experiences, *Dream on Monkey Mountain* and *Spell #7*, I borrow Eve Sedgewick's notion of queering texts¹¹ to argue that McClintock's productions quared these respective plays. This quaring can be seen in how McClintock created one season that speaks across Afro-Caribbean, womanist, and gay identities and how, in performance, the actors "articulated identities." The audience could then consider the relationship between and across these bodies, which both raise up the community and critique hegemonic oppression.

Considering McClintock was not the only outlier in the Black Theatre Movement, the quare framework in this chapter is in conversation with both queer scholarship and Black feminist studies. For example, scholar Cherise Pollard explores the misogynistic tendencies of Black Arts Movement poetry: "As [leaders] articulate manhood through the pen, the gun, the penis, and the microphone, male poets in the Black Arts Movement defined and reified revolutionary black male identity."¹² However, as Pollard argues, poets such as Sonia Sanchez and Nikki Giovanni, similar to McClintock, worked both inside and outside the ideological lines of Black Power philosophy: "[Many women poets]... worked both within and against the men's assumptions about the relationship between race and gender and art and politics."¹³ Pollard's argument that these women poets adopted an oppositional stance, using heterosexist and homophobic language to undermine hypermasculine authority, offers important insights into McClintock's productions of Amiri Baraka's revolutionary dramas.[14] Many of Baraka's early one-acts included homophobic and misogynistic slurs. However, in directly interrogating a brand of Black nationalism that excluded rather than included, McClintock quared these plays. He also recognized the complicated politics of Black nationalism, understanding that supporting the principles of Black agency, power, and community building did not have to necessarily contradict his lived experience as a gay man.

When looking at McClintock's productions, quare theory can help situate McClintock's positionality as a gay Black nationalist and also analyze the significance of intersecting identities within the 127th Street Repertory Ensemble. Quareness therefore "speaks across identities, but *articulates* identities as well,"[15] such as the "illegible black body" Marc Anthony Neal refers to in *Looking for Leroy*. Neal points to the importance of Gene Anthony Ray's portrayal of Leroy in *Fame* (1980) to his own development as an adolescent: "As a teenager growing up in the Bronx, I had few available examples of masculinity that didn't play to basic heteronormative assumptions."[16] I contend that Neal's notion of "illegible black males" can be applied to McClintock. Neal defines "legible" Black male bodies as "continually recycled to serve the historical fictions of American culture... Here black male bodies continue to function as tired and tested props."[17] Conversely, Leroy's body challenged popular stereotypes of bourgeois masculinity as embodied by characters such as Heathcliff Huxtable in *The Cosby Show*.[18] Neal notes that Ray's portrayal of Leroy related to queerness in representation but also in "a radical rescripting of the accepted performances of a heteronormative black masculinity."[19] Likewise, McClintock did not fit into heteronormative or homonormative assumptions perpetuated in popular culture.

McClintock's place in the Black Arts Movement can also be paralleled with the ways Black nationalist's positioned James Baldwin's politics and sexuality. Analyzing the work of figures such as McClintock and Baldwin, Dwight A. McBride finds that methodologies rooted in cultural and Black queer studies engenders critical thought without essentializing "racial blackness; or fixing, reifying, and/or separating race, gender and/or sexuality in the name of their political serviceability to racial blackness."[20] As acknowledged in Chapter 3, Amiri Baraka was a critical figure in the Black Arts Movement, bringing radical politics to theatre and the arts. He was also an emblem of "Black authenticity" tied to hypermasculinity and power. Baraka revered James Baldwin's work as an activist but had trouble reconciling Baldwin's sexuality. He said, "Jimmy Baldwin was neither in the closet about his sexuality, nor was he running around proclaiming homosexuality."[21] As McBride points out, Baraka accepted Baldwin as a "race man" because his "sexual identity [was] unlocatable."[22] Baldwin was certainly strategic about his speeches, amalgamating his racial and sexual identities to yield "rhetorical ambiguity" about his sexuality.

FIGURE 4.3 Ernie McClintock and Amiri Baraka, indoors.
Credit: Private Collection of Geno Brantley.

FIGURE 4.4 Ernie McClintock and Amiri Baraka, outdoors.
Credit: Private Collection of Geno Brantley.

Similarly, McClintock was ideologically aligned with Black Power activism, yet was an out-gay man living in Harlem producing an eclectic collection of plays. As mentioned in Chapter 3 in the discussion of *Slave Ship*, Marc Primus points out that Baraka did not frequent the Afro-American Studio for Acting Speech, but he did not publicly reject their productions either. In fact, there are several photos in the archive of McClintock and Baraka from what appears to be the late 1960s or early 1970s (Figures 4.3 and 4.4).

Chapter 4 explores how McClintock subverted the English repertory model to create a Black repertory ensemble in a jazz idiom within the context of 1980s Reaganomics. Through archival research, interviews, and reviews of these productions, I demonstrate how effective Jazz Acting is when applied to a diverse production season. I use a quare framework, which acknowledges "difference within and between particular groups,"[23] to examine how McClintock successfully implemented a strategy promoting a kaleidoscopic view of Blackness that challenges the presumption of a singular Black experience.

Reaganomics: the Sociopolitical Context of the 1980s

With the election of Ronald Reagan in 1980, American society became subject to Reaganomics. While capitalism and white conservatives flourished under this system, this federally sanctioned economic structure proved to be devastating for marginalized and arts communities. Arts communities like the Black Theatre Movement companies struggled to sustain themselves. In the 1960s, social programs and artistic initiatives funded by the government had expanded rapidly, benefiting the economy and providing optimism and support for many communities. Through this support, theatre became a prominent aspect of the Black Arts Movement.[24] However, under Reagan, both the National Endowment for the Arts (NEA) and Expansion Arts Division (EAD) lost substantial funding, resulting in the disbanding of the Black Theatre Alliance (BTA). All the theatres of the BTA had benefited from federal support, particularly through the NEA/EAD's Comprehensive Employment and Training Act (CETA), which accounted for half of their $475K budgets in 1979.[25] However, even before the funding was slashed, McClintock and Walker's approach to theatre centered on resourcefulness and creativity. Despite the loss of funding in the 1980s, McClintock's company continued to produce innovative plays.

The Reagan administration's replacement of CETA with job training bills impacted funding to the BTA, which included a host of theatres such as the Afro-American Studio for Acting and Speech, the Afro-American Singing Theatre, the Bed Stuy Theatre, the Brownsville Lab Theatre, the New Heritage Repertory Theatre, the Afro-American Total Theatre, and Theatre Black.[26] Changes to the CETA were made swiftly, within the first month of the conservative administration: "The Reagan Administration, which has cut CETA's funds by a third for the current fiscal year and has terminated its public works section, says it wants to continue job training for disadvantaged youths next year."[27] The intention was to integrate job training for youth, but the result was the reduction of governmental financing for social programs, which fell in line with Reagan's overall goals:

> Reagan... delivered on his pledge to combat the social philosophy, programs, and regulations.... Although affirmative action had produced significant gains for both Blacks and women, Reagan ordered his attorney general to fight such programs in the federal courts, and packed the Civil Rights Commission and EEOC with individuals dedicated to reversing the racial policies of previous administrations. Reagan slashed food stamp benefits, eliminated 300,000 CETA jobs, cut AFDC funds and lowered the benefits of an additional 300,000 families receiving welfare assistance.[28]

Therefore, in addition to the slashed government funding to the BTA, the surrounding community in Harlem experienced an abrupt change in progress for social programming, while incomes largely declined and poverty increased.[29] African Americans living in densely populated cities such as Harlem and Newark presumably could not focus on their collective whole because they were struggling individually with poverty. These changes affected McClintock's work, and this lack of support for Black theatre and the accompanying closure of institutions of the Black Theatre Movement in Harlem was part of the reason McClintock and Walker moved out of New York in 1990. However, throughout the 1980s, they continued to establish a repertory ensemble and broadened the scope of inclusion in the American theatre.

From a theoretical point of view, Reagan's conservative political philosophy was diametrically opposed to the principles of McClintock's Afrocentrism, which accessed self-expression in service of the collective common good. Reagan's philosophy rested on the individual's inherited privilege and drive for corporate success as a conduit for economic success. This hyperindividualistic mentality leaves little room for government funding of social programs. Political historian William Chafe notes that "the American spirit of individualism, competition, and personal pride would be restored, and with the shackles of government bureaucracy removed, individual citizens would once again be liberated to maximize their abilities and aspirations."[30] However, this individualistic approach assumes that all Americans are on an equal playing field, an assumption the civil rights and Black Power movements exposed as falsehood. Despite these radical cuts and the shifting gestalt that heralded the supremacy of conservative politics, McClintock's ingenuity and perseverance allowed them to forge ahead, establishing a model of theatre that disrupted the white mainstream.

Though McClintock did fundraise and make pleas for donations in programs and newsletters, the company was resourceful and, even on a shoestring budget, impressed audiences. Even before these cuts, the Studio operated on a modest budget, which required ingenuity since sets, costumes, and lights can eat up a large portion of any production budget. Jazz Actor Shantell Dunnaville recalls McClintock telling his students "If you don't have what you need, build it."[31] While McClintock was resourceful throughout his career, it was Ronald Walker, the technical director, lighting and set designer, who was the unsung hero keeping the company afloat. Walker's apprentice, Geno Brantley, recalled that one year, the electricity went out at the 127th Street space and Walker instructed Brantley to fuse wire to a breaker box and run it through a grate in the basement and up a light pole. This crafty (and illegal) way of accessing electricity lit up the Studio for about three years. Brantley described sourcing pieces for production sets:

> Ron and I used to go out during the day or in the evening with a shopping cart and dumpster dive. Collect things, bring it back to our theatre and it was on set the next day. He was so creative.[32]

Walker was an artist and would not be rushed in his process; rather, he worked at his own pace, carefully arranging the found pieces and expertly curating the lighting design. According to Jazz Actor J. Ron Fleming, Walker's methods "express the resourcefulness that Black folks had to have to survive,"[33] using a minimalist yet powerful aesthetic. Brantley further noted that Walker's design approach was of his "own invention"[34] and atypical of mainstream design practices. In this way, Walker remained steadfast regardless of the amount of federal funding provided.

Afro-Caribbean Representation: *Dream on Monkey Mountain*

Quaring the English repertory model, revising it according to an Afrocentric framework and using Jazz Acting techniques, subverts Anglo storytelling and acting methods by privileging African diasporic storytelling. This is what McClintock did with his productions of *Dream on Monkey Mountain*, *Spell #7*, and *Equus*, which were hosted by the Theatre Renny on Adam Clayton Boulevard in Harlem from July 7 to August 1, 1982.[35] Understood within a quare framework, the bringing together of these three distinct perspectives highlights versatility within Black culture and avoids "the reduction of multiple identities into a monolithic identity or narrow cultural nationalism."[36] From an acting perspective, circulating these three plays in rep required actors to play a range of characters, echoing the notion that quare theory "engenders a kind of identity politics,"[37] in that the actors would have to acknowledge and embody the differences between the constituency each play represents.

In a *New York Amsterdam News* interview, Marc Primus observes, "This venerable acting school has specialized in controversial themes and in what director McClintock calls 'The Black Classics.' Of the three productions this season, though, McClintock considers only one of them to be a classic: *Dream on Monkey Mountain*."[38] Aside from the fact that Walcott was known as a "certified genius" and was the recipient of the Nobel Prize in Literature, McClintock recognized the themes of contradiction, nationalism, and self-hatred all mediated through dream sequences that would "stretch an audience's imagination."[39] Indeed Walcott's play is widely analyzed and understood as a prolific piece of literature and theatre that wrestles with postcolonial rule in the Caribbean, where West Indian folk culture is blended with an array of cultural expressions, including European forms.[40]

Dream on Monkey Mountain takes place on a nameless Caribbean island and centers on the character Makak. The protagonist arguably experiences self-hatred because of his skin color. He causes destruction at a local market and is in jail throughout the play. While in prison, a white apparition encourages him to return to Africa. Throughout the play's dream sequences, Makak becomes a great African warrior, gaining followers along the way but neglecting his people. In the end, he beheads the white apparition, wakes up free from his infatuation with whiteness, and resolves to return to Monkey Mountain. The play is a complex and poetic piece of dramatic literature, playing with language, imagery, and dreams versus reality.

In terms of content and form, *Dream on Monkey Mountain* is well suited for Jazz Acting in that the play itself is a subversion of European language and stereotypes. Through a quare lens, the play acknowledges the specificity of experience in an Afro-Caribbean context. The play is rooted in West Indian character and speech paired with an ebullient subversion of European language and stereotypes about Black bodies. For example, the protagonist's name "Makak" is pronounced like the French word "macaque" which translates to "monkey," also referenced in the title. In the history of colonialism, Black bodies have been compared to apes in efforts to dehumanize and stereotype. Corporal Lestrade, the colonial official who throws Makak in jail, is a biracial character who walks the line between Black and white. He is "the straddler, neither one thing or the next, neither milk, coal, neither day or night, neither lion or monkey, but like a mulatto, a foot-licking servant of marble law."[41] In the end, when Makak kills the white apparition and proclaims that his name is Felix Hobain, he liberates himself from the animal name, rejecting Corporal Lestrade's definition of himself reflected in his dream.

The inclusion of *Dream on Monkey Mountain* in the rep season is significant in that it challenges monolithic notions of Black identity, but also because it makes space for Afro-Caribbean actors to connect with and perform the material. McClintock essentially quared the make-up of his acting company by bringing a multiplicity of cultures and identities into the studio itself, including Lola Louis, an actor from the Republic of Trinidad and Tobago who was nominated for several AUDELCOs, including best actress for Errol John's *Moon on a Rainbow Shawl* (1957). McClintock asked Louis to devise a silent character for *Dream on Monkey Mountain* that integrated Jazz Acting's character observations.[42] Louis developed the character by observing homeless folks in Harlem, describing this mysterious and looming character as "fishing through things and looking at people," and constantly in motion.[43] According to Louis, the audience recognized this character as part of their community. Hence, although the play was culturally specific to the Caribbean, McClintock infused elements of Harlem to connect with the audience. Notably, the cast of characters is overwhelming male, by including a female character on the margins of society McClintock further complicates and enriches Walcott's play. Jazz Acting realized in performance created palpable connections between the audience, the actor, and the playwright's postcolonial tale.

In the archives, next to a photocopy of Lionel Mitchell's *New York Amsterdam News* review titled "'Dream on Monkey Mountain' reveals a fine rep company," is a description of the 127th Repertory Ensemble that includes the tagline "Individually Exceptional—Collectively Phenomenal" presumably typed by McClintock himself. From this point on, the 127th Street Repertory Ensemble's publicity materials included this tagline, which speaks to the individual and collective identity of a jazz orchestra. Mitchell reported that the ensemble was "an excellent group that has done a tremendous amount of homework, and who, despite slim grants and money problems, persist in doing some the best theatre going!"[44] In revising the English repertory model into a Black repertory theatre, McClintock highlighted individuality and differences within Black culture, while the technique and productions were firmly rooted in Black nationalist precepts of self-determination and community building. In his quote, Mitchell also points out that McClintock was undeterred by the financial setbacks caused by the Reagan administration. McClintock upends the English repertory model, founded in British theatrical practices and populated by Eurocentric playwrights, to present a multiplicity of identities to the audience and challenge the actors to navigate the nuances of various demographics through Jazz Acting. In practice, then, this Black repertory model reflects a quare strategy to highlight difference, and in so doing, reveals a critique of hegemonic systems.

"Antidote for Abuse of Black Image": *Spell #7*

For mainstream audiences, Ntozake Shange's *for colored girls who considered suicide, when the rainbow is enuf* (1975) is more well-known and more often produced than *Spell #7*, which centers on a specific group of artists living in Harlem. Shange describes *Spell #7* as "in the throes of pain and sensation experienced by my characters responding to the involuntary constriction of their humanity."[45] Shange's piece is about three actors, one musician, one amateur performer, and two singers who are guided by a magician to come to terms with their identity in the context of a white supremacist society. They learn, as they confront horrifying stereotypes, that the magician's spell is the magic and richness of their Blackness. As Shange notes in her forward, white critics and audiences were overwhelmed by the intensity and grotesque nature of the piece. She asserts these opinions were formed because of her overt distortion of English "with the intentions of outdoing the white man."[46] Scholars such as Tejumola Olaniyan, Mikell Pinkney, and Karen Cornacher have analyzed Shange's use of poetry and language, a critical component in her writing, which disrupts the Aristotelian structure and denounces the western conception of beauty. *Spell #7*, identified as a choreopoem, confronts the oppression of the western gaze on the characters so that they might self-heal. As discussed in Chapter 2, healing was a fundamental part of an actor's training with McClintock, and in the case of *Spell #7*, impacted live audiences at the Theatre Renny in 1982 and revealed the social concerns of Black folks, from fashion trends to accessing their self-worth in the face of the oppression inflicted on them by the capitalist, heteropatriarchal hegemony.

In reaction to a trend of processed hair in the 1940s and 1950s, the 1960s saw a reawakening of Africanity where many women and men yearned to celebrate their African roots, fashioning dashikis and pan-African styles along with natural Afros and textured hair. This departure from the straight processed style resulted in debates about issues well beyond style. In 1969, Nikki Giovanni reminded her readers that "Our enemy is *Look* and *Life*, not *Ebony*" and insisted that all women with or without a natural and dashiki should be welcomed.[47] Giovanni's call echoes the aspect of quareness that invites difference and challenges essentialism. Shange explores this dilemma of beauty as it relates to Black authenticity and femininity, and, as Yusef A. Salaam points out in his review, McClintock highlighted this in the production:

> One, powerful revealing scene in the play dealt with the Black woman's hangups about her hair. Here, Shange, the poet, flings metaphors, similes and word rhythms that sizzled like Betty Carter's scats. The good hair/straight-curly-long hair syndrome has plagued the African woman in America for centuries, driving many to the point of psychosis.[48]

Salaam is referencing a moment in the play when the character Lilly brushes her hair 100 times a day. In the same review, Salaam writes that McClintock directs the actors "without hardly missing a beat." He sums up McClintock's production as "an antidote which says that the African woman/African nation must look in the mirror and start liking what she/it sees."[49] While McClintock did not have the lived experience of being a Black woman, many of the performers were Black women, and Jazz Acting asks the actors to integrate their lived experiences in New York City. The trends in fashion capitals like New York and Paris uphold standards based on Anglo-European, white, thin, able-bodied beauty. McClintock's lived experience as a gay man who is a proponent of Black nationalism provided a marginalized lens as he straddled these binaries under white supremacist oppression.

A play that addresses the complexity of living in a Black body in a white heteropatriarchal society necessitates a technique, such as Jazz Acting, to develop trust among the ensemble and find ways to foster the cultural and ontological experiences of the actors. Specifically, McClintock's breathing and articulation exercises went beyond learning how to project their voice on stage, working also to help actors develop self-confidence and find their individual voice. Bolanyle Edwards, who portrayed maxine [sic] in *Spell #7*, observed about the voice training: "The one exercise the La-ta-da-da. It was part of his technique to loosen up the articulators and to breathe. It's getting in touch with who you are. And believing in that character and that you are that character."[50] Edwards, who teaches at the Tupac Center in Atlanta, still teaches these breathing and articulation exercises, which attests to the effectiveness and legacy of McClintock's technique. Edwards teaches young actors to find their own voice, rather than conforming to the estimations of a "good voice" perpetuated in white mainstream training programs. McClintock stated, "Contrary to the beliefs of some, it is not 'white' or 'European' to speak well. At the same time, the Black idiom should be used as much as possible but the actor should theatricalize his vocal efforts."⁵¹ By "theatricalizing," the actor is focusing on rhythm and tempo to emphasize the Black idiom for an audience. The fundamentals of voice and speech at the Studio focused on the actor's responsibility to learn to control his or her instrument, with the ability to apply vocal variety, diction, and vocal flexibility, projection, and word value.⁵²

The actors who either trained with McClintock and/or worked with him on previous seasons were advanced in the technique and cast in *Spell #7*. In McClintock's estimation, a Black actor playing a role that was strikingly similar to their own lived experience would require a technique to achieve freedom on stage and trust the ensemble to riff within Shange's story. Edwards reflected on McClintock's deliberate choice to produce *Spell #7*:

> A lot of the characters that were in *Spell #7* were us. He cast us. He felt I was maxine.... The characters we played are who we were in real life. The characters did things that we did. They hung out at the bar. There was a bar across the street from us called the Lucky Spot on 127th street and that's where we all hung out. That play was who we were and I think that's why he chose it.⁵³

For an actor, playing a role that is so similar to one's own life is arguably a challenging feat that makes one vulnerable, especially when the director requires an authenticity that is theatricalized and stylized in front of a live audience.

Through the Jazz Acting technique, the production reflected familiar characters to the Harlem audience and, in turn, promoted self-acceptance and self-healing as well as community building. McClintock quared this production not only by including Shange's play in the season, but by recognizing the diversity of Black life in New York and encouraging actors to bring their unique perspectives, tastes, and talents to their character portrayal. Jerome Preston Bates played ross [sic], the musician, and based his character on his own devotion to and love for Jimi Hendrix. Salaam described his performance as "heaving the breadth of life into the play."⁵⁴ Bates notes that ross can be interpreted in myriad ways:

> You could take it to a folk place, you could take it to a blues place, or you can take it to a rock and blues place. I was a Jimi Hendrix madman, so I took it to that space.⁵⁵

The other cast members included Shola Gabby Olaye as the magician, Pat Matthew as lily, Robin Thorne as dahlia, Bruce Jenkins as alec, and Ed Sewer as lou. The level of trust and sophistication in the ensemble work in *Spell #7* communicated the actors' self-acceptance and McClintock's healing techniques as evidenced by Salaam's headline, "Antidote for abuse of Black Image." Through Jazz Acting, the production reflected the variety of experiences among Black men and women as well as the shared experience of being Black in Harlem. As part of the rep season, McClintock's production subverted white heteropatriarchal notions of beauty and sustained that fundamental quare critique of hegemonic systems of oppression.

"McClintock's *Equus* in Theatrical Mane-Stream": Jazzing a Western Narrative

The 127th Street Repertory Ensemble's production of Peter Schaffer's *Equus* was an unlikely choice to answer Baraka's call to destroy western storytelling and assault the mainstream theatre. But in the jazz tradition, McClintock revised this white European play to tell a story, instead, of Black queer sexuality. In 1982, there was a paucity of plays exploring Black queer sexuality. Due to the lack of material in this genre, McClintock appropriated Schaffer's successful Broadway hit and transformed the play through Jazz Acting. As Marc Primus remarked, "By the time Ernie got to *Equus* the story changed."[56] McClintock's *Equus* became a story about Black repressed sexuality, and, in certain moments, visually showed audiences the beauty of male queer sexuality and the inner struggle of a gay teenage boy living in a fundamentalist household. This vision was executed through Black actors engaging in ensemble work and creating characters from their individual self-expression. McClintock conducted and staged the production, embodying the musicality of a jazz ensemble orchestra and ultimately quaring the Black Theatre Movement.

Based on a true story from the early 1970s, *Equus* is about a young stable hand in the English countryside who attacked six horses and cut out their eyes. That the boy apparently worshipped horses added to the bizarre and macabre event. Shaffer was interested in unpacking the psychology of this event as well as the protagonist's love for the horses. As critic Clive Barnes notes, "the spirit that Mr. Shaffer calls Equus, a deification of the horse as life force... the boy has entered realms of passion and, in a sense, reality, that his own humdrum existence has never known."[57] Broadway director John Dexter's approach was similarly described as part court drama, part mystery thriller, and part philosophical exposition.[58]

The play included homoerotic overtones that were glossed over by the majority but acknowledged by members of the queer community. Shaffer was a gay man who did not publicly discuss his sexuality, which journalist Mark Lawson suggests was understandable as Shaffer was part of "a generation of writers who, even after the removal of the legal jeopardy to homosexuality, neither wrote about the subject directly nor spoke about his private life in interviews."[59] Additionally, in a *New York Times* interview, John Firth, the original Alan Strang, distanced himself from any discussion of homosexuality in modern society, to the point of disparaging sexual liberation:

> I'm beginning to feel that too much of this so-called liberation business can get out of hand. Just think of the Roman empire at its peak. There was a lot of promiscuousness, a lot of homosexuality, a lot of excessive luxury. That's when Rome started to crumble. One should think about that. Anyway, I'm not really like that. Right now, I'm involved with someone. She's in London.[60]

In addition to frowning upon the exploration of sexuality, Firth is quick to affirm his heterosexual identity. By categorically affirming his heterosexuality, he implicitly reveals discrimination and a problematic attitude toward queer folk. Although, in the twenty-first century, *Equus* is widely regarded as "a homoerotic classic,"[61] reviews of the premieres at the British National Theatre and Broadway focus on how the play is a psychological thriller and attempt to understand Alan Strang's motivation and repression within the context of his religious upbringing. Within gay communities, however, there was a recognition that Alan Strang was contending with his sexuality.[62] And certainly, the story is that of a white British family; it had not been conceived of as an American story about Black queer sexuality until it was reworked by McClintock.

Though McClintock rarely accommodated a strategy of avoidance, the onset of the AIDS epidemic in the early 1980s meant that queer sexuality continued to be a taboo subject in Black communities. Because of the complex relationship with queer sexuality and the belief that AIDS was a "white, gay disease," Black political leadership initially ignored "the threat of HIV and AIDS in black communities."[63] As AIDS began to impact Black and Brown communities, many of these leaders pursued aggressive strategies to deny and distance, but this changed drastically in the next decade.[64] Nevertheless, the topic of same-sex relationships is complex in Black communities, especially within religious households. However, as E. Patrick Johnson explains in *Sweet Tea: Black Gay Men of the South, an oral history* "Despite the South's history of racial segregation and religious fundamentalism, black gay men have carved out a space in which to live productive and fulfilling lives."[65] Johnson mentions that there is a constituency of Black gay men who participate in the church choir to "adhere to the religiosity of southern culture," but that it's also an outlet for their creativity and a space to meet other queer men.[66] Marc Anthony Neal asserts that "homosexuality in some communities mirrored a don't ask don't tell policy."[67] Ernie McClintock's refusal to abide by such a policy made him the subject of rumors. As referenced in Chapter 3, in the late 1970s, McClintock was labeled a sexual deviant who required participation in orgies for admittance into his company, a patently false accusation. Levy Lee Simon, who portrayed one of the stallions in *Equus*, asserts that

> in all the years I knew Ernie he never disrespected me or anyone else I know with any sexual aggression or anything like that. Never. The rumors were false to my knowledge. So if anyone even began to mention something like that I'd shut them down with a quickness.[68]

Through Schaffer's story, McClintock folded in the Black queer perspective that Marc Primus explains escaped some of the audience members due to their shortsightedness.[69] "People didn't get it. But they absorbed it without getting. They never got it, but they were excited by something about it is what I think. In that way his theatre was subtle."[70]

Amidst the tensions and complexity about queer sexuality in Black communities, the production was hailed as a success by both white and Black critics. Critic Abiola Sinclair wrote, "Ernie is directing like a person who doesn't give a damn. Who's been to hell and back. And the direction is the best I've seen in a long time."[71] Sinclair also postulates that McClintock may have chosen this play because he saw a bit of himself in the story. The 127th Street Repertory Ensemble's *Equus* was a "must-see" production in 1982 and theatre patrons made the pilgrimage to Harlem to witness Wallace, as a young Black teenage Alan Strang, and the ensemble of horses, played by six nearly naked Black men, reinterpret the British classic. The jazz revision of Shaffer's play reimagined in the context of Black agency laden with queer overtones echoes a "rhetorical ambiguity." The production won five AUDELCO awards including for Best Actor, which Gregory Wallace shared with a young Denzel Washington, who won for his portrayal of Malcolm X in Lawrence Holder's *When the Chickens Come Home to Roost* (1982). Having two recipients of the coveted award is unusual as best (Figure 4.5). Wallace, former director of UC San Diego's MFA program (2011–2016) and current professor of acting at the Yale School of Drama, attributes the beginnings of his success to McClintock's mentorship. His career started with *Equus*, which propelled the young actor into the New York theatre scene.

Unlike the commercial standard of producing a repeatable performance night after night through the vision of a director, McClintock provided ample space for the actors to discover their own melody within the foundation of the script. In the British version, John Firth summarized his approach as exacting: "I know that in order for my role to have the right kind of passion, the performance has to be very controlled, very quiet, very disciplined. Otherwise, it would be imprecise."[72] Precision and control help actors establish consistency in performance in a methodical, measured way, and Firth's portrayal revealed "a cumulative technical prowess."[73] Gregory Wallace's process was different; he explained that McClintock tapped into something quite personal but allowed him the space to make his own discoveries:

FIGURE 4.5 Denzel Washington and Gregory Wallace at the 1982 AUDELCO Awards.
Credit: Private Collection of Geno Brantley.

> He recognized a process going and he should leave me alone. He would whisper in my ear. I realized the role was someone who was off-center. Someone who had an offbeat way of looking at the world and not understanding. I knew what that was—I am off-center—that's how we connected.[74]

The image of a Black adolescent living in a fundamentalist religious household discovering his sexuality with six barely clothed, dark-skinned Black men titillated many and frightened others. Strong reactions to the production illuminate assumptions about Black male aggression and gay stereotypes in the 1980s. As Cornel West explains, "White fear of Black sexuality is a basic ingredient of white racism."[75] I propose that part of the awe associated with the production is attributed to the absence of a Black buck[76] stereotype, which suggests that the angry Black man is barbaric and feral. Instead, McClintock conceives of the relationship between Alan and his favorite horse, Nugget, as a tragic story of repression and societal oppression interspersed with moments of reverence for the Black body. In McClintock's direction and conception of *Equus*, he was perhaps able to reflect his own experience of queer identities as a place of love and intimacy as opposed to sinful and unnatural. McClintock never explicitly discussed how he saw himself in the story per say, but through the production he countered skewed narratives of gay couples and brought to light the trauma and societal pressures imposed on queer folk. In providing space for actors to make their own discoveries and in unmasking the ensemble of horses, McClintock created nuance and humanity instead of one-dimensional stereotypes (Figure 4.6).

In an important departure from the Broadway version, and in a move that was crucial to subverting the Black buck stereotype, the horses had simple

FIGURE 4.6 Ensemble of Horses in *Equus*.
Credit: Private Collection of Geno Brantley.

costumes and no masks. Most productions take a puppeteer approach, with actors wearing large symbolic horse masks. Having the horses unmasked underlined the actors' humanity as well as their impressive acting skills. The actors embodied the horses solely by gaze, neighs, and an exacting physicality, astounding audiences. They focused on the upright nature of the horse, the gait, the sounds, and kept their arms locked behind their backs. In the sexual climax of the play, when Alan mounts Nugget, Wallace climbed onto Jerome Preston Bates' shoulders with legs hanging, whipping the Black horse. According to Bates, this moment gave Alan Strang the confidence to escape from his suppressed self.[77] Wallace says of this moment: "The wildest thing about it was six Black men in leather, and incredible and unabashedly sexual and sensual, and being with me completely... touching and embracing and sensing Jerome. The show clicked—everyone's jaw dropped." It was a story of Black male sexuality, and the horses were true stallions.[78] Unmasking the actors playing the horses created intimacy between Wallace and Bates, while it simultaneously avoided painting the actors portraying animals as feral. Rather, they are symbolic of Alan Strang's repressed queer sexuality.

The discovery process between Bates and Wallace took weeks of experimentation that both actors reflected on as "luxurious." Bates won two AUDELCOS for *Equus*, Best Choreography and Best Supporting Actor, despite not uttering a single word. Bates' approach differed from Wallace's in that McClintock insisted on a physical creation of Nugget through Jazz Acting's observations. Being a company member cast in a production was just as much an education as a student enrolled in the Afro-American Studio. Bates expressed he felt blessed to be part of the 127th Street Repertory Ensemble:

> It was like going to school, acting school. It was more than putting on a play, it was putting life on stage. Living and eating it. He gave us the

opportunity to...understand our craft, see what we had and didn't have and how we could include what we had in our work."[79]

The actor-choreographer and five horsemen spent weeks observing horses in Central Park to create majestic characters. They even slept in the stable. When I interviewed Bates in a Brooklyn coffee shop in 2015, he embodied the horse's neigh without missing a beat. The actor's immediate recall 30 years later demonstrates the effectiveness of McClintock's technique.

The weeks of rehearsal, experimentation, and physical exploration culminated in a complex production that turned the Broadway run on its head. This climactic scene with Bates and Wallace quared Shaffer's play manifested a profound connection between two cis Black characters, offering a revision of the Black buck stereotype. Bates insists that McClintock taught the importance of leaving your blood on the stage where

> Ernie took you place where you gave it everything you got- the work you had to do and to realize you always had. Put two feet on the ground, stand naked on the stage and deliver. The audacity to have the freedom to be an artist and do what artists do.[80]

As a raw and provocative Black Arts institution, McClintock's theatre was one of the last few standing from the Black Theatre Movement and so this production not only subverted the mainstream but perhaps quared the remains of the Black Theatre Movement in Harlem.

The staging of the production is reflective of McClintock's theoretical grounding in jazz aesthetics and harkens back to William J. Harris's theory that jazz aesthetics is a procedure converting white poetic and social ideas into Black ones.[81] Beyond the selection of the play, the directorial style incorporated notions of jazz into the production value and acting style, and most importantly, process. The process of creation, rather than the end result, is an essential component of jazz. McClintock's actors recall that rehearsals and experimentation with the work never stopped, even in production. For example, the day the actors rehearsed in the theatre, one week prior to performance, he blasted a jazz album to create a sexually charged environment. Wallace said, "Jazz: I love that. It was so much about the musicality. In the way that he approached work and language and staging. I can tell you—the way he encouraged me was deeply sensorial."[82] McClintock's decision to play music in the rehearsal hall just days before opening demonstrates how his aesthetic valued process over product, a stark contrast to the commercial theatre with rigid blocking that creates a repeatable performance night after night. Although each actor is deeply grounded in the sensorial, the physical creation of character, there is a simultaneous emphasis on the ensemble manifested in the staging of *Equus*. McClintock's staging reinforced the idea of the ensemble by having all the actors remain on stage, sitting on the edge of the stage in plain sight of the audience for the duration of the performance. This staging choice also emphasizes McClintock's focus on ensemble rather than individual stars. To McClintock's mind, the individual might be exceptional, but the collective was indeed phenomenal.

McClintock's staging both revises the original production and challenges prevailing notions of the1980s individualism reflected in the Broadway premiere. McClintock's *Equus* quares Shaffer's original British play by integrating a Black gay perspective through an Afrocentric approach to theatre-making. The 127th Street Repertory Ensemble's *Equus* therefore speaks "across identities" and yet "articulates identities as well." In the Broadway version, some audience members sat on the stage, which parallels McClintock's staging choice in that it evokes a kind of voyeurism. However, as Barnes's *New York Times* review states, "[*Equus*] is essentially a Broadway vehicle for star actors."[83] The Times also wrote a featured piece on how *Equus* made an unknown 20-year-old actor, John Firth, "a star."[84] The way the play was originally produced, then, reinforces individualism, whereas McClintock's focused on ensemble-building and collectivity. By placing the actors on stage, watching the action unfolding as actors as opposed to characters, McClintock created community and connection with the audience.

At varying points in child development and identity formation, children become aware of race and gender, and in a heteropatriarchal society, they also become aware of racial stereotypes, gender inequality, and homophobia.[85] In *The Souls of Black Folk*, Du Bois chronicles his own experience: "Then it dawned upon me with a certain suddenness that I was different from the others; or like, mayhap, in heart and life and longing, but shut out from their world by a vast veil."[86] In McClintock's *Equus*, Strang struggles with his own identity as a Black queer teenager in a Christian home. The very presence of six muscular glistening Black men with a godlike presence paired with erotic homosexual overtones celebrates the beauty and complexity of Black queer identity. In exploring Strang's identity crisis and sexual repression, McClintock challenged "black nationalist claims of 'black authenticity,'"[87] which categorically excluded queer identities. McClintock's directorial approach and the actors' application of Jazz Acting in performance resonates with E. Patrick Johnson's quare theory framework, which is "grounded in a critique of essentialism," and strategically embraces "identity politics while also acknowledging the continency of identity."[88]

Conclusion

Through a quare lens, Ernie McClintock established a Black repertory theatre according to jazz aesthetics, creating a pathway to include distinct perspectives under one roof at the Theatre Renny. The 1982 summer season of *Dream on*

Monkey Mountain, *Spell #7*, and *Equus* instituted bold, unorthodox programming in the Harlem community, garnering 19 AUDELCO nominations and critical praise from mainstream and Harlem-based journalists. The variety of themes and identities explored in the 1982 season demonstrate how, as a visionary, McClintock challenged monolithic notions of Blackness. These often-overlooked factions of the Black community—Afro-Caribbean men and women, Black women, and Black gay men—dispelled the myth of a Black authenticity that is tied to American militancy and heteronormativity. The impact of these productions on both the actors and audiences further demonstrated the versatility of the company and McClintock's mastery of directing and teaching.

However, as a Black gay figure in Harlem's theatre scene, McClintock's inclusive programming, his persona, and his acceptance of varying perspectives and identities established an "illegible black masculinity" much like James Baldwin and Leroy from *Fame* had done. In being an enthusiast of hypermasculine Black Revolutionary playwrights such as Amiri Baraka and Ed Bullins, McClintock does not fit neatly into the role of queer progressive because, as discussed in Chapter 2, the foundational tenets of his technique and aesthetic, community building and self-determination, emanated from Black Power philosophy. His paradoxical programming and complex belief system became illegible during his lived moment and were largely excluded from the Black Arts Movement historical accounts.

In the 1980s, Reagan's administration starved the arts, impacting even those like Ernie McClintock and Ronald Walker who were tenacious and steadfast in their devotion to Black arts. The following chapter, "Rebel in Richmond" will explore McClintock's last years in Harlem and his transition to establishing the Jazz Actors Theatre in Richmond, Virginia. In the mid- to late-1980s, McClintock explicitly associated his technique and production aesthetic with jazz. Despite financial challenges and the devastation the AIDS epidemic had on his people, he forged ahead, evolving Jazz Acting and producing Afrocentric plays within the context of 1990s Richmond.

Notes

1 Harrison, "Praise/Word," 7.
2 Rowell and Jackson, *Repertory Movement*, 1.
3 Rowell and Jackson, *Repertory Movement*, 177.
4 Publicity Materials from the Private Collection of Geno Brantley.
5 Johnson, "'Quare' Studies," 129.
6 Johnson, "'Quare' Studies," 136.
7 Johnson, "Appropriating Blackness," 48.
8 Butler, "Critically Queer," 169.
9 Butler, "Critically Queer," 170.
10 Johnson, "'Quare' Studies," 129.
11 Queering is a literary technique that emerged in the 1980s as a way to upend heteronormative works by identifying challenges to gender, sexuality, masculinity, and

femininity in the text. For an extensive study, refer to Eve Sedgwick "Queer and Now" in *The Routledge Queer Studies Reader*, eds. Donald Hall and A. Jagose (New York: Routledge, 2013), 3–16.
12 Pollard, "Sexual Subversion," 173.
13 Pollard, *Sexual Subversion*, 173.
14 Pollard, *Sexual Subversion*, 181.
15 Johnson, "'Quare' Studies," 127.
16 Neal, *Looking for Leroy*, 1.
17 Neal, *Looking for Leroy*, 4.
18 Neal, *Looking for Leroy*, 3.
19 Neal, *Looking for Leroy*, 4.
20 McBride, "Straight Black Studies," 74.
21 McBride, "Straight Black Studies," 75.
22 McBride, "Straight Black Studies," 76.
23 Johnson, "'Quare' Studies," 135.
24 Chafe, "Unfinished Journey," 459.
25 Hill and Barnett, *Historical Dictionary*, xlix.
26 Williams, *Black Theatre*.
27 King, "Job Training Bills."
28 Chafe, "Unfinished Journey," 458.
29 Chafe, "Unfinished Journey," 458.
30 Chafe, "Unfinished Journey," 458.
31 Dunnaville, Interview.
32 Brantley, interview.
33 Fleming, interview.
34 Brantley, interview.
35 Primus, "Ernie McClintock," 29.
36 Johnson, "'Quare' Studies," 135.
37 Johnson, "'Quare' Studies," 135.
38 Primus, "Ernie McClintock," 29.
39 Primus, "Ernie McClintock," 29. For more analysis and context on Walcott and *Dream*, refer to Edward Baugh's scholarly biography "Derek Walcott" and Jan Uhrbach's "A Note on Language."
40 Baugh, "Derek Walcott," xiv.
41 Uhrbach, "A Note on Language," 579.
42 For a thorough explanation of Jazz Acting's observations, please refer to Chapter 2.
43 Louis, interview.
44 Mitchell, "Dream on Monkey Mountain," 36.
45 Shange, *Three Pieces*, 69.
46 Shange, *Three Pieces*, 3.
47 Giovanni, "Black Poems," 110.
48 Salaam, "Spell No. 7," 34.
49 Salaam, "Spell No. 7," 34.
50 Edwards, interview.
51 McClintock, "Perspective on Black Acting," 83–84.
52 Simon interview. Word value refers to the emphasis or weight an actor gives to any given word. This becomes more specific as the technique evolved at the Jazz Actors Theatre.
53 Edwards interview.
54 Salaam, "Spell No. 7," 34.
55 Bates, interview.
56 Primus, interview.
57 Barnes, "'Equus'," 26.

58 Barnes, "'Equus'," 26.
59 Humm, "Peter Shaffer's."
60 Gruen, "Equus Makes a Star," 1.
61 Billington, "Peter Shaffer's homoerotic classic."
62 Shewey, "Equus—A Horse of a Different Color." In *Gay Community News*, Don Shewey reviewed a 1975 revival of the play at the Wilbur Theater in Boston in which he both unpacks aspects of the text and draws comparisons to experiences that he, and he assumes, other gay folks have experienced when recalling heterosexual encounters. He blatantly connects Alan's desire for a horse with a desire for a man. Other reviews of this same production in mainstream publications gloss over any homosexual overtones in the play.
63 Neal, *Looking for Leroy*, 157.
64 Neal, *Looking for Leroy*, 157.
65 Johnson, *Sweet Tea*, 2.
66 Johnson, *Sweet Tea*, 3.
67 Neal, *Looking for Leroy,* 158.
68 Simon, interview.
69 Primus, interview.
70 Primus, interview.
71 Sinclair, "McClintock's 'Equus'," 50.
72 Gruen, "Equus Makes a Star," 1.
73 Gruen, "Equus Makes a Star," 1.
74 Wallace interview.
75 West, "Race Matters," 86.
76 Bogle, *Toms, Coons*, 10. Donald Bogle traces stereotypes from their inception to contemporary manifestations. Bogle argues that Griffith's *The Birth of a Nation* cemented this stereotype in the social conscience.
77 Bates, interview.
78 Primus, interview.
79 Bates, interview.
80 Bates, interview.
81 Harris, *Poetry and Poetics*, 13.
82 Wallace, interview.
83 Barnes, "*Equus* a New Success," 26.
84 Gruen, "Equus Makes a Star," 1.
85 Eccles, "The Development of Children." For an extensive study in the development of identity and self-awareness in early childhood development refer to Jacquelynne S. Eccles's research.
86 Du Bois, *Souls of Black Folk*, 8.
87 Johnson, "'Quare' Studies," 136.
88 Johnson, "'Quare' Studies," 129.

Bibliography

Barnes, Clive. "'Equus' a New Success on Broadway." *New York Times*, October 25, 1974, 26.

Bates, Jerome Preston. Interview by Elizabeth Cizmar, August 31, 2015, Brooklyn, NY.

Baugh, Edward. "Derek Walcott." *Caribbean Quarterly* 38, no. 4 (December 1992): xiii–xv.

Billington, Michael. "Peter Shaffer's Homoerotic Classic Is Exhilarating." *The Guardian*, February 24, 2019. https://www.theguardian.com/stage/2019/feb/25/equus-review-peter-shaffer-horse-blinding-theatre-royal-stratford-east-london-ned-bennett.

Bogle, Donald. *Toms, Coons, Mulattoes, Mammies, and Bucks: An Interpretive History of Blacks in American Films*, 4th ed. New York: Continuum, 2001.
Brantley, Geno. Interview by Elizabeth Cizmar, September 9, 2015, Richmond, VA.
Butler, Judith. "Critically Queer." In *The Routledge Reader in Politics and Performance*, edited by Lizbeth Goodman with Jane de Gay, 167–71. New York: Routledge, 2000.
Chafe, William. *The Unfinished Journey*, 3rd ed. Edited by Nancy Lane. New York: Oxford University Press, 1995.
Du Bois, W. E. B. *The Souls of Black Folk*. Edited by Brent Hayes Edwards. Oxford: Oxford University Press, 2007.
Dunnaville, Shantell. Interview by Elizabeth Cizmar, June 15, 2022, Zoom.
Eccles, Jacquelynne S. "The Development of Children Ages 6 to 14." *The Future of Children* 9, no. 2 (Autumn 1999): 30–44. https://doi.org/10.2307/1602703.
Edwards, Bolanyle. Interview by Elizabeth Cizmar, August 25, 2015, Atlanta, GA.
Fleming, J. Ron. Interview by Elizabeth Cizmar, September 9, 2015, Richmond, VA.
Giovanni, Nikki. "Black Poems, Poseurs, and Power." In *Call and Response: Key Debates*, edited by Henry Louis Gates Jr., and Jennifer Burton, 711–15. New York: Norton, 2001.
Gruen, John. "'Equus' Makes a Star of Firth." *New York Times*, October 27, 1974, 1.
Harris, William J. *The Poetry and Poetics of Amiri Baraka: The Jazz Aesthetic*. Columbia: University of Missouri Press, 1985.
Harrison, Paul Carter. "Praise/Word." In *Black Theatre: Ritual Performance in the African Diaspora*, edited by Paul Carter Harrison, Victor Leo Walker II, and Gus Edwards, 1–12. Philadelphia: Temple University Press, 2002.
Hill, Anthony D., and Douglass Q. Barnett. *Historical Dictionary of African American Theater*. Lanham, MD: The Scarecrow Press, Inc., 2009.
Humm, Andy. "Peter Shaffer's Coming Out Celebration." *GayCityNews.com*, April 13, 2017.
Johnson, E. Patrick. *Appropriating Blackness: Performance and the Politics of Authenticity*. Durham, NC: Duke University Press, 2003.
Johnson, E. Patrick. "'Quare' Studies, or (Almost) Everything I Know About Queer Studies I Learned From My Grandmother." In *Black Queer Studies: A Critical Anthology*, edited by E. Patrick Johnson, and G. Henderson, 124–57. Durham, NC: Duke University Press, 2005.
King, Seth S. "Job Training Bills to Replace CETA Prepared." *New York Times*, January 17, 1982. http://www.nytimes.com/1982/01/17/us/job-training-bills-to-replace-ceta-prepared.html.
Mayfield, Julian. "You Touch My Black Aesthetic and I'll Touch Yours." In *The Black Aesthetic*, edited by Gayle Addison, 24–31 Garden City, NY: Doubleday & Company, 1971.
McBride, Dwight A. "Straight Black Studies: On African American Studies, James Baldwin, and Black Queer Studies." In *Black Queer Studies: A Critical Anthology*, edited by E. Patrick Johnson, and G. Henderson, 68–89. Durham, NC: Duke University Press, 2005.
McClintock, Ernie. "Perspective on Black Acting." *Black World* (May 1974): 79–85.
Mitchell, Lionel. "'Dream on Monkey Mountain' Reveals a Fine Rep Company." *New York Amsterdam News*, July 24, 1982, 36.
Neal, Mark Anthony. *Looking for Leroy: Illegible Black Masculinities*. New York: New York University Press, 2013.

Pollard, Cherise. "Sexual Subversions, Political Inversions: Women's Poetry and the Politics of the Black Arts Movement." In *New Thoughts on the Black Arts Movement*, edited by Lisa Gail Collins and Margo Natalie Crawford, 173–87. New Brunswick, NJ: Rutgers University Press, 2006.

Primus, Marc. "Ernie McClintock Talks of the Goals of 127th St. Rep." *New York Amsterdam News*, July 10, 1982, 29.

Primus, Marc. Interview by Elizabeth Cizmar, August 25, 2015, Atlanta, GA.

Radford-Hill, Sheila. *Further to Fly: Black Women and the Politics of Empowerment*. Minneapolis: University of Minnesota Press, 2000.

Rowell, George, and Anthony Jackson. *The Repertory Movement: A History of Regional Theatre in Britain*. Cambridge: Cambridge University Press, 1984.

Salaam, Yusef A. "'Spell No. 7': Antidote for Abuse of Black Image." *New York Amsterdam News*, July 13, 1982, 34.

Shaffer, Peter. *Equus*. New York: Scribner, 1973.

Shange, Ntozake. "Spell #7." In *The Metheun Drama of Anthology of American Women Playwrights 1970–2020*, edited by Wesley Brown and Aimée K. Michel, 57–88. New York: Metheun Drama, 2020.

Shange, Ntozake. *Three Pieces*. New York: St. Martin's Griffin, 1992.

Shewey, Don. "EQUUS—A Horse of a Different Color." *DonShewy.com*. Accessed September 11, 2020. https://www.donshewey.com/theater_reviews/equus_1975.html.

Simon, Levy Lee. Interview by Elizabeth Cizmar, September 18, 2015, phone.

Sinclair, Abiola. "McClintock's 'Equus' in Theatrical 'Mane-Stream.'" *New York Amsterdam News*, August 7, 1982, 50.

Uhrbach, Jan R. "A Note on Language and Naming in Dream on Monkey Mountain." *Callaloo*, no. 29 (1986): 578–82. http://www.jstor.com/stable/2930916.

Walcott, Dereck. "Dream on Monkey Mountain." In *Dream on Monkey Mountain and Other Plays*, 207–326. New York: Farrar, Straus and Giroux, 1970.

Wallace, Gregory. Interview by Elizabeth Cizmar, September 16, 2015, phone.

West, Cornel. *Race Matters*. Boston, MA: Beacon Press, 2001.

Williams, Mance. *Black Theatre in the 1960s and 1970s: A Historical-Critical Analysis of the Movement*. Portsmouth, NH: Greenwood Press, 1985.

5
REBEL IN RICHMOND (1987–1993)

In 1987, Ernie McClintock renamed the 127th Street Repertory Ensemble the Harlem Jazz Theatre acknowledging and signifying the importance of the jazz aesthetic in his pedagogical and artistic vision. By the mid- to late-1980s, the vibrancy of the Black Arts Movement and the majority of theatre institutions in Harlem closed their doors due to financial strain. As explored in Chapter 4, Reaganomics benefited Americans who were born into privilege and focused on an individual's drive for success rather than building community. The policies slashing funding for the arts as well as other social programs impacted the survival of the Black Theatre Movement. However, the spirit and commitment to forge ahead, create meaningful work responding to a surrounding environment, and evolve the Black Aesthetic to be more inclusive was undeterred. McClintock was a tenacious arts leader where he lived and breathed Black Theatre without the aims of fame and fortune. He did, however, become infamous for his unorthodox style, strict approach in the classroom, and refusal for any performance to be less than extraordinary. And so, he established the Harlem Jazz Theatre to meet those standards and further develop his production aesthetic.

McClintock's decision to include jazz in the name of his Harlem-based company also extended to when he moved to Richmond establishing the Jazz Theatre of Richmond and then the Jazz Actors Theatre. The Jazz Actors Theatre in particular also includes the term "actors" harkening back to his first days in the 1960s analyzed in Chapter 2 where his main objective was to fill a lacuna in acting methods to develop an Afrocentric technique. In an invitation for a showcase on December 20, 1987, in bold print it states: "WHY JAZZ THEATRE? It's different, it's daring, it's unpredictable." (Figure 5.1) This description is consistent with McClintock's conception of theatre, in for example, subverting *Equus*. The invitation also includes definitions of style and jazz

DOI: 10.4324/9781003187448-6

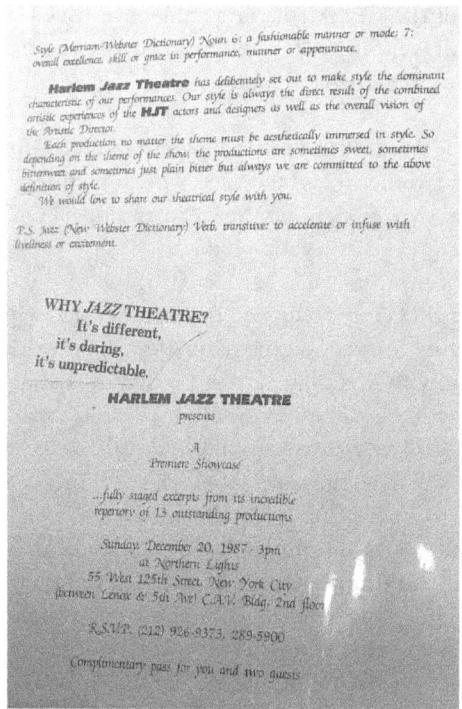

FIGURE 5.1 Invitation for Harlem Jazz Theatre Showcase.
Credit: Private Collection of Geno Brantley.

demonstrating his intentional choice in renaming the company. It notes that they have "…deliberately set out to make style the dominant characteristic,"[1] infused with the electricity of jazz and, of course, high standards of excellence. This piece of archival material demonstrates that regardless of a production's genre, they were committed to this definition of style requiring overall excellence, skill, and grace. Jazz Actor Shantell Dunnaville describes McClintock's jazz theatrical style as an explosion on the stage where the cast is so spiritually connected that they are acutely attuned to one another.[2] These standards reflect the level of sophistication and mastery it takes to become a bona fide Jazz Actor.

In his transition from Harlem to Richmond, McClintock remained centered in jazz aesthetics. However, McClintock adjusted his teaching and productions based on his student population, further rebelling against a one-size-fits all approach reflected in Stanislavsky training, analyzed in Chapter 2. In Richmond, his acting students were mostly young folks in their late teens to early twenties, many of whom were enrolled in surrounding colleges such as Virginia Commonwealth University and University of Richmond. The devotion of these young artists is impressive in that they were fully committed to the Jazz Actors Theatre while simultaneously pursuing degrees and working part-time jobs.

To be a member of the Jazz Actors or a student in McClintock's class would require tireless hours of study both inside and outside the classroom. As articulated by Jazz Actor Dr. Christel Temple,

> His technique was driven in that we spent so much time with him. Class could last for two hours and then you'd get something to eat, so there was fellowship as well as training. Strict in training but fellowship [where] you could laugh and everybody sighed.[3]

Temple noted that McClintock applied the Jazz Acting technique to every aspect of life—listening to songs on the radio, discussing world phenomena, and that every moment with McClintock was a lesson in Jazz Acting.

In continuing with the methodology of the previous chapters, based on firsthand interviews with Jazz Actors, original archival research, and play analysis, the following demonstrates how McClintock's technique and aesthetic continued to develop from 1987 to 1993 where, by 1991, he and Ronald Walker settled in Richmond, Virginia, with a large population of Black folks, yet few options in terms of Afrocentric performance. Prior to his move, the New York landscape was changing and he engaged in more guest directing gigs. In 1989, he was appointed as a board member for the first National Black Theatre Festival, which demonstrates his importance in the 1980s American Black Theatre. In Richmond, with his new, eager student population, he continued to develop Jazz Acting in which he subverted not only western storytelling, but the white mainstream theatre scene in Richmond. McClintock developed his craft and aesthetic in the heart of the Black theatre scene in the 1960s and 1970s, a hub of Black art and culture. He was surrounded by his people and his work spoke to the Harlem-based community. When he moved to Richmond, he confronted a very different population, which had a robust Black population, but lacked Black Theatre. Based on interviews of those who lived in Richmond in the 1980s and 1990s, the city seemed to be quite segregated. According to Temple, "Richmond is a conservative place."[4] The remnants of the antebellum south circulated Richmond, with statues of confederate soldiers watching over the city. And so, in the capital of the confederacy, he ventured to create a Black Theatre presence filling a gap of representation, forever changing the landscape of Richmond Theatre.

Harlem Jazz Theatre

By the late 1970s, McClintock's reputation was established nationally in which he was often asked to be a guest director at various regional theatres training actors in what Monica White Ndounou refers to as on-the-job-training (OJT).[5] For example, in 1978, he was a guest artist resident at the Elma Lewis School of Fine Arts in Roxbury, MA for 12 weeks culminating in a production of Phillip Dean Hayes' *Freeman* (1973). In Harlem in the 1980s, McClintock was presented with guest directing gigs to supplement his income, such as The Boys Choir of Harlem (1968–2007) founded by Dr. Walter Turnbull and Ruth Nixon.[6] McClintock also took on guest directing jobs at various regional theatres disseminating his aesthetic across the country by implementing OJT, a paradigm that is part of the tradition of Black performing arts institutions.[7]

OJT had been part of McClintock's approach since the early 1970s when actors would audition for the 127th Street Repertory Ensemble and learn the technique during rehearsals. Actors who learned in this tradition include Jerome Preston Bates, Gregory Wallace, and Levy Lee Simon. The difference is these actors during rehearsals for *Shango de Ima* and *Equus*, would be working alongside actors who had trained at the Afro-American Studio. When McClintock went on the road, he encountered an entire cast of actors new to Jazz Acting, or what he called a Common Sense approach in the 1970s. The technique evolved to meet the needs of his students and the needs of the times. Therefore, when the Harlem Jazz Theatre was founded, McClintock was splitting his attention between his own company and guest directing work to make ends meet. Presumably, the lack of funding for the arts that had been cut during the 1980s required McClintock to find outside work. Taking on contract jobs would be a consistent practice in order to supplement his income and continue to cultivate the Jazz Actors Theatre.[8] Although McClintock may have preferred to stay focused on his companies, these guest directing opportunities allowed for artists in various pockets of the country to learn Jazz Acting.

Contextually, in the late 1980s, the George H.W. Bush versus Michael Dukakis election highlighted growing racial tensions across the country. Essentially, the Bush Dukakis election hinged on a Black inmate, Willie Horton, who had been convicted of rape and assault, and when he was granted a weekend furlough, raped again. The leftist presidential nominee, Dukakis, among many of his liberal policies, endorsed weekend furloughs for prisoners who had committed violent crimes. With Horton's breach of furlough, the Republican strategists created Horton as a poster-boy for leftist liberalism as a tactic to sway voters that a vote for Bush was a vote for a safer country. All other issues such as globalization of the economy, Mikhail Gorbachev's revolution in the Soviet Union, and homelessness fell to the wayside and Bush won. Therefore, this election and strategy capitalizing on racial polarization set the stage for the decade and was the backdrop of McClintock's work in the 1990s.

The sociopolitical circumstances of the election that exacerbated the racial divide did not deter the Black Theatre community from creating provocative theatre, celebrating the tenacity of a people, and honoring the accomplishments of Black artists. In McClintock's partnerships with other theatres, his reputation as an important figure in the Black Theatre Movement preceded him. In particular, Larry Leon Hamlin, the founder of the North Carolina Black Repertory (est. 1979) in 1989 hired McClintock to direct the anti-apartheid play

The Island (1973) written by Athol Fugard, John Kani, and Winston Ntshona. Based on a true story, the play is set in an unnamed prison, presumably based on South Africa's Robben Island prison, where two prisoners rehearse scenes from Sophocles' *Antigone* in which parallels are drawn between Antigone's narrative and unjust oppression of Black political prisoners. During this historical moment in the United States, there was growing awareness and outrage with the apartheid. McClintock had included this piece for the 1978 127th Street Repertory Ensemble season alongside Richard Wesley's *The Sirens* (1975), Lonnie Elder III's *Ceremonies in Dark Old Men* (1969), and Joseph Walker's *The River Niger* (1973). Notably, well-known actor Richard Gant, a member of the 127th Street Repertory Ensemble, directed The *Island* during the 1978 season. In an interview about the production in Winston-Salem, McClintock stated:

> I think the play, as performed in the United States, is a play that gives us a particular kind of information that we don't really get in our day-to-day lives in terms of the information on television and in the newspaper... The play gives a more in-depth view of what living under racist, South African apartheid is like. The acts of heroism that the people display on a daily basis in defiance of that government give us an insight into the loneliness that many of those men and women have to suffer.[9]

The opening of the production was in conjunction with the South African Crisis Coordinating Committee in Winston-Salem holding anti-apartheid initiatives. The production, then, was tied to a tangible political act to engage with the community and join the effort to dismantle apartheid in South Africa. In the words of Hamlin, "...we want to move people to stimulate the people of Winston-Salem to fight apartheid."[10] Although the crux of the production was meant to "stimulate the people," McClintock noted that it was a very theatrical production, not "a weighty political lesson."[11] Therefore, even with a production with a clear political agenda, he maintained the mission of the Harlem Jazz Theatre to maintain style with high standards of excellence related to skill and grace.

In 1989, McClintock became part of one of the most "historical and culturally significant events in the history of Black theatre:"[12] the founding of the National Black Theatre Festival. The 1989 festival's theme was "A celebration and reunion of spirit," produced by Larry Leon Hamlin and hosted by the North Carolina Black Repertory Company. The aim of the festival, which is still active today, is to bring together Black theatres from across the country for performances, workshops, and seminars. It draws thousands of participants and spectators where in the first year, nearly 200 Black Theatres traveled to Winston-Salem. For the first festival, Dr. Maya Angelou served as the chair of the National Advisory Board where Ernie McClintock joined renowned figures such as Debbie Allen, Ed Bullins, Vinette Carroll, Ossie Davis, Ruby Dee, Arsenio Hall, Rosemary Harris, Robert Hooks, Woody King, Jr., and others.[13]

One of the objectives of the National Black Theatre Festival aligns with McClintock's tenet of community building, an overlapping concept in the African Diaspora. Additionally, there were urgent concerns over the future of Black performing arts: "Black theatre in America may very well become non-existent in the next ten years if steps are not taken now on a national level to ensure its longevity."[14] Hamlin's objective for the festival was, therefore, to highlight for the nation the importance and plight of Black Theatre in the twentieth century. And although community is one of the principles of Afrocentricity, Hamlin noted that during that moment, prior to the Festival, there were not many opportunities for Black Theatre artists to convene and establish strategies to succeed. The Black Theatre Movement as well as the Harlem Renaissance were certainly two movements in which Black Theatre exploded from an institutional standpoint. In fact, two theatres born of the Black Arts Movement, the Harlem Jazz Theatre and the Negro Ensemble Company, performed at the festival in 1989. McClintock brought the Contemporary Black Classic *Do Lord Remember Me*, fully explored in Chapter 3, to the inaugural event. The National Black Theatre Festival, with seminars and workshops, provided the time and resources to work together, exchange ideas culminating in a "celebration and reunion of spirit," as opposed to the competitive nature inherent in mainstream, capitalist theatre. McClintock and Walker's goals were to be able to support themselves financially, sustain a company of actors producing quality Black Theatre, develop the Jazz Acting technique, and maintain artistic autonomy absent of the white gaze. His aims were not centered on reaching celebrity status; otherwise, he would have gone the mainstream route. At the same time, he would have to take freelance gigs across the country to remain afloat.

The Move to Richmond

Due to the changes in the New York theatrical landscape, financial challenges, and devastation of 57 company members and friends dying from the AIDS epidemic,[15] Ernie McClintock and Ronald Walker left New York in 1989 seeking change:

> We have fifty seven of our members who died from AIDS and did their eulogies and it has to be included and that devastated the studio and no one talks about it. Everyone at the studio seemed to arrive at themselves so we are all human beings.[16]

The couple wanted to settle in a new town and pursue art with a new group of young, driven actors.[17] They initially went to Atlanta, an already established theatre community, where McClintock had many connections in the industry. However, the tight-knit clique of theatre artists was not accepting of outsiders like McClintock and Walker. The couple left discouraged and briefly considered Norfolk, VA before landing in Richmond. Temple observed "The Black world of the City of Richmond has an interesting identity complex. For example, that's how we became the murder capital of the nation in the early 1990s."[18] In that time period, Richmond consisted of a 60 percent Black population, yet there was a major deficit of Black Theatre in the community.[19]

When McClintock and Walker moved to Richmond, the country witnessed the beating of Rodney King bringing what Black folks had experienced on a daily basis to the living rooms of white America. On March 3, 1991, Rodney King was driving while intoxicated on I-210 in Los Angeles and after a high-speed chase, four police officers savagely beat and terrorized Rodney King. The police officers were tried on charges of use of excessive force where three of the assailants were acquitted and the jury failed to reach a verdict on the fourth police officer. Police brutality was recorded on video, but the all-white jurors ruled in favor of the cops. Riots ensued eerily resembling the Watts Rebellion from 1965 where "Chief Daryl Gates frequently indulged in racist remarks where police acted without restraint and ignored the rules."[20] What emerged from this incident was a demonstration of the police acting like a southern lynch mob of the late nineteenth century. The all-white jury also mirrored trials from centuries past in which they had irrefutable evidence of the police's wrongdoing and, "It was as though they had taken a hallucinogenic drug that altered their reality—and the drug was race."[21] As a result, in April and May of 1992, riots erupted in Los Angeles forcing the white public to contend with systemic racism.

Despite the divisions in Richmond and friction across the country, Geno Brantley asserts that Richmond received McClintock and Walker with open arms; and even with programming challenges, the Jazz Acting technique continued to evolve, impress audiences, and change the lives their students. Regarding the challenges, McClintock stated,

> It was extremely difficult because it is something new. In the last ten years, Black theater has not been traditional in Richmond... except for professional theater. There are some white theaters that do major Black productions a few times per year, but there is little more than that.[22]

At this unlikely location, McClintock filled a void not just in terms of productions, but also in terms of providing a culturally specific acting technique for Black actors in a town with a history of racial divide. Ernie McClintock introduced his inclusive Afrocentric approach, which subverted mainstream theatre, yet cultivated community building. Temple observed, "I hadn't met anyone in Richmond so committed to [a Black] institution beyond the church."[23] Through these efforts, his theory and technique continued to develop in the tradition of jazz aesthetics, bringing to fruition the Jazz Actors Technique: A Common Sense Approach to Acting, an OJT paradigm, which lives in perpetuity.

In Richmond, McClintock had to restructure the curriculum and structure from the Afro-American Studio because the faculty he worked with in New York pursued other interests. Therefore, while there were some basic technique classes in Richmond, they were geared toward production, both scripted and collectively-authored work. McClintock was not affiliated with any institution at this point—his pedagogy from Harlem had not changed—he aimed to create a company of actors where he could develop his acting technique and directorial aesthetic. The student population, however, did shift. Richmond is a college town with institutions that offer Bachelor of Fine Arts and Master of Fine Arts in theatre. Consistent with other mainstream institutions, these students were taught primarily Stanislavsky-based methods. Young actors of color got wind of Ernie McClintock, a seasoned director and acting teacher, who brought an Afrocentric approach to theatre-making (Figure 5.2). In Harlem, in the 1960s–1980s, many of his students were closer to their 30s and had full-time jobs outside of pursuing acting. In Richmond, students would study at the institution they were enrolled in including Virginia Commonwealth University and the University of Richmond, and then study in the evenings with McClintock, whose standards were high and expected discipline and commitment. The classes were more like workshops that lasted several weeks with the intention of fully realizing a show, as opposed to an eight-week curriculum like in New York. For various reasons, such as financial, logistical, or artistic, some productions would not reach an audience. While at other times, their work yielded staged readings, workshop productions, and fully staged work.

FIGURE 5.2 Still of Jazz Actors: Top Row L to R: Mia Burdie, Cheryl Sullivan, dl Hopkins, Linwood Jones, Ed Broaddus, Jakotora Tjoutuku, Mary Hodges Bottom Row L to R: J. Ron Fleming, Toni McDade-Williams, Derome Scott Smith.
Credit: Private Collection of Geno Brantley.

"Two Jazz Theatres? Ludicrous!"

The establishment of the Jazz Theatre of Richmond in 1992 demonstrates how the New York-based director's theoretical foundation and aesthetic had persisted beyond the period considered the Black Arts Movement (1965–1975). In studies on this time period, when the federal funding and grants were halted and the Black Theatre Alliance dismantled, the assumption was that the movement had ended. However, given the continued success of Barbara Ann Teer's National Black Theatre, Woodie King Jr.'s New Federal Theatre, Robert Hooks' Negro Ensemble Company, and Ernie McClintock's Harlem Jazz Theatre and subsequent Jazz Actors Theatre, the movement defies "neat" historical narratives. McClintock's ability to connect to any given community from 1960s Harlem to 1990s Richmond, proves how his technique and productions serve the diverse makeup of artists across the United States.

In 1992, McClintock instituted the Jazz Theatre of Richmond where from the get-go, he aimed to change the landscape of Richmond Theatre. Through Richmond Department of Parks and Recreation, S. Allison Baker, director of the city agency, McClintock was hired to create a theatre program by teaching classes to children and seniors as well as direct full-scale productions. In McClintock's inclusive vision, he believed this space would be, "For everyone who has dreamed of performing...this will provide an opportunity."[24] The lack of inclusivity of another local theatre, Dogwood Dell Productions, was noted by anonymous source in the Richmond Free Press:

> ... essentially it has catered to white suburban family audiences, and we're finding that many Richmond residents don't feel so comfortable with these shows. We aren't looking for only African-American works, but we need a better mix in the selections. We need a more inclusive outlook.[25]

McClintock's arrival to Richmond filled a much-needed gap in art and representation. Baker presumably recognized this and supported the establishment of a board of directors for the Jazz Theatre of Richmond to raise money so that McClintock could focus on program development. He was given a dedicated studio in the Mosque, which was a well-established theatre space that booked "high end productions."[26] The proximity of the Mosque was in central downtown Richmond, on the campus of VCU, shops and restaurants nearby. This was an ideal location to draw in crowds and establish his presence in Richmond.

McClintock actively recruited and instituted programming to change the landscape of Richmond Theatre evidenced by his personal writings. One entry appears to be a draft of a report for the board of directors and/or the Department Recreation because he entitled it "Theatre Program Monthly Report." He visited high schools, such as John Marshall, to introduce the technique to children and adults. In these mini workshops, he also created feedback forms for the participants. This feedback process provided an opportunity to assess the specific makeup of the community and how he could connect with them. In his writings, he observes the enthusiasm for Jazz Acting in Richmond: "It should be noted that practically every student expressed a desire to attend more advance classes in the fall."[27] This reveals a hunger for alternative acting methods during this time in Richmond where a visionary brought diverse production offerings to the community and infused the theatre scene with new energy. In the draft of the monthly report, he lists a wish list including hiring an administrative assistant, a computer, additional phone line, water fountain, transportation for kids, more personal contact with parents, and, most importantly, increased communication between the department of Parks and Recreation and his team.

The Jazz Theatre of Richmond lasted only a year after McClintock split from the board of directors and founded the Jazz Actors Theatre. The board had apparently wanted to keep the Jazz Theatre of Richmond running while McClintock took his faithful students to form the new company. However, it seems without McClintock, and after his departure, the Jazz Theatre of Richmond proved to be "ludicrous."[28] In *The Richmond Afro-American and The Richmond Planet*, J.W. Robinson Horne wrote a piece about the absurdity of having two jazz theatres. Horne explains that the genesis of the Jazz Theatre of Richmond was born of McClintock's Jazz Acting technique, the same impetus that sparked the Afro-American Studio in Harlem in the 1960s. He states:

> With this knowledge of the Jazz Theatre Technique, conceived and taught by Mr. McClintock, it is inconceivable how the Board of Directors could take Jazz Theatre of Richmond when they decided to form their own group... Why use the name which is an integral part and description of a theatrical technique created by someone else? In my opinion it borders on plagiarism![29]

Horne's outrage also stems from the fact that he was named to the advisory board, but more importantly, he states that this division in the Black community is distressing because unity, not division should be stressed.

Based on interviews, newspaper articles, and correspondence, McClintock was not receiving the support he needed from the board of directors. Horne also emphasized that prior to the split, Ernie McClintock's directorial expertise and two decades of producing during the Black Theatre Movement, afforded four successful seasons in Richmond.[30] McClintock was accustomed to a New York-pace and drive in which the board did not have the experience in "the type of institution-building or financial patronage that could sustain Ernie's vision."[31] At the same time, McClintock was known as rigidly uncompromising and wanted things done his way. This is a reason why he never aimed to become a celebrity on the Great White Way—the necessary evil of losing some artistic autonomy.

In 1992, the Richmond Free Press published an article that the Richmond City Department of Parks and Recreation hired McClintock to build a theatre program for the city. Essentially, the city provided space and resources for McClintock to develop his company and school to benefit all age groups at various community centers in the city. Although the Jazz Theatre of Richmond would be part of the Department of Parks and Rec, McClintock's company was a "virtually independent operation although it...nominally [fell] under the city-wide arts programs run out of Pine Camp,"[32] the Richmond Parks and Rec activity center.

For reasons that seem unclear, the Department of Parks and Rec asked him to direct Errol John's *Moon on Rainbow Shawl* (1958). In a letter to S. Allison Baker recounting reporting on the split from the Jazz Theatre of Richmond McClintock wrote "You may or may not be aware of my sincere and intense professional reluctance to direct "Moon on a Rainbow Shawl" as the first production this summer. It was only after extensive dialogue...that I consented. I was promised exceptional support but it was not hand has not been extended."[33] In the play that takes place during the US occupation of Trinidad in which Dr. Christel Temple played Mavis, a sex worker, white soldiers entered and exited Mavis' shack with "brazen insinuations of sex."[34] According to Temple, it seemed like a bold choice because "it was a very Afro-culturally mature play for a lightweight Richmond City Parks and Rec audience."[35] McClintock made it a priority to know the community and the audience, and when he first arrived in Richmond, his goal was to create a thriving theatre ensemble with a permanent location, something that he yearned for his whole life. Directing John's play, however, did supply him with the much-needed income. Despite his reservations and the audience demographic, the show received rave reviews.

Another way in which McClintock was mistreated was the directive to abruptly move from the dedicated theatre space at the Mosque to Pine Camp. The Mosque Theatre opened its doors on October 27, 1927, marking the "farewell performance of opera legend Madame Ernestine Schumann-Heink."[36] The city bought the Mosque in 1940 with a renovation in the mid-1990s, seating 3565 spectators. According to Stage Manager Donna Pendarvis,

> It has undergone several renovations of varying budgets, named the Landmark by the city in 1995 to coincide with a $5.4 million renovation for expansion of dressing rooms and the fly rail to accommodate larger touring Broadway shows, and in 2014 Altria (Philip Morris) donated $10 million for naming rights as part of a $50 million renovation.[37]

The Altria regularly hosts Broadway tours and celebrity headliners. Initially, McClintock's office was in the Mosque, a massive space with offices, rehearsal space, a pool, a bowling alley, and "at one time had secret rooms."[38]

The City of Richmond has owned and operated this space since 1940 and the Department of Parks and Rec was also run by the city. On Thursday, June 3, 1993, administrator Flo Grigg met with McClintock at the Powhatan Recreation Center at Pine Camp where she said he was to vacate the Mosque and move into Pine Camp, a large playground with indoor facilities and used primarily for kids' after school and summer programs. The location was the farthest northern Parks and Rec facility off of I-95. In McClintock's estimation, the move was not conducive to creating the kind of change he aimed to have in Richmond. Namely, it was a far cry from the center of Richmond, especially for McClintock who did not have a driver's license, and those with limited access to transportation and financial resources:

> In terms of demotion in space, to go from the Mosque to a dusty little playground camp area was visually symbolic. But, by this time, it seemed that Ernie had a steady income with Rec and Parks. It wasn't a bad place, though. The theatre was intimate and cute, and it was an answer to Ernie's need for space that was not in super high demand from others. Ernie didn't drive.[39]

The reasoning behind the move from the Mosque to Pine Camp was never specified, but ostensibly McClintock was being physically and symbolically edged out of Richmond. McClintock produced a successful production of *Moon on a Rainbow Shawl,* despite the content of the play that could have turned off Richmond audiences. He was building a theatre program and company to bring more inclusivity to the Richmond Theatre scene, and yet, he was asked to move out of the major theatrical institution in the city. Perhaps his work was too subversive and would invite theatre administrators to seriously think about programming that up to that point had been largely exclusive. Based on the types of productions and artists that come through the doors, they brought in shows and stars where they can make a handsome profit, rather than consider the identities and artistic perspectives of those artists living right in Richmond. McClintock felt this was a decision that disrespected his "30 years of accomplishments as a theatre professional."[40] This, however, did not deter his mission and in a letter to Baker, even after mistreatment, he said "I can and want to be part of a great theatre effort. I believe I can be a major asset to its success. I believe I am working in the direction that meets your approval"[41] (Figure 5.3). McClintock continued to bring his mission and aesthetic to the Richmond community and shifted his technique to meet the needs of his students. His students were loyal to McClintock who followed him to Pine Camp because they knew they had so much to learn under his tutelage. Even though he was not making massive profits from his teaching and directing, he shaped the lives of hundreds of actors. Although he had a reputation for being quite ornery in rehearsals and strict in the classroom, the work of his students and his productions

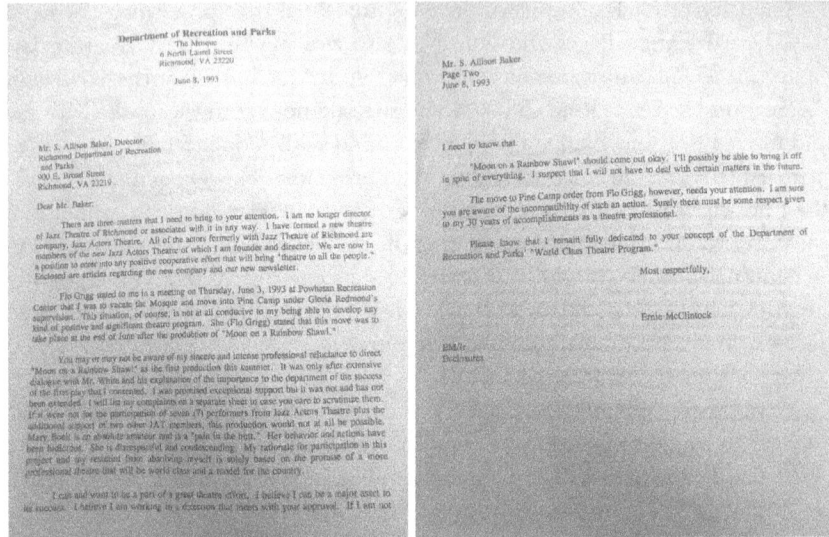

FIGURE 5.3 Letter from Ernie McClintock to S. Allison Baker June 8, 1993. *Credit*: Private Collection of Geno Brantley.

spoke for themselves. He was unmatched in terms of his excellence in actor training and his company realizing an ensemble aesthetic in performance.

The Technique

The structure and approach adapted to align with the needs of a younger student demographic in a southern city where the Jazz Acting technique continued to evolve. In one of McClintock's notebooks, written in the last few years of his life, he reflected on the purpose of creating the Jazz Actors Theatre:

1. To offer opportunity for select Black actors to significantly enhance their acting skills in a culturally based environment.
2. To provide Mr. McClintock a forum to further evolve his Jazz Actors Technique: A Common Sense Approach to Acting, which has since 1966 been an important tool for actors interested in the pursuit of artistic excellence in performance.
3. To present to diverse audiences a variety of plays by Black writers focusing most on those of social significance, challenging aesthetics, and outstanding literary achievement.[42]

McClintock maintained his core beliefs from 1966. He advanced the original mission to establish a technique for Black actors, to develop a directorial aesthetic aligned with the principles of jazz, and to challenge the status quo through performances that spoke to a particular cultural moment. Aspects of the technique developed in the days of the Afro-American that carried over to the Jazz Actors Theatre include gestures, habits, community observations, and activities, detailed in Chapter 2. In Richmond, however, McClintock placed a greater emphasis on language and script analysis alongside the physical portrayal of character.

In Jazz Acting script analysis, the question that is posed and answer is, "What is my objective and what am I willing to do to achieve it?" Just as the actor is fully committed to the physical life of the character, the actor must be at all times fully aware of their objective. McClintock did not use "beats" for scenes, as commonly used in Stanislavsky-based systems. Rather, he referred to "units" within scenes, which according to Jazz Actor Mary Hodges was "more than a beat. It's part of entrances and exits. A palpable shift."[43] The actor should write out the objectives for each unit and the means to achieve that objective, to enforce the performance. The actor may not achieve the objective. The objective statement is "I want to _____ (to whom or to what) in order to (words that I choose to define)."[44] The objective is accomplished, detained for later, or defeated. Once one of those three happens, a new unit for the actor begins with a new objective. Jazz Actor Derome Smith noted with this analysis you focus on character, relationship, environment, place, and objective. All these elements are important and at play, "You have to work that way as a Jazz Actor, understand where you are and what moves you to the next thing."[45] These objectives are predetermined, however, in performance or in rehearsal if something happens in the live moment, a unit could end earlier or perhaps the objective is detained for later, as opposed to rejected. Smith acknowledges, however, that the technique is "Based on what is happening on stage at that time. There are things of course, common sense, that govern everything you do."[46] His comment is particularly important in understanding the discipline and complexity of Jazz Acting—all the elements McClintock considered throughout his teaching. At different moments in the classroom and across decades, his teaching might emphasize one aspect of the technique, based on the needs of the students.

McClintock often referenced Paul Carter Harrison's *The Drama of Nommo* (1972), which identifies the relationship between the African concept of Nommo and Black Theatre. Carter Harrison argues that Black Theatre is a site for exploring and discovering Black experiences. Nommo defines the human body and mind as being one with the life force, in rhythm with the earth and the first ancestors. In terms of language and speech, Nommo informs the delivery and cadence: "...the power of the *word*, that Nommo force which manipulates all forms of raw life and conjures images that not only represent his biological place in Time and Space, but his spiritual existence as well."[47] In a nondenominational sense, therefore, Jazz Acting has a spiritual component that manifests through the spoken word. Although McClintock did not specifically identify Nommo as part of his pedagogy in 1966 (prior to when the book came out), there was certainly a component of connecting with the ancestors in courses like Black History and Culture and in productions like Baraka's *Slaveship*, analyzed in Chapter 3.

Language was connected to this idea of Nommo—that when a word is spoken, its image is realized in the theatrical space. When working on poetry, the first step a Jazz Actor would engage in, McClintock would say, "See it, say it, see it say it,"[48] to take the words of a poem and make it alive in the rehearsal hall. McClintock adopted the notion of Pronouns and Absolutes from his work with Helen Espie, referenced in Chapter 1. Regarding pronouns, actors certainly had to "See it, say it," in that every time they uttered a pronoun, they need to know exactly how the character feels about that person, place, or thing, and clearly communicate that feeling to the audience. Jazz Actor Sheldon Woodley who attended Juilliard after working with McClintock observed, "To stress pronouns sounds more poetic, [Juilliard] concentrated more on verbs to move the text."[49]

McClintock developed Espie's notion of absolutes through an Afrocentric framework. For Espie, absolutes such as never, always, don't, etc. were considered guideposts of language. Actor Thaddeus Daniels particularly uses these concepts in his acting today. He contends that McClintock's evolution of Espie's approach to absolutes evolved so that the actors could connect language to the music and rhythm of a sentence. Each word in the script was loaded, each word of the script required the power of Nommo to effectively communicate with the audience and result in a performance of magnitude and certainty. The concentration on verbs is a common method in Stanislavski-based training, which perhaps one would assume creates a more embodied performance. However, with Jazz Acting, the gestures, habits, and activities do not rely on the text to create theatricality or drama. The actor needs to create their own agency and choices, to be as McClintock articulated, "more than a shell, a body and a voice that moves around..."[50]

In the spirit of one ensemble and a community, McClintock established the First Word, which served to create a distinct, fully realized character from the first moment an actor appears on stage. The actor now has a detailed and thorough understanding of the character based on both the text and imagination, and they transition into scene work. This moment is the first time the character is seen on stage by the audience. The actor must do or say something that establishes who the person is in a flash.[51] After the First Word, there should be a pause and then the actor "goes for it."[52] Initial possibilities are a particular emphasis of the First Word of text, gesture, or even a facial expression. The audience is meant to connect to the actor and then move forward in the scene. Actor Thaddeus Daniels referenced the late Michael Jackson as a prime example of the First Word in performance. Jackson's First Word occurred the first moment with a flash of choreography. He drew the audience in with this flash of movement, paused, and proceeded. As Derome Scott Smith contends, "You just don't turn on the lights and I'm there. What can you do to unpack for the audience when they first see you?"[53] The First Word allows the actor to consider the theatricality of the work. In other words, this is not actually real life or pure "naturalism." McClintock would say that the person in the back row needs to connect with the First Word, and the actor must create a perfect balance larger than life yet still grounded in humanity. Thaddeus Daniels recalls that the First Word in vocalization had to be strongly and effectively pronounced. In his role in *Before It Hits Home*, when his first line was "Excuse me, I have an appointment with Dr. Weinberg," McClintock boldly said to him, "Open your fucking mouth. Don't murmur. I want to hear what you are saying."[54] Geno Brantley, lighting designer, pointed out that the First Word had to be reflected in the lighting design as well. Therefore, the First Word in gesture, language, and design had to strike the audience both visually and aurally.

As part of McClintock's evolving jazz directorial aesthetic with a primacy on ensemble cohesiveness, he created the concept of actors "Jazzing It" in performance.[55] "Jazzing It" relates to McClintock's definition of ensemble established in 1978: "a group of actors, intensely working with the same technique and philosophy over an extended period of time, resulting in a creative communications process that allows for a harmonious and identifiable style in production."[56] Mary Hodges explained the notion of Jazzing It in performances, which she still applies to her acting and directing work:

> Choose an ensemble moment and collectively do something together. The audience may not necessarily pick up on it. But we decide as a group that moment for the story or play… It could be something like we all look up and look out and see the sunset…It could be something such as each actor doing the same gesture at different points throughout the play… The ensemble as a collective planned it.[57]

Jazzing It moments depend on all the character work that precedes it. The actor must be prepared to alter preplanned moments, and allow the performance to be a living, breathing entity. McClintock's primacy on ensemble work dated back to the Afro-American Studio for Acting and Speech and the 127th Street Repertory Ensemble. Jerome Preston Bates, who played Nugget in *Equus* explored in Chapter 4 recalls his own education on McClintock's concept of ensemble:

> He gave me the tenacity and patience to embrace ensemble work. A company of actors, not just individuals who want to stand out. Being a part of a company, to tell a story – ensemble work does that. Ensemble work is what tells the story.[58]

These particular moments as an ensemble bring the actors together as one voice, one community, and within the riffing of the melody, resulting in an ever-evolving discovery process.

Jean Genet's *The Blacks* in Unconventional Theatrical Spaces

Prior to the 1993 productions of *The Blacks: A Clown Show* (1958), Ernie McClintock had not mounted Genet's absurdist play in New York. In New York, *The Blacks* premiered at St. Marks Playhouse in the Lower East Side where it ran for 1408 performances.[59] The plot of the controversial play tells the story of 13 Black characters who put a White Queen on trial, essentially revealing that if Black folks came to power, the white population would be oppressed. Based on the forward of the play, Genet aimed for white audiences to consider and reflect on stereotypes. He wrote that it

> ...is intended for a white audience, but if, which is unlikely, it is ever performed before a Black audience...Then let white masks be distributed to the black spectators as they enter the theatre. And if the Blacks refuse the masks, then let a dummy be used.[60]

As scholar Mance Williams notes, although Genet's play challenges minstrelsy and racial discrimination, the question of stereotypes was already in society's consciousness.

McClintock's two performances of *The Blacks* were set in unconventional spaces: one was a performance of protest outside the Altria Theatre, at that time known as the Mosque (and in 1995 became the Landmark theatre) where McClintock was asked to leave for a residency at Pine Camp, and the other staged in a tent outside the Virginia Commonwealth University's Performing Arts Center. The performance of protest was not related to the friction between him and the administration as far as being as to move from the Mosque. It was not a petty protest, but, rather, a demonstration against a touring company that was set to perform at the Altria. This touring company is what he referred to as the Chitlin Circuit. The Chitlin Circuit is a performance genre that targets Black audiences but often uses stereotypically Black characters that resemble racial tropes in minstrel shows designed to entertain white audiences. In August Wilson's iconic speech "The Ground On Which I Stand," Wilson considers the Chitlin Circuit a modern version of the enslaved Africans performing for the benefit of the master on the plantation: "An important part of Black Theatre that is often ignored but is seminal to its tradition is its origins on the slave plantations of the South. Summoned to the 'big house' to entertain the slave owner and his guests, the slave that reached its pinnacle for Whites consisted of whatever the slave imagined or knew that his master wanted to see and hear. This tradition has its present life counterpart in the crossover artists that slant their material for White consumption."[61] Conversely, Henry Louis Gates Jr. argues that the Chitlin Circuit is meant as entertainment for Black audiences to laugh at themselves, and create a reprieve from the political and social relatives of African Americans, and not mean to be considered "high art" but rather entertainment for their community.

McClintock took the stance of August Wilson in that he opposed this kind of entertainment, especially within the context of Richmond—at the commercial white theatre with primarily white audiences. Mary Hodges recalled that McClintock told his students "we have evolved from that. Stereotypical Black Theatre that was buffoonish."[62] Therefore, his demonstration was an advertisement for their upcoming production of *The Blacks*, but also served to resist the mainstream theatre for promoting stereotypes and making money off this type of entertainment.

> Ernie said, you know what, "We are going to picket, we are going to protest." We had a show coming up, *The Blacks* so it was a way of advertising. We dressed up in our costumes and we marched. And he wanted us to get a sense of pride and privilege to do the theatre we did. And there are these people paying all this money for the stereotypical, buffoonish entertainment. So he was really livid about it and he wanted us to see why. We were marching, singing songs, doing scenes, monologues. It was an educational process in the capital of the confederacy.[63]

A Chitlin Circuit production performed in Richmond's landmark theatre that typically hosts "high culture" white Broadway shows to primarily white audiences highlights August Wilson's critique. Therefore, the white Richmond audience experience of Black characters is through their white gaze. Moreover, these characters more commonly seen in Tyler Perry's productions both on stage and on screen, are not necessarily meant for white consumption. The irony of the characters that Gates argues is lost in this mainstream performance context and stereotypes are affirmed in the white imaginary.

The protest served as advertising for their own production, which VCU slated to be performed on May 1 and 2 in 1993, but due to McClintock's unconventional process, midway through rehearsals, the university administration denied the cast and crew access to the indoor space. Presumably, due to this conflict as well as his protest of the Altria, McClintock was not well-liked by all, especially those in administrative positions. He was unwavering in his vision, his standards, and his commitment to Black Theatre. The actors were not privy to the details of the disagreement but dl Hopkins who played Diouf and assisted with the logistics of the production recalls:

> ...we had an agreement with VCU to put on a production at their theatre. Because Erie has an unorthodox rehearsal, process, everything, he did not adhere to the rules in which they wished to confine him in. But he agreed to do a show. So we did a show. We went from the theatre to a tent outside.[64]

The production was J. Ron Fleming's introduction to the Jazz Actors Theatre in which he insists that the chaos surrounding the production was part of McClintock's genius.

The Jazz Actors noted that they were rehearsing up to opening in which the process-driven play was about creating tension. McClintock's directing and teaching philosophy required the actors to swim in the confusion of the play aligned with the conundrum of Black actors struggling against the white mainstream. They played ridiculous characters (McClintock made some characters even more outrageous—such as J. Ron Fleming as a gay valet akin to a Liberace-type[65]) and as college students were prohibited from performing inside their university theatre. Despite the cast's recollection of confusing process, the makeshift tent outside on the grounds of VCU, J.W. Horne Robinson's review in the "The Richmond Planet" called the production a "tour de force" ensemble.[66] The review acknowledges the talent of the 12 actors, but notes that McClintock "craftily solved the dilemma"[67] exploring nontraditional space and setting a new precedent in Richmond, inspiring out of the box thinking. Horne ends his review by identifying the "artistic audacity" for this troupe to stage such a performance, a description that speaks to McClintock's ventures throughout his career.

In the program for the show, the reviewer picked up on this revolutionary act in Richmond. The director's note, "...for the audience as to...what this play is about, [McClintock] answers the question with the question... what do you think it's about?..." Robinson concludes,

> ...my most prevalent view is that it's about a group of talented, developing African American actors who-with no place to perform was available to them- craftily solved the dilemma by performing in a tent next to the very 'nice' VCU Performing Arts Center.[68]

McClintock's unwavering negotiation with the rules of a university's Performing Arts Center and demonstration of a commercial theatre promoting stereotypes demonstrates how he applied this resistance to the mainstream, to create space and a voice for young actors within the particular context of Richmond.

McClintock's commitment to the local Richmond community is grounded in an Afrocentric worldview, which he passed along to his pupils. This worldview is based on Molefi Asante's establishment of the very notion of Afrocentricity. As fully explored in Chapter 2, Asante's perspective is a moral and intellectual engagement to posit Africans as subjects, rather than objects of human history.[69] In other words, "since an art grows out of a culture and reflects and perpetuates the values of the culture from which it emerges, the values of an art are inextricably connected to the cultural identities of the creators of the art."[70] With regard to *The Blacks*, McClintock's worldview within the context of Richmond essentially adapted Genet's text in production and practice, addressing the dominant Eurocentric commercial culture in this local community.

Collectively-Authored Performance in Richmond

As opposed to the Afro-American Studio, whose community was rich in Black culture and all worked in their own way to create revolutionary theatre, Richmond's particular context and student body shaped McClintock's repertoire in both scripted and collectively-authored work. In Harlem, he established a poetry theatre for and by women, directed primarily by Helmar Cooper, and, in Richmond, he recognized the need to give a voice to the womanist perspective, and also create a theatre to educate African American youth. Beyond just theory and history, the very plays he chose and created for the actors in conjunction with the technique, educated the artists and the audiences. Although the education he provided his students did not provide a degree and much of the unorthodox learning happened in rehearsals rather than a "traditional" classroom, they collectively-authored productions such as *The Collard Greens and Cornbread Divas* and *Sense of Pride*. *The Collard Greens and Cornbread Divas*, a theatrical piece, centered on Black women's experiences so who better to create his piece, but the women themselves. *Sense of Pride* was a children's show based on the African Diaspora experience:

> One of the most brilliant things he came up with… We just did the show like that as an ensemble. We found these stories and put it together as one show. We called it *Sense of Pride* because they were plays based on the African American diaspora experience. Some of them were boring until we thought of it like a children's show… This story about how the sky became the sky.[71]

The production highlighted McClintock's commitment to education and community for the next generation of African Americans in Richmond, where the established curriculum did not include histories and narratives about African folktales promoting Black Pride.

Part of the theoretical grounding in Afrocentricity is the connection to the African Diaspora that really came into full fruition in the 1970s. It was the efforts for "Black Consciousness" that gave way to Pan-Africanism. Jazz Actor Iman Shabazz considers himself a Pan-Africanist and considers his Jazz Acting education beyond the mechanics of theatre:

> The interesting thing is that I stayed with Ernie in his home and looked at his books. He had Franz Fanon, Askia Touré, things I had never seen. All these things helped me to see a sphere of thought around how important connecting theatre to the culture and the culture to the people.[72]

The ensemble dynamic encouraged a community-based focus rather than commercial aspirations, which is also grounded in an Afrocentric worldview encountered throughout the African Diaspora. For example, in a performance of *The Collard Greens and Cornbread Divas*, Thaddeus Daniels recalls that in performance, the women would pick a man from the audience and rub his feet with oils to create a real connection to the ancestors.[73]

By creating a unified story on stage that used the cultural perspectives and related practices in the preparation and performance, McClintock's approach to training actors to engage with audiences accentuated the importance of African ancestry and culture for the performers and audiences. According to Levy Lee Simon, McClintock's primary influence also relates to McClintock's notion of integrating the African ancestry in the work, connecting theatre to the community, and connecting the work to the political and social issues of the day.[74] Part of that unified story is the African Diaspora where McClintock promoted pride within African American culture, and a connection to African ancestry.

Conclusion

The move from New York to Richmond was certainly a culture shock for McClintock and Walker in which they faced administrative and programming challenges. However, consistent to McClintock's character, he never wavered from his "high artistic standards" or commitment to developing Black actors no matter if he was in Harlem, the epicenter of the Black Theatre Movement, or in Richmond, VA, where there was a paucity of Black Theatre. The Jazz Acting technique was not stagnant, but rather it was an ever-evolving artistic endeavor that remained rooted in the fundamental precepts of Black Power. Because he was true to his beliefs and expected nothing but the best from his actors and collaborators (including the board members), he was not entirely "liked," but he was effective. It stands to reason that a gay Black man who was uncompromising would ruffle feathers no matter where he goes, in Harlem or Richmond.

He gained a reputation in Richmond as the premier acting teacher, as McClintock scribbled in one of his journals, "if you want to act, McClintock is the cat."[75] Chapter 6, "The Persistence of a Living Legend," will explore how with the Jazz Actors Theatre firmly established, he continued to promote the values of Black Power in his productions such as Richard Wesley's *The Mighty Gents* (1979), within the context of the 1990s. The messages and efforts of the Black Arts Movement were and still are relevant. In the Jazz Actors Theatre, he also produced queer narratives in one of his most well-known productions of Cheryl L. West's *Before It Hits Home* (1993). McClintock's resistance to mainstream theatre would have meant having to compromise with producers whose goals would be centered on profit rather than excellence in Black Theatre.

Throughout his career, McClintock consistently focused on community building, the agency of African American artists, and the representation of Black life on stage. His work inspires an acting approach that recognizes the role of representation on self-perception, self-determination, and self-actualization for actors and their audiences.

Notes

1 Invitation for Harlem Jazz Theatre Showcase, Private Collection of Geno Brantley.
2 Dunnaville, interview.
3 Temple, interview.
4 Temple, interview.
5 Ndounou, "Being Black on Stage and Screen," 125.
6 The Boys Choir of Harlem (1968–2007) was a major performing arts institution with an international reputation.
7 Ndounou, "Being Black on Stage and Screen," 125.
8 Temple, interview.
9 Barksdale, "N.C. Black Repertory to Present Anti-Apartheid Work, 'The Island'," B4.
10 Barksdale, "N.C. Black Repertory to Present Anti-Apartheid Work, 'The Island'," B4.
11 Barksdale, "N.C. Black Repertory to Present Anti-Apartheid Work, 'The Island'," B4.
12 "The 1989 National Black Theatre Festival," 8.
13 "National Black Theatre Festival: An overview," D2.
14 "The 1989 National Black Theatre Festival," 8.
15 Primus, Interview.
16 Primus, Interview.
17 Rodriguez, "Black Theatre Finds a Voice in Richmond at the Second Annual Black Theatre Festival," 5.
18 Dr. Christel N. Temple, email message to author, January 15, 2021.
19 Hopkins, interview.
20 Chafe, 519. The Watts Rebellion, which is sometimes referred to as the Watts riots or Watts Uprising, occurred in the Watts neighborhood of Los Angeles from August 11–16, 1965. Marquette Frye, a 21-year-old Black man was pulled over for drunk driving. When he resisted arrest, a police officer struck him in the face with a baton. Rumors ensued around the police's use of excessive force to tame the onlookers where a pregnant woman was kicked. Six days of civil unrest erupted resulting in 34 deaths and over 40 million dollars in property damage.
21 Chafe, 519.
22 Rodriguez, "Black theatre finds a voice in Richmond at the second annual Black Theatre Festival,"5.
23 Temple, Interview.
24 "McClintock to Create City Theater Program," no page/no author, Dec 17–19, 1992.
25 "McClintock to Create City Theater Program," no page/no author, Dec 17–19, 1992.
26 Temple, interview.
27 "Theatre Program Monthly Report; Ernie McClintock, Instructor" How Do I Cite – From the Private Collection of Geno Brantley.

28 Horne, "Two Jazz Theatres? Ludicrous!," B3.
29 Horne, B3.
30 Horne, B3.
31 Dr. Christel N. Temple, email message to author, January 15, 2021
32 "McClintock to create city theater program" December 17–19, 1992.
33 Letter to Mr. S. Allison Baker, from the Private Archives of Geno Brantley.
34 Dr. Christel N. Temple, email message to author, January 15, 2021.
35 Email Correspondence Dr. Christel N. Temple
36 "History," Altria Theater, https://www.altriatheater.com/about-us/history.
37 Donna Pendarvis, email message to author, April 2, 2021.
38 Donna Pendarvis, email message to author, April 2, 2021.
39 Temple, interview.
40 Letter to Mr. S. Allison Baker, from the Private Archives of Geno Brantley.
41 Letter to Mr. S. Allison Baker, from the Private Archives of Geno Brantley.
42 From the Private Collection of Geno Brantley.
43 Hodges, interview.
44 Smith, interview.
45 Smith, interview.
46 Smith, interview.
47 Harrison, *The Drama of Nommo*, xvi.
48 Temple, Interview.
49 Woodley asserts that at first when he attended Julliard there was a conflict at first, but with time and experience was able to use both techniques, which are of equal value in his experience. Other popular techniques include teachings of Lee Strasberg, Stella Adler, Sanford Meisner, Harold Clurman, Michael Chekhov, and Konstantin Stanislavsky. Sheldon Woodley, interview.
50 McClintock, "Perspective on Black Acting," 79.
51 Daniels, interview.
52 Ibid.
53 Smith, interview.
54 Daniels, interview.
55 Hodges, interview.
56 Bailey, "Rapping with Ernie McClintock," 1.
57 Hodges, interview.
58 Bates, interview.
59 Hatch, "From Hansberry to Shange," 388.
60 Genet, *The Blacks: A Clown Show*, 4.
61 "The Ground on which I stand, A Speech on Black Theatre and Performance, A speech delivered by August Wilson (1996, Princeton University McCarter Theatre)," accessed March 12, 2017, //aas.princeton.edu/blog/publication/thegroundonwhichistand/.
62 Hodges, interview.
63 Hodges, interview.
64 Hopkins, interview.
65 Fleming, interview.
66 J. W. Robinson Horne, "Aspects of the Arts: 'The Blacks' ensemble 'Tour de Force," *The Richmond Afro-American and the Richmond Planet*, May 22, 1993, B3.
67 Horne, B3.
68 Ibid.
69 Asante, *Afrocentric Idea Revised*, xll.
70 Molette and Molette, "Black Theater: Premise and Presentation," 12.
71 Hodges, interview.

72 Shabazz, interview.
73 Daniels, interview.
74 Levy Lee Simon is a poet, director, playwright, and actor. His most celebrated work in the American theatre is *For the Love of Freedom* (2001) about the Haitian Revolution and Independence 1791–1820. This play received 17 nominations from the NAACP and Ovation Award Committees, and in 2001 he won the NAACP award for Best Playwright.
75 From the private collection of Geno Brantley.

Bibliography

Asante, Molefi Kete. *The Afrocentric Idea Revised*, 2nd ed. Philadelphia, PA: Temple University Press, 1998.
Bailey, A. Peter. "Rapping with Ernie McClintock." *Black Theatre Alliance Newsletter*, February 1978, 1–2.
Barksdale, Robin. "N.C. Repertory to Present Anti-Apartheid Work, 'The Island.'" *Winston-Salem Chronicle*, June 1, 1989, B4.
Bates, Jerome Preston. Interview by Elizabeth M. Cizmar, August 31, 2015, Brooklyn, NY.
Daniels, Thaddeus. Interview by Elizabeth M. Cizmar, August 12, 2015, Jersey City, NJ.
Dunnaville, Shantell. Interview by Elizabeth M. Cizmar, June 15, 2022, Zoom.
Genet, Jean. *The Blacks: A Clown Show*. New York: Grove Press, 1960.
Harrison, Paul Carter. *The Drama of Nomo*. New York: Grove Press, 1972.
Hatch, James V. and Errol Hill. "From Hansberry to Shange." In *A History of African American Theatre*, 375–429. Cambridge: Cambridge University Press, 2003.
"History," Altria Theater, https://www.altriatheater.com/about-us/history.
Hodges, Mary. Interview by Elizabeth M. Cizmar, August 29, 2015, New York, NY.
Hopkins, dl. Interview by Elizabeth M. Cizmar, September 9, 2015, Richmond, VA.
Horne, J.W. Robinson. "Aspects of the Arts: 'The Blacks' Ensemble 'Tour de Force.'" *The Richmond Afro-American and the Richmond Planet*, May 22, 1993, B3.
Horne, J.W. Robinson, "Two Jazz Theatres? Ludicrous!" *The Richmond Afro-American and the Richmond Planet*, June 19, 1993, B3.
"McClintock to create city theater program." *Richmond Free Press*, December 17–19, 1992.
Molette, Carlton W. and Barbara J. *Black Theater: Premise and Presentation*. Bristol: Wyndham Hall Press, 1986.
"National Black Theatre Festival: An Overview." *Winston-Salem Chronicle*, August 10, 1989, D2.
Primus, Marc. Interview by Elizabeth M. Cizmar, August 25, 2015, Atlanta, GA.
Rodriguez, Holly M. "Black Theater Finds a Voice in Richmond at the Second Annual Black Theatre Festival." *Style Weekly*, August 14, 2002, 5.
Shabazz, Iman, Interview by Elizabeth M. Cizmar, September 9, 2015, Richmond, VA.
Simon, Levy Lee. Interview by Elizabeth M. Cizmar, September 18, 2015, phone.
Smith, Derome. Interview by Elizabeth M. Cizmar, September 9, 2015, Richmond, VA.
Temple, Christel. Interview by Elizabeth M. Cizmar, September 25, 2020, Zoom.
"The 1989 National Black Theatre Festival." *Black Masks*, August 31, 1989, 8.

Wilson, August. "The Ground on Which I Stand, A Speech on Black Theatre and Performance." A Speech Delivered by August Wilson (1996, Princeton University McCarter Theatre)". Accessed March 12, 2017, //aas.princeton.edu/blog/publication/thegroundonwhichistand/.

White Ndounou, Monica, "Being Black on Stage and Screen." In *The Routledge Companion to African American Theatre and Performance*, edited by Kathy A. Perkins, Sandra L. Richards, Renée Alexander Craft, and Thomas F. DeFrantz, 124–27. New York: Routledge, 2019.

Woodley, Sheldon. Interview by Elizabeth M. Cizmar, September 27, 2015, phone.

6
THE PERSISTENCE OF A LIVING LEGEND (1994–1997)

In the early to mid-1990s, 30-year theatre veteran Ernie McClintock continued his mission to train Black actors and carry forth the Black Power notions of self-determination and community building. In Richmond, McClintock's actors were known for their electrifying character portrayals and dynamic ensemble performances in scripted and unscripted work. McClintock was exacting in his play selection as he wanted to establish a Black presence in the Richmond Theatre scene, serve his students, and create more awareness of Black cultures past and present.

The mid-1990s brought a new context to McClintock's work; as America witnessed Clinton liberalism, police brutality, the exposure of a flawed justice system, and the AIDS epidemic, self-determination, and community building were as relevant as they had been in the 1960s. From the 1960s to the 1980s, Americans had experienced extremes of optimism and cynicism from the hope of the Kennedys, the civil rights movement, and creating a democratic ideal, to violence, racial unrest, assassinations, and wars abroad. According to historian William Chafe, the 1990s became a decade with a giant question mark as the conflicts that ensued were a summing up of what had occurred in the previous three decades.[1] At this time, America was figuring out how to proceed amid history repeating itself.

This chapter examines the political and cultural milieu of the mid-1990s in relation to two of McClintock's productions: his 1994 production of Richard Wesley's *The Mighty Gents* (1979) and his 1996 production of Cheryl L. West's *Before It Hits Home* (1993). Although Wesley's play was written in 1979, it looks at the aftermath of the 1960s and examines the lives of those who fought for Black liberation and were subsequently left behind in the inner city. During this period, people of color were disadvantaged due to economic, political, and cultural

DOI: 10.4324/9781003187448-7

policies in the United States. The "glory days" of the Black Power Movement had faded and many folks who had fought for economic and political equality continued to be oppressed through both violent and nonviolent means. Wesley's play aligns with the gestalt of the 1990s, as identified by Chafe, which asked in which direction the country should proceed; it exposes a flawed system made apparent in inner cities. West's play centers on AIDS and the impact of the epidemic on the Black community in the 1980s. Through Jazz Acting, McClintock's actors performed these class- and community-specific works and responded to their lived moment while remaining centered in Afrocentricity. McClintock brought the play *Before It Hits Home* to the National Black Theatre Festival in 1997, when he was presented with the Living Legend Award (Figure 6.1).[2]

Using similar methodologies as the previous chapters—including first-hand interviews, archival evidence, and contextual research—this chapter also engages with critical race theorists such as Cedric Robinson, Cathy Cohen, and Roderick A. Ferguson, in tandem with close textual readings of the plays. Robinson introduced the term "racial capitalism" to describe how the socialist ideal developed from Marx and Engels presumed that "the European bourgeois society would rationalize social relations."[3] Ferguson's work in *One-Dimensional Queer* unpacks

FIGURE 6.1 The Living Legend Award 1997.
Credit: Private Collection of Geno Brantley.

how the struggle for gender and sexual equality is inextricably tied to racial and class disparities. Finally, Cohen's groundbreaking article "Punks, Bulldaggers, and Welfare Queens," published in 1997, engages with intersectionality. In this article, she contends that queer activism must not assimilate to the incumbent structures that are the very systems that allow oppression to operate.[4]

McClintock's selection of plays was significant in this period in that, whether they were Contemporary Black Classics (see Chapter 3) or more recent works, they addressed the intersectional dilemma in a post-Black Arts Movement world. *The Mighty Gents* and *Before It Hits Home* query incumbent systems, whether the welfare office or the Christian church, that are built on racially heteronormative ideals and feed a racially capitalist system. Thus, the political and cultural backdrop of the 1990s is critical to understanding McClintock's play selection process and instruction during his residency in Richmond. Through *The Mighty Gents*, the community looked at questions of the past: what worked, what didn't, and who was left behind. In this case, the Gents—a former Newark gang, some of whom were veterans—attempted to take the straight-and-narrow path through the local unemployment office. However, the failing welfare system and violence within their communities demonstrate both state violence and social abandonment, which links to Michel Foucault's concepts of sovereign power and biopower. Foucault defines sovereign power as originating in monarchies: "The right which was formulated as the 'power of life and death' was in reality the right to *take* life or *let* live."[5] Sovereign power is not only the right to let someone live or die, but it works with "deduction,"[6] taking away wealth, services, and labor. As Chloë Taylor has written, "Sovereign power's right over life is merely the right of subtraction, not of regulation or control."[7] According to Foucault, in the seventeenth and eighteenth centuries, a new form of power emerged to regulate and manage life, known as biopower. Biopower, defined as the power over a life or lives, works primarily through the state in the form of institutions and population regulation. Foucault also identifies disciplinary power, which works through institutions, but as Taylor notes, "the state is also involved in many institutions, such as the prison."[8] Social abandonment, a form of biopower, is glaring in West's *Before It Hits Home*, which deals with the pressing issue of AIDS in terms of who has access to medical attention. It also demonstrates how religious institutions can function as a form of sovereign power and influence familial and societal dynamics. Black gay and bisexual men at this time were often left behind—by religion, by family, and by their community—yet West provides the possibility of change and acceptance within this particular Black community.

Racial Divide: The Center of American Politics

By 1994, McClintock and Ronald Walker were firmly planted in Richmond. Here, in the historical capital of the Confederacy and a city divided along racial lines, they established a reputable theatre company. In the 1990s, several watershed moments in American history and politics occurred, including the 1994 Crime Bill, the Welfare Reform Act, the O. J. Simpson trial, and the continuing devastation of HIV/AIDS. Given the context of the mid-1990s, McClintock's play selection responded to the dilemmas of class disparity, systemic racism, and homophobia. He took a direct approach to confronting these issues by choosing plays with characters whose experiences were similar to those within many Black communities at this time. He continued to workshop and produce the classic works of Amiri Baraka, like *Madheart* and poetry theatre, but he emphasized gritty realism. As fully explored in Chapter 3, Baraka's work remained a staple in McClintock's repertoire because of the artistic and political potential within the plays to showcase a multitude of Black perspectives rooted in the Black Power Movement.

Like in the 1960s, in the 1990s, prior to McClintock's foray into the New York theatre scene, the country seemed to experience optimism. With the election of William Jefferson Clinton in 1992, it seemed as if the idealism of the early 1960s and Camelot were alive yet again.[9] Much like John F. Kennedy, the attractive and charismatic Clinton promised to work for all Americans. According to Chafe, for Democrats, tolerance of people from diverse backgrounds and lifestyles became a positive value. This contrasted with seeing multiple cultures negatively, as a source of tension, or as un-American.[10] Conversely, the Republican National Committee (RNC) featured fundamentalist Christians, such as Pat Buchanan and Pat Robertson, who demonized Democrat rhetoric and proclaimed that feminism and homosexuality were un-American. Idealism won the American people over, yet Clinton wavered on his liberal social policies; for example, he instituted the Don't Ask, Don't Tell policy in the military. This prohibited military officers from asking about homosexuality while barring openly gay, lesbian, and bisexual applicants from serving their country. The policy did not include all queer-identifying folks as it addressed only homosexuality and bisexuality. In his effort to win over centrists, Clinton signed the controversial 1994 Crime Bill to give the impression that he was hard on crime, endorsing "law and order." The Crime Bill, officially known as the Federal Violent Crime Control and Law Enforcement Act of 1994, is a discriminatory piece of legislation against African Americans that exacerbated an already flawed prison system. The Crime Bill brought an additional 100,000 police officers to the streets and endorsed the "three strikes and you're out" provision, incentivizing "Mandatory Life Imprisonment for Persons Convicted of Certain Felonies."[11] The bill outlines that a person will receive a life sentence if they have been convicted of certain felonies on three separate occasions. This includes two or more serious violent felonies or one or more serious violent felonies and one or more serious drug offenses.[12] The bill ignores the history of racism within law enforcement that results in innocent Black folks being convicted and imprisoned for crimes they did not commit. Overall, this bill resulted in communities of color being directly and disproportionately targeted with unnecessary criminalization. Although *The Mighty Gents* does not directly address the Crime Bill, the play exposes how someone might be convicted of a felony not because they are a "super predator"[13] but because the system is designed to imprison Black men.

Another piece of legislation from the Clinton era connected to how McClintock wrestled with class disparity and discrimination in his productions was the 1996 Personal Responsibility and Work Opportunity Reconciliation Act (PRWORA). PRWORA reforms intended to assist those in need by quelling welfare dependency through promoting work and heterosexual marriage, reducing the number of births out of wedlock, and rewarding heteronormative two-parent families.[14] Clinton promised to "change welfare as we have come to know it."[15] The Act reinforced heteronormativity and targeted Black families. In a 2020 reflection on the complicated and discriminatory history of welfare reform in the United States, journalist Marguerite Ward critiques Clinton's policies because "at a time when Black Americans were given significantly more access to public assistance, measures were enacted to make assistance harder to access."[16] The way this system has played out is that white folks still make up the majority of those on welfare while the gap between the rich and poor has become wider. Moreover, as an interviewee of Ward's stated: "When we do get included in the welfare state, in the Great Society programs, we are stigmatized for it."[17] As a result, unemployment is increasingly racialized and the limitations of welfare and the privatization of federal housing programs have "deepened the poverty in black families."[18] The catch 22 of being stigmatized if they do, stigmatized if they don't, as well as the cycle of poverty within inner cities, is directly addressed in *The Mighty Gents*. McClintock deliberately brought these concerns to the Richmond community.

The stereotyping of African Americans through demonizing the Black body persisted into the 1990s. McClintock's work continued to subvert stereotypes like the Black Brute, defined as a seething savage who raises havoc. According to historian Donald Bogle, in portrayals of the Black Brute, his physical violence serves as an outlet for his sexual repression and uncontrollable rage.[19] In 1996, during a campaign speech at Keene State College, Hillary Clinton blatantly perpetuated this stereotype.[20] She outlined the seven principles of President Clinton's second-term campaign and stated that one of the country's challenges was to take back the streets from "crime, gangs, and drugs."[21] Referring to the makeup of gangs, she said, "they are often the kinds of kids called super-predators, no conscience, no empathy."[22] The Crime Bill was, in part, intended to initiate community policing and for the police to create more of a connection with communities. However, within Clinton's speech, the flagrant comparison of young, Black children to the Black Brute trope stands out. There is an underlying suggestion that everyone associated with gangs is sociopathic, and that engaging in crime is an inherent characteristic rather than a survival tactic. McClintock's productions of the work of Ed Bullins and Wesley directly challenges Clinton's assertion.

Another event underlining the racial divide in America at large in the 1990s was the O. J. Simpson trial, which can be summed up by one Los Angeles barber's remark following Simpson's acquittal: "They framed a guilty man—that's all it was."[23] Simpson, a football player and TV and film personality, was a "national treasure." On the evening of June 12, 1994, Simpson's ex-wife, Nicole Brown Simpson, and her friend, Ronald Goldman, were murdered in Los Angeles' Brentwood neighborhood. After attempting to dodge the police in a white Bronco driven by his former teammate Al Cowlings, Simpson was arrested at the home of Robert Kardashian on June 17, 1994. Simpson's DNA was found at the scene of the crime, directly tying him to the murders. He also had a track record of domestic abuse. However, the police handled evidence carelessly, in particular a black glove that was a crucial piece of evidence for the prosecution—it was too small for Simpson's hand and, as Johnny Cochran famously said, "If it doesn't fit, you must acquit."[24] The defense then revealed the racist remarks and rogue procedures of a police officer, Mark Fuhrman, who was recorded saying the N-word repeatedly and routinely manipulating evidence for convictions. Simpson was acquitted on all charges and Cochran was accused of using the "race card." However, as Chafe points out, "Cochran did not have to play the race card. The entire trial—the entire deck of cards—had race written all over it."[25] The general consensus is that Simpson did indeed commit these crimes. However, the exposure of corrupt and racist law enforcement officers who planted evidence provided ample room for reasonable doubt for the mixed-race jury.

This trial captured the attention of the entire country, who watched the trial on CourtTV for eight months. It brought to life what Black Americans experienced daily, and it exposed racial and class inequity. Many white folks across the country were outraged with the outcome and thought Simpson was acquitted because of his celebrity status and financial ability to hire top attorneys. Both may be true. Simpson's case came after the Rodney King uprisings discussed in Chapter 5, where justice was not served and white police officers were exonerated for their abuse of King. King did not have celebrity status and was not afforded the same privileges as Simpson to hire top criminal defense attorneys. Nevertheless, at the same time, Simpson's experienced attorneys who understood the institutional racism of Los Angeles exposed the racist underpinnings of the Police Department. McClintock took into consideration the nuanced class distinctions within the Black community into his season planning. His move to Richmond forced him to deal with a community that was quite different from the Black artistic hub of Harlem in the 1990s. Specifically, McClintock and Walker lived on Broad Street in Richmond, a city with a robust Black population but theatres that were dominated by white voices.[26]

As well as Black Americans being disproportionately treated unfairly by law enforcement, Black men and women were prominent victims of the AIDS epidemic. Chapter 5 discusses how many of McClintock's company members lost their lives to AIDS, and one of the reasons the couple left New York was to escape the devastation. Research and therapies were being developed in the 1990s, but Black folks did not typically receive these medical advancements. This can be attributed to a lack of resources to pay for the expensive therapies, as well as "the more generalized reality that blacks remained relatively invisible objects of public concern and government health programs."[27] McClintock confronted daily the racialized lack of healthcare resources for HIV-positive people, the negative implications of testing positive, and the religious right's claim that the HIV/AIDS was punishment to queer folk. Friends, colleagues, and students that he cared about perished, and not many conversations about the epidemic were happening in his Black community.[28] McClintock directly addressed these issues in works like *Before It Hits Home* and *Miss Evers' Boys*, explored in Chapter 7.

An identifiable shift in McClintock's work during this three-year period of 1994–1997 is a sense of urgency; he was responding to the watershed moments happening around him. He also responded to the context of the 1960s, but then he was in Harlem and selected plays that were more symbolic in nature, rather than narratives grounded in realism. Regarding Chafe's assertion that there was a giant question mark facing the country in the 1990s, McClintock was answering that question through his productions. He indicated that communities needed to discuss the controversial, uncomfortable topics Black people faced and that affected the social and political welfare of the entire country. By doing so, there could be a reckoning with inequity from an intersectional understanding of how certain bodies, races, and sexual orientations are relegated to second-class status.

The work of playwrights like Wesley and West, among others, examines what Young refers to as the "Black habitus" in the African Continuum from two distinct perspectives: the inner city and a Christian household. Young draws on sociologist Pierre Bourdieu's theory of habitus to understand how performance presents the Black body as both singular and collective.[29] This duality is identified by Young as critical memory, explored in Chapter 3 in relation to McClintock's approach to *Do Lord Remember Me*. Critical memory "assists in the process of identifying similarities—shared experiences and attributes of being and becoming—among black folk not by presuming that black bodies have the same memories but by acknowledging that related histories create experiential overlap."[30] Bourdieu's theory of habitus analyzes how social expectations are projected onto bodies and how those expectations then become a model for society and other individuals. Young explains that the theory of habitus, in terms of Black habitus,

> allows us to read the black body as socially constructed and continually constructing its own self. If we identify blackness as an idea projected across a body, the projection not only gets incorporated within the body but also influences the ways that it views other bodies.[31]

These projections can occur in the family unit, the classroom, the community, and the media. In the mainstream media, Black bodies are often depicted in poverty-stricken neighborhoods, furthering stereotypes. As Young explains, although Black habitus is painful and dangerous, Black communities are never completely trapped by it. McClintock's career and his productions of *The Mighty Gents* and *Before It Hits Home* demonstrate liberation from Black habitus in performance. Exposure to complexity and variety in the human experience can redefine social expectations and become an entry point to understanding multiple perspectives. Plays like *The Mighty Gents* educate audiences and performers to connect with street life, and, as Jazz Actor J. Ron Fleming notes, plays like *The Mighty Gents* "were selected to show the culture and humanity of a people."[32] *Before It Hits Home* ruptures stereotypes of Black bisexual men and assumptions that straight, Christian, Black men are incapable of accepting queer Black family members.

The Mighty Gents: Reflections on the Past and Implications in the Present

During the 1990s, McClintock continued to produce plays from the Black Theatre Movement, including works by Wesley, Bullins, and Baraka. Educating his acting students and the broader Richmond community was an eye-opening experience. Jazz Actor Derome Scott Smith stated in an interview that when he met McClintock, he met the Black Theatre Movement.[33] Although *The Mighty Gents* was published in 1979, four years past the commonly defined end of the Black Arts Movement, playwright Wesley had been a substantial voice in the movement.

In the context of the events of the mid-1990s, *The Mighty Gents* wrestles with what happened to those who fought for Black Power and were then caught in the cycle of Black habitus as it relates to upward mobility and white hegemony. The King uprising occurred in 1991, triggering memories of the rebellions of the 1960s. This explosion of violence and outrage resulted from increased racial polarization, a plummeting economy, and high unemployment in a city run by white politicians.[34] Additionally, three white Los Angeles police officers were acquitted on all charges by an all-white jury. Through Young's concept of Black habitus, as well as his notion of critical memory,[35] he considers institutions of oppression that have trickled down from slavery and have limited Black peoples' opportunities and put Black lives at risk. In McClintock's production of *The Mighty Gents*, audiences and actors alike are encouraged to empathize with a community that is perhaps unfamiliar and are encouraged to better understand various responses to white hegemony.

McClintock produced *The Mighty Gents* in Richmond from 1992 to 1994 and used excerpts from the play for scene study classes. Wesley's play centers on the former gang, "the Mighty Gents, from Newark, New Jersey, who had been a major force on the streets. Their gang was called "the Mighty Gents." The play begins 30 years after their heyday, and the Gents are unemployed. Two characters, Zeke and Braxton, represent opposite ends of the American success spectrum. Zeke is a homeless alcoholic and Braxton is a racketeer who claims to be an embodiment of the American Dream. Frankie, the leader of the Gents, takes his crew on one last raid, to rob Braxton. Zeke follows Frankie and confronts him during the heist; they struggle over a gun and Zeke accidentally shoots and kills Frankie. Throughout the play, Frankie yearns to change his circumstances but cannot escape the burdens imposed on him by the government and ultimately fails to change his habitus. The "straitjacket" is how the system disproportionately disadvantages African Americans. Despite the play's narrative ending, through Jazz Acting, McClintock's actors discovered the nuances of these characters and explored the complexity of these individuals within the context of the 1990s, giving voice to those left behind by the government.

In this particular sociopolitical context, the idea of poor Black men being left to fend for themselves by a government that was built on the backs of their ancestors, including men who fought in the US military, reflects Foucault's notion of biopower. In this scenario, biopower, or social abandonment, can be distinguished from sovereign power, which is an active attack on Black bodies in the form of police brutality. In the mid-1990s, both were happening simultaneously through the ongoing targeting of Black bodies on the streets, senseless shootings, and the failings of the welfare system. When Black bodies are left behind, there is a sense that the country is "moving forward," but as the old cliché tells us, history repeats. We can never fully move forward if we continue to abandon all the marginalized at various intersections, such as "Punks, Bulldaggers, and Welfare Queens" Cathy Cohen identifies in her work.

Through the detail-oriented Jazz Acting technique, working on *The Mighty Gents* challenged the actors to connect with the often-stereotyped "ghetto" characters, and reveal that despite poverty, these characters are fully human and complex. As explored by Elijah Anderson in "The Iconic Ghetto," the ghetto is an idea that white people often used to mean "where Black people live."[36] It conjures images of poverty, drug-infested streets, violence, and crime.[37] McClintock was always cognizant of how Black characters were stereotyped, and also of how mainstream acting techniques fed into those stereotypes. In his article "White Imitations Dropped by Acting School in Harlem," William Glover states that "breaking out of racial cliché is the reason for the Afro-American Studio that McClintock manages in Harlem."[38] McClintock continued this fight in Richmond two decades later. In his productions of *The Mighty Gents*, McClintock's technique directly challenged Black stereotypes with the aim of pushing audiences and actors to understand multiple perspectives and various socioeconomic statuses, as well as the aim of stimulating awareness of those left behind by federal programs by bringing to light the deeply flawed and racialized system of governance.

Given Jazz Acting's emphasis on language, the text provides a pathway for actors to empathize with their characters and embody the musicality of a culture. Actor Sheldon Woodley articulates the approach of playing roles outside of his experience by researching the contextual circumstances and the struggle of their everyday lives. He states that

> when people struggle, they use language and rhythm to interpret what they are feeling. They use art.... When you hear people in economic backgrounds when they speak and have a way, it just doesn't come from nowhere, it comes from rhythm, and the way certain cultures speak.[39]

As explored in Chapters 2 and 4, this level of specificity ties to McClintock's emphasis on voice and speech training to feature the Black idiom, as opposed to a whitewashed Standard American English.

In *The Mighty Gents*, Wesley's characters are caught in a cycle of drugs, crime, alcoholism, and unemployment due to racial and class discrimination perpetuated by oppressive systems. Their relationship with the white hegemony prevents them from liberating themselves from their habitus. For example, the former gang members begin the play discussing their unemployed status, a significant issue discussed and debated by the federal government at the time of McClintock's performance. To this day, conservatives and liberals debate over whether or not unemployment (especially during the COVID-19 pandemic) is a useful tool to support Americans. However, perhaps dependency on unemployment checks reveals that the minimum wage does not constitute a living wage. Tiny, a war veteran, expresses disdain and embarrassment as his peers expose the inefficiency of an unemployment office meant to serve the community:

FRANKIE: How much you make, Eldridge?
ELDRIDGE: (*Evasive*) Enough.
TINY: Betcha that turkey's lucky if he made ten dollars.
  (Tiny begins to laugh.)
ELDRIDGE: Well, whatever I got more than *you* got, Tiny, so you shut up.
TINY: That's okay, man. I got me some money. My veteran's disability check's comin' tomorrow. I'll be richer than alla you chumps put together.
  (Eldridge laughs.)
FRANKIE: Looks like the war did somebody good after all.
TINY: Yea, some good.
FRANKIE: Come on, man, you know what I mean.
TINY: Yea... sure. (*Pause.*) You shudda seen me in the unemployment office. I felt like I was in a circus doin' tricks. I hate that place.
ELDRIDGE: Then why keep goin'? You know if they got no jobs for able-bodied civilians, they ain't hardly holdin' no jobs for war vets with gimpy legs.
TINY: (*Quietly*) Hey man, lighten up. You know I don't like to talk about that.[40]

Wesley's nuanced dialogue criticizes the US government for disparaging African Americans who served their country and promoted democracy. The play demonstrates the reality explored in Chapter 1 that much like after World War II, Black soldiers came home defending a country and touting the ideals of a government whose democracy was laden with institutional racism. This issue of neglecting those who served in the military continues to resonate in the twenty-first century, as veterans who suffer post-traumatic stress disorder require medical attention and are often left on the margins of society.

Regarding audience identification, the play addresses these issues in a way that further exposes stereotypes, such as that of the "welfare queen." The welfare queen stereotype, popularized in the 1960s by Democrat Daniel Patrick Moynihan and revived throughout the 1980s and 1990s by both Republicans and Democrats, is a late-twentieth-century version of the "pure coon" stereotype, defined as a "no-account roustabout," and an "unreliable, crazy, lazy, subhuman creature... good for nothing more than eating watermelons, stealing chickens, shooting rap, or butchering the English language."[41] The welfare queen figure is usually represented as "an overweight, hyperfertile, openly sexual, and improperly aggressive black woman who obtains benefits that she does not deserve while lazing around and enjoying luxury consumer goods."[42] Eldridge articulates his futile daily visits to the unemployment office, visits that yield "pennies" and damage his self-worth. The exchange of dialogue between Braxton and Eldridge challenge the stereotypes of the lazy coon and the welfare queen propagated by conservative politics in the 1980s and 1990s.

In Jazz Acting, actors approached characters such as Eldridge through understanding the historical context of the play, which still held relevance in their lived moment, and exploring the musicality of text. The musicality of the text was connected to McClintock's reverence for language, a concept he learned from Helen Espie in the 1960s (see Chapter 1). Actors like Woodley emphasized pronouns to connect to the rhythm and language of the text. Woodley distinguishes McClintock's approach from Julliard training: "To stress pronouns sounds more poetic, [Juilliard] concentrated more on verbs and moves the text."[43] The concentration on verbs is a common method in Stanislavsky-based training, as explored in Chapter 5.

McClintock's First Word, analyzed in Chapter 5, provided an entry point for dl Hopkins, who played Frankie, to challenge the stereotype of the parasitic coon.[44] Hopkins, raised in Virginia, was not intimately familiar with the urban environment depicted in *The Mighty Gents* and initially did not think he was equipped to play a character from the "urban ghetto."

> The black ghetto is distinguished by the local boundaries that physically separate it from the rest of the city, including wide streets, thoroughfares or freeways, some of which were deliberately constructed to contain the ghetto. The demarcation is often a wide swath of a "no man's land,"

although sometimes white areas fade into homogenously black neighborhoods. Today the ghetto is commonly regarded at best as the home of those black people who have been left behind by racial progress and, at worst, as a place inhibited by those who have failed to assume personal responsibility for themselves and their families.[45]

Hopkins notes the immense responsibility actors take on when they play roles that are outside of their lived experience, especially when certain "ghetto" characters are represented as stereotypes like the Black Brute and welfare queen. Although both the characters in this play and the actors who played them experienced discrimination, their lived experiences are quite different: urban versus rural, middle class versus lower class, formally educated versus street smart. One can only imagine what the audience in Richmond may have assumed about these characters from the "urban ghetto" of Newark prior to seeing the production. Not only was there a lack of Black theatre in Richmond prior to McClintock's arrival in the city but staging plays about "the underbelly" of America was not a particularly appealing option to Richmond's commercial theatres. However, McClintock's anti-assimilationist aims in bringing this play to Richmond, and his subsequent impact on the community, shows how radical tactics and unorthodox practices are as effective as Cohen proposes. Specifically, Cohen encourages queer activists to challenge "vehicles of power that render them at risk"[46] and exaggerate anti-normativity. McClintock's rehearsal processes, play selections, and brazen attitude all challenged a priori practices in theatrical institutions.

To ameliorate Hopkins' concerns about playing such a role, McClintock integrated his character analysis (fully broken down in Chapter 5) and his concept of the First Word. Hopkins was able to find an entry point of authenticity and connection to Frankie:

> [Ernie] really impressed upon us that you have to start before you start. So depending on the piece and what we are doing, you have to deal with what happened before. You can't just show up and start talking. An hour before, whatever it is you set up in your character analysis. When I did *The Mighty Gents*, everyone in it gave me a moment. I get choked up when I think about it.... I didn't see myself as an actor. Ernie without saying it said you will be leading this show. We read it and then I realized this is the guy. Ernie said you will be fine. I don't know what he saw in me. But everyone gave me what I needed. Because I'm not a street guy. But you start off with whatever had to happen to get you to that first monologue. That first word had to inform everybody, whatever it was where the hell you came from and why you are here.[47]

Through Hopkins's detailed biography as part of character analysis, he was able to establish the First Word to embody a character outside of his lived experience. He was able to connect with Frankie yet acknowledge the differences in their lived experiences and, in doing so, subverted the coon stereotype perpetuated in the mainstream media.

Like Frankie, Zeke, an elderly homeless alcoholic character portrayed by Wally Brandon, also attempts to liberate himself from the Black habitus but cannot break the cycle. The playwright paints Zeke as a compassionate, desperate character who, despite his shortcomings, shows great humanity. The character is a haunting prophecy of what the younger generation in Newark could become. At the conclusion of the play, when Zeke accidentally shoots Frankie, he claims the gang's recently acquired loot and retreats into the alley. Zeke wavers between liberation and entrapment, which demonstrates the ongoing struggle to break out of Black habitus within the context of an economically depressed city where survival takes precedence.

In McClintock's production, the Jazz Acting technique showcased the nuances of Zeke's humanity, further upending stereotypes in performance. According to Fleming, part of the education of this production (and Wesley's canon) emphasized the richness in overlooked cultures. Toward the end of the play, Scene 10 consists of a lengthy monologue where a disheveled, intoxicated Zeke addresses the audience. He tells a story from his youth in which, after being kicked out of home by his father at 17, he befriended drug users who protected him. They never allowed young Zeke to partake in drugs. After a night of heroin, his caretakers overdosed and died in front of him. He remembers in great detail:

> The stuff was pure, man, an' their bodies couldn't take it. They gagged an' fell on the floor twitchin', their eyes bulgin' outa their sockets, their tongues was stickin' out an' saliva was just flowin' outa their mouths. Well, I sat there for the longest time tryin' my best to deal with what was happenin'. I got drunk and sat some more an' finally, I realized why I hadn't run away. I got up an' propped alla their bodies up in real, dignified manners: legs crossed, heads titled back, cigarettes in hands. They couldn't have an' respect in life, then I'd see to it they had it in death.[48]

An actor or director could easily gloss over such a monologue in a way that does not consider the humanity within the character, even though the playwright's melody lends itself to nuance. Fleming notes that,

> it turns out [Zeke] was a brilliant human being. So one of the things I learned from the art that Ernie taught us, and the works he selected, was that we have to show the brilliance of culture even in spaces where people don't see it... we have so many examples of people who have been traumatized by life and they are extraordinary people.[49]

Although the play's narrative concludes with the Gents unable to escape their Black habitus, liberation can occur in the actor's process, which can also awaken an audience's compassion. Jazz Acting provides space for actors to connect with a collective memory and relate to institutions of oppression to reach audiences, regardless of their social class or proximity to Newark. As Fleming notes, "the work we did showed the humanity in every one of us."[50]

Braxton, the racketeer and rival of the Gents, reveals this notion of the humanity in every one of us by exposing the white capitalist system that breeds "survival of the fittest." Braxton is more financially successful than the Gents but is reliant on maintaining crime and poverty in the city, to halt the upward mobility of the less fortunate. When the audience meets Braxton more than half way through the play, the Gents have been referencing him as their target for the robbery. Braxton's first words are

> I am the American Dream. I read the *New York Times* and subscribe to the *Wall Street Journal*. I drive a Seville... and a Mercedes. I have a comfortable home in the suburbs and a spacious apartment.... I wear only the finest suits.[51]

These items are signifiers of wealth and whiteness. However, he proclaims, "I stand at the gates between the caveman and civilization. My job is to keep them contained."[52] The "them" Braxton refers to are the folks in Newark who are scraping by. Therefore, he has become a pawn of white capitalist hegemony. He insists that the audience should be grateful for his violent tactics to control the containment of this community.

Braxton is an authority who polices and brutalizes weaker members of the community; he is part of the system that keeps poor Black neighborhoods immobilized by rewarding so-called "Black-on-Black crime."[53] The play posits that the capitalist system is the real impetus for violence in Black communities. Part of the Black Power Movement was about uplifting communities and creating a collective-based social justice initiative. Capitalism emphasizes the individual and the community is not a priority. In this system, where some are born into privilege but the global majority are not, there is a desire to keep the poor, poor and the rich, rich. By incentivizing Black-on-Black crime, capitalism continues to prevail. According to Robinson,

> The historical development of world capitalism was influenced in a most fundamental way by the particularistic forces of racism and nationalism. This could only be true of the social, psychological, and cultural origins of racism and nationalism both anticipated capitalism in time and formed a piece with those events that contributed directly to its organization a of production and exchange.[54]

Braxton, who perpetuates this organization of "production and exchange," protects the massive gap between the poor and the rich. The structure imposes pressure on Braxton and he is also a victim of the system he is manipulating.

As far as McClintock's relationship with capitalism, he never explicitly critiqued the system in his writings but his season selection and unorthodox practices reveal an artist who was anti-assimilationist and focused on restructuring the creative process. As Cohen points out, "activists of color, have through many historical periods, questioned their formal and informal inclusion and power in prevailing social categories."[55] McClintock knew that his work challenged the prevailing commercial system and, in almost every interview I conducted, his students and collaborators claim he never wanted to be part of mainstream theatre because he would have to compromise. His way of creating theatre and his acting theory clashed with white, straight ways of theatre-making. Moreover, as a queer Black artist, McClintock recognized how the capitalist system that supports commercial theatre used Black folk as "surplus labor in an advanced capitalist structure" and/or saw them as expendable, denied them resources, and locked them up in prisons.[56] His exclusion from Black Arts Movement narratives can perhaps be attributed to his difficult personality, but labeling him as such contains an undercurrent of homophobia and reflects a lack of recognition for his subversive practices in upending heteronormative capitalist systems.

As a pioneer of the Black Arts Movement, McClintock addressed the discriminatory shortcomings of capitalism and gave agency to the economically depressed. For actors and audiences, *The Mighty Gents* "opens your eyes and forces you to deal with, make some decisions, embrace or at least consider what is happening around you."[57] In practice, McClintock welcomed overlooked members of society and gave them a voice. Thaddeus Daniels remembers that McClintock often wandered the streets of his community to connect and "be with [his] people... feel, smell, breathe, and taste."[58] McClintock's inclusion of street life in his repertoire and his efforts to know the community—observe their body language and listen to the rhythm of their speech—all contributed to the way Jazz Acting serves the characters in *The Mighty Gents*.

Black Queer Theatre Hits Richmond

In 1996, when the Jazz Actors Theatre produced West's *Before It Hits Home*, conversations around Black gay and bisexual men and AIDS circulated. With the spread of HIV in the 1980s and 1990s, Black queer men went from twice marginalized[59] to thrice marginalized: "queer Black bodies were no longer simply to be tolerated, excused, and humored, but were now going to be culturally and politically quarantined as diseased Black bodies."[60] This marginalization built on the association of whiteness with purity and Blackness with evil, which Malcolm X explains in his autobiography.[61] Through

McClintock's production of *Equus* (unpacked in Chapter 4), many actors, audiences, and critics came to know the beauty and complexity of the Black male body on stage. However, by the time McClintock produced *Before It Hits Home* in the mid to late 1990s, many other connotations had become associated with Black queerness. Through this initial production, McClintock asserted self-determination in a conservative and divided community.

Before It Hits Home left lasting impressions on the audience and actors through illuminating issues avoided by many Black communities: bisexuality, AIDS, and the implications of Black masculinity. The play follows the story of Wendal Bailey, a jazz musician, who struggles with his sexuality in the context of a Christian household. He is unfaithful to his pregnant fiancé, Simone. Wendal's lover, Douglas, is HIV-positive and passes the virus to Wendal. The musician's health quickly deteriorates. Dwayne, Wendal's teenage son, lives with Wendal's strict Christian parents, Reba and Bailey, because Wendal is most days of the year touring with his jazz band. Throughout the play, Wendal's body deteriorates. Bailey defies society's call to shun his son and, in the final moments of his son's life, demonstrates compassion and love for his dying son. The play's intensity and engagement with questions of sexuality, AIDS, and Black masculinity shook audiences and critics to the core through the Jazz Acting technique.

McClintock's production queried notions of Black masculinity and queerness, using the Jazz Acting technique to rupture heteronormative assumptions about AIDS and bisexuality, much like the Black Arts Movement ruptured assumptions about Blackness. During the course of the play, Wendal and his father Bailey are able to break out of the Black habitus and connect with each other. Wendal's mother, Reba, and Wendal's ex-girlfriend, Simone, are unable to find freedom from their habitus. This stark contrast provides the audience the opportunity to think about their own assumptions as they relate to their constructed identities, and how they are perceived in their own communities. Aligned with Cohen who calls for real people who are cast as "Punks, Bulldaggers, and Welfare Queens," to establish a radical queer politics that rejects respectability, racism, and classism, the play introduces a narrative to the theatre that challenges assumptions about Black queer culture and brings attention to the HIV/AIDS epidemic that was a shameful subject. Cohen expresses the need for queer communities of color to establish their own political agenda and restructure society instead of working within a racist, homophobic, and classist system. As explored by Robinson through his concept of racial capitalism and discussed more fully in Chapter 2, the root of America's success lies in the foundation of the heteronormative family and slave labor. A radical queer politics aims to destroy the system that upholds these homophobic and racist values. Along the lines of Cohen's call for action, McClintock's play rejects assimilation and "pursues a political agenda that seeks to change values, definitions, and laws which make these institutions and relationships oppressive."[62]

By bringing this play to Richmond, McClintock queried institutions such as the Baptist church, making race, class, and sexuality more visible. Despite the controversial subject of *Before It Hits Home*, audiences who saw McClintock's production in New York, Richmond, and Winston-Salem praised the ensemble. McClintock's directing spoke to local and national communities and also brought together the older Afro-American Studio for Acting and Speech generation from New York and the younger generation in Richmond to forge a familial relationship, carrying on the legacy of African ancestry.

In the 1980s and 1990s, Broadway featured subversive plays such as Larry Kramer's *The Normal Heart* (1985) and Tony Kushner's *Angels in America* (1991), which gained much attention. The Broadway musical *Rent* (1996) was produced at this time and includes a multiracial cast, yet the first character to die of AIDS in the show is Angel, a Latinx character, while Mimi almost dies in the end. The white characters in the Broadway musical, which aimed to be a diverse cast, appear healthy and rehabilitated, although one is HIV-positive. Jonathan Larson, *Rent*'s creator, was a well-intentioned, white heterosexual artist who was nonetheless shortsighted about how various races and sexual identities were presented in his musical. In varying ways, *The Normal Heart* and *Angels in America* included narratives centered on white gay men, leaving a gap in representation and illustrating Ferguson's assertion in *One-Dimensional Queer* that "the rise of a single issue (i.e., one-dimensional) model of queer politics has inspired several political developments concerning the meaning and itineraries of queer politics."[63] Although Ferguson addresses politics in particular, we can draw connections to the theatre industry, where the plight of white middle class gay men has eclipsed the struggles of queer artists of color. *Angels in America*, *Rent*, and *The Normal Heart* all reached commercial and financial success via Broadway and films in which these narratives continue to benefit white bodies. Black actors and theatre-makers are largely familiar with *Before It Hits Home*, but within white theatre circles, it is an unknown play. Building on Ferguson's analysis that ties together race, class, and sexuality as they intersect with queer politics, I suggest that *Before It Hits Home* offers opportunities to educate audiences and create dialogue in all communities of various cultures and backgrounds. It is not only meant for Black audiences and the discussions around the play can resurrect those Black queer bodies that have been left behind in the realms of both theatre and politics.

McClintock directed *Before It Hits Home* in Richmond, New York, and at Winston-Salem's National Black Theatre Festival, bringing the director's aesthetic front and center on a national platform. The play, written by a Black woman ignited conversations around queer sexuality, the AIDS epidemic, and prejudices within Black religious households. McClintock's productions of *Before It Hits Home* demonstrated how he supported Black women playwrights who posed disruptive sociopolitical questions on the stage. McClintock was awarded the Living Legend Award in 1997 for his contributions as an actor, director, and educator where he chose West's play as emblematic of Jazz Acting.[64] Among the other recipients of the award that year were prominent Black Theatre Movement playwrights Douglas Turner Ward and Ed Bullins. Artists such as August Wilson and Amiri Baraka participated in festival workshops and seminars under the theme "the Black Family on Stage."[65] It is unclear whether or not McClintock chose *Before It Hits Home* for the festival or included the play in his repertory seasons, but the productions at the festival explored relevant subjects affecting Black families and communities.

One aspect of the narrative deals with Wendal's inability to live an authentic life as a bisexual Black man, with the added pressure of his church deterring self-determination for those who identify outside of heteronormativity. From interviews and impressions gleaned through archival work, I surmise that McClintock's outspoken and unapologetic attitude suggests he found ways to cope with societal pressures and created a loving community around him and his partner, Ronald Walker. However, discrimination and hate crimes against queer folk were part of daily life in the 1980s and 1990s, whether or not they were documented. Lola Louis, who played Maybelle, the neighbor, in McClintock's production of *Before It Hits Home*, recalls not knowing many gay directors in McClintock's era. She said she never saw him hide in the shadows and that he was independent and "did not conform or compromise."[66] Conversely, in Black Christian circles, churches are complicated entities that serve communities but are known to subscribe to a policy of silence:

> Typically, the stance taken by the Black church is one of 'don't ask, don't tell,' referring to the military policy signed in 1994. In other words, gays and lesbians may actively participate n the church as long as they are silent about their homosexuality... [which] also perpetuates the most oppressive and repressive aspects of fundamentalist Christianity.[67]

McClintock's uncompromising stance and bold persona led him to produce West's controversial play in a town that was not known for queer or Black representation in the theatre before his arrival. His self-determined spirit, born from the Black Power Movement, shaped his attitude and provided a platform for marginalized individuals to tell their stories. His refusal to adopt an assimilationist approach answers Cohen's call to restructure white heteronormative institutions.[68] As such, his bold and provocative theatre undoubtedly made uncomfortable those who embodied white privilege, and it brought promise to those in Richmond who sought plays foregrounding race, class, and sexuality.

In McClintock's performance, the prejudicial nature of Christian fundamentalism that prevented Wendal from living his truth revealed itself in an exchange between Wendal, played by Thaddeus Daniels, and Reba, played by Joan Green. Reba exposes her prejudice against and disgust over her son's sexuality, exploding:

My son! And I took such pride... but last night you made me realize I hadn't made nothing, not a damn thing... been walking around fooling myself.... It's hard to look at something.... I mean I look around here and it's like somebody came in and smeared shit all over my walls.... I'm scared to touch anything.... I can't stay here and watch it fester, crumble down around me... right now I can't help you.... I can't hardly stand to even look at you.[69]

In Reba's mind, Wendal's HIV-positive body has contaminated the house to the point where she cannot face him or his bisexual identity.

Referring to the Jazz Actors version of the play in 1997 at the National Black Theatre Festival, Daniels recalled Green's performance as a quintessential manifestation of Jazz Acting. When she entered the scene, she carried a bottle of holy water, a prop that had never been integrated into rehearsals or previous performances. In sects of Christianity including Catholicism, priests sanctify water for the purpose of blessing people, places, and objects, or as a means of casting out evil.[70] When Wendal confessed that he has contracted HIV and Reba shamed him, Daniels "snatched it from her and slathered it over [his] face."[71] In the scene, Wendal pleads with his mother to understand, and her unabashed vitriol attempts to emasculate Wendal and his quest for self-determination. For Daniels, smearing the holy water on his face was an attempt to defy Reba and the homophobic fundamentalist Christian church. Not even holy water can "cure" him of his bisexuality. This powerful moment came about through the Jazz Acting process and is not stipulated in the playwright's stage directions. The actors stayed in line with the intentions of the playwright and found their riffs, a key improvisational element of the technique.

Through the lens of Black Power, the issue with Black masculinity conflicts with a father accepting and loving his bisexual son. However, McClintock's aesthetic in this production ruptures the traditional definition of Black masculinity via the father's acceptance of his son, and Bailey is liberated from his particular Black habitus. Patriarchy associates masculinity with heterosexuality and machismo, but in an analysis of Marlon Riggs's influential documentary *Tongues United*, E. Patrick Johnson argues that masculinity is not more of a signifier of Blackness than femininity and heterosexuality is no Blacker than gayness.[72] As he suggests, "Some people view black homosexuality as the final break in masculinity and don't see the love, don't see the empowerment, don't see the caring, the sharing, don't see the contributions."[73] *Before It Hits Home* concludes with a father demonstrating passion for his son, despite Christian doctrine and the pressures of Black masculinity. Bailey breaks down in tears—an action associated with femininity—and comforts his son as Wendal dies.

Jazz Acting applied to West's play culminated in a powerful theatrical experience, so much so that in August 1996, McClintock brought the cast to New York, where the play was offered as an official event of Harlem Week '96.[74]

Within the contexts of the AIDS epidemic, Black masculinity, and 1990s Harlem, McClintock's and the Jazz Actors' audacious statement cannot be overstated. Abiola Sinclair's review of the production at the Victoria Five Theater opens with: "Ernie McClintock's directing goes without saying."[75] This shows that McClintock's return to Harlem was like a homecoming—his artistic reputation preceded him, and while he still encountered some resistance, he embraced it.

> According to Ernie McClintock who recently returned to Harlem after an almost eight-year absence. '... Since Harlem is a conservative community, I guess we'll go against the grain.' Whoop! There it is! Iconoclastic McClintock is back to rock the boat. Hunh![76]

This writer refers to McClintock's arrogance: "Doesn't he know what we've been through these last few years?" At the same time, there is an expectation that McClintock will wow audiences and shake up the system. In addition to *Before It Hits Home*, Walker and McClintock brought the Contemporary Black Classic *Do Lord Remember Me*, explored in Chapter 4, and two original pieces: *Two Thousand*—a hip-hop futuristic piece addressing police brutality, sexuality, AIDS, mental health, and pop culture—and *The Collard Greens*—a ritualistic piece focusing on the writings of Black women, including Alexis De Veaux, Zora Neale Hurston, Winnie Madikizela-Mandela, Toni Morrison, Paula Marshall, Gloria Naylor, and Alice Walker. He continued this tradition of the quaring repertory theatre (see Chapter 5) into the 1990s, and even to this Harlem tour.

Sinclair's observation of Daniels's performance in *Before It Hits Home* reflects the effectiveness of McClintock's First Word technique: "Wendal's entrance into this situation is strained, largely because he strains it himself. And the stress of putting on a glad face when he's not feeling well adds to the tension."[77] Sinclair highlights the fact that before the actor even opens his mouth to speak in a scene, there is a flash of past, a whole history coursing through the actor's body and communicated to the audience. Daniels asserts that the First Word provides this detailed information to the audience but also connects the actor to the audience, before the actor moves forward with the scene.

The close-knit ensemble family dynamic established by the rigorous Jazz Acting technique allows the actor in performance to access theatricality and imagination. Dr. Indira Etwaroo, who played the nurse at the 1997 National Black Theatre Festival, recalls that the process for all productions, and the rehearsal process, never began with a table read. A table read is a typical practice in mainstream theatre and is when the cast, director, and design team read through the play while seated at a table. Presumably, McClintock viewed table reads as "boring" and an ineffective way to begin unpacking character. This presumption ties to the fact that in rehearsals, McClintock expected actors to be fully prepared with character analyses and character choices, both physical and vocal. A table read typically is when actors are reading the play aloud for the first time and haven't made any bold acting choices. Actors reading a play without physical embodiment is not a productive way of creating electricity on stage. Rather, Jazz Acting supports risk-taking on stage due to the discipline and trust established by the actors.

Such risk-taking paid off in the case of Lola Louis's portrayal of Maybelle; she applied Jazz Acting's "Secrets" and attributes her choice to have a Secret to McClintock's ability to encourage actors to make bold and imaginative yet grounded choices. Jazz Acting's Secrets asks the actor to identify one piece of critical information about their character that no one knows on stage—the characters or their fellow actors. This can aid in bringing urgency and motivation in character portrayal. Louis's bold choice centers on the friendship between Maybelle and Reba: "I brought an edginess to the scene, so I brought a subtle tone of lesbianism to the relationship.... You can have a best friend and have a crush and nothing happens, but I only brought it to life in a scene."[78] The technique, therefore, invites actors to access their imaginations and consider the possibilities between characters. She based her Secret on the character's relationship history with Reba. In this respect, the technique requires all actors—whether on stage for the duration of the play or just a couple of scenes, like Louis—to create fully realized characters because each actor is of equal importance in the ensemble.

Since the days of the Afro-American Studio, McClintock's insistence on laborious rehearsal hours resulted in a genuine community and the actors ended up living together, eating together, and talking for hours beyond rehearsal time. Daniels recalls:

> We would always be together and it was more than just rehearsal and everyone goes home. He forced us to become an ensemble even though we came to him at difference points, we each felt a throughline because of Ernie.[79]

McClintock insisted that Thaddues Daniels and Zaria Griffin, who played Bailey, travel by train to North Carolina. At the end of the play, Wendal utters in his last breath,

> I'm riding Dad. I'm on the train. I see you... Junior... Mama. Simone (*Gasping for breath*) She's pregnant. Oh my God no.... I'm so sorry Simone.... I'm sorry.[80]

Daniels connected with this moment in terms of the character but also in terms of the bond he had formed with Griffin.[81]

For characters Wendal and Bailey, liberation from Black habitus occurs in this reconciliation and in the recognition of a shared humanity. Assumptions about the legibility of gayness or the bigotry of a devout southern Christian are ruptured in these final moments. Wendal and Bailey's liberation from their habitus is juxtaposed with Reba and Simone, who are caught in the cycle of what society projects on them. Reba refuses to accept Wendal's bisexuality and ends up demonizing and abandoning him. Simone's character takes a fascinating, haunting turn in the final moments of the play. The playwright notes that the same actor should play Simone and Angel Peterson. Wendel encounters Angel, an HIV-positive pregnant woman, in the waiting room of his first doctor's visit in Act I, Scene I. In this office—which is presumably not in the best part of town—Angel, with her brash dialect, could be seen as embodying the welfare queen stereotype. For instance, she tells the nurse to "Tell this sick mutherfucker he's got AIDS and put him out of his misery... so he can stop walking around foolin' himself."[82] However, the purpose of Angel's appearance is revealed at the very end of the play, when Bailey stays with his dying son. For that scene, the stage directions read *"Lights on Simone. Simone takes off her earrings, then her wig and then the robe and transforms into Angel Peterson from Act One."* Simone transforming into Angel represents the notion of a character tragically unable to liberate herself from Black habitus. However, this event in the performance dispels myths and assumptions about stereotypes, sexuality, and the class structure in which racial capitalism thrives.

Conclusion

In Richmond in the mid-1990s, McClintock established a career as the premier acting teacher and director. His notoriety extended nationally. He was awarded the Living Legend Award at the National Black Theatre Festival and continued to maintain connections with his former students and colleagues in New York. Bringing *The Mighty Gents* and *Before It Hits Home* to Richmond exposed audiences and actors to the history and remnants of the Black Arts Movement, as well as to the taboo subjects of bisexuality and the AIDS epidemic. Thirty years after the founding of his studio in 1966, in 1996, he continued to promote an inclusive theatre that was representative of diverse perspectives within the Black community. Through the Jazz Acting technique, actors were able to connect with characters that seemed like distant people in unfamiliar environments. They rooted their character creation in self-expression and found the dynamic of the ensemble through the principles of the jazz aesthetic.

Chapter 7, "To See Another Day," focuses on the last years of McClintock's life, specifically 1998–2003, when he continued to raise up the voices of the socially marginalized through scripted productions, like *From the Mississippi Delta* and *Miss Evers' Boys*, and through poetry theatre, like the devised piece *Ndangered*. In his final years, McClintock also created Richmond's Black

Theatre Festival, to ensure the continuation of his life's work. Unfortunately, the festival was short-lived and ended after his death. The theme of the third and final festival was "To See Another Day," which McClintock described as "the ability to move forward when the odds are against you,"[83] encouraging artists and teachers alike to persist.

Notes

1. Chafe, *The Unfinished History*, 482.
2. It is quite a feat to win this award. Moreover, McClintock was discriminated against throughout his life because of his openly queer sexuality, and he made the decision to bring this play as an emblem of his success. Alongside McClintock, Douglas Turner Ward and Ed Bullins were also recipients, yet the history books write far more about these two figures of the Black Theatre Movement than about McClintock.
3. Melamed, "Racial Capitalism," 76.
4. Cohen, "Punks, Bulldaggers," 437.
5. Foucault, *History of Sexuality*, 136. Emphasis is in the original text.
6. Foucault, *History of Sexuality*, 136.
7. C. Taylor, "Biopower," 42. For more information see Foucault, *History of Sexuality*, and D. Taylor, *Michel Foucault*.
8. C. Taylor, "Biopower," 45.
9. After Kennedy's assassination, Jacqueline Kennedy referred to her husband as the "American Camelot," referencing the (presumably fictional) twelfth-century castle of King Arthur that embodies idealism and is a symbol of his glory.
10. Chafe, *The Unfinished Journey*, 492.
11. Crime Bill, Title VII, Sec 7001.
12. Crime Bill, Title VII, Sec 7001.
13. Gearan and Phillip, "Clinton regrets 1996 remark on 'super-predators' after encounter with activist," https://www.washingtonpost.com/news/post-politics/wp/2016/02/25/clinton-heckled-by-black-lives-matter-activist/.
14. Personal Responsibility and Work Opportunity Reconciliation Act of 1996.
15. Ward, "How Decades."
16. Ward, "How Decades."
17. Ward, "How Decades."
18. Anderson, "The Iconic Ghetto," 14.
19. Bogle, *Toms, Coons*, 10.
20. Gearan and Phillip, "Clinton Regrets 1996 Remark."
21. Clinton, "Hillary Clinton Campaign Speech."
22. Clinton, "Hillary Clinton Campaign Speech."
23. Martel, "The Media and Race."
24. Deutsch, "OJ Simpson Murder Trial."
25. Chafe, *The Unfinished Journey*, 520.
26. Hopkins, interview.
27. Chafe, *The Unfinished Journey*, 522.
28. Primus, interview.
29. Young, *Embodying Black Experience*, 20.
30. Young, *Embodying Black Experience*, 18.
31. Young, *Embodying Black Experience*, 20.
32. Fleming, interview.
33. Proctor, "Stage Presence," D5.

34 Mazzola and Yi, "50 Years Ago."
35 Through his concept of critical memory, Young acknowledges the overlap of experience across the African Diaspora yet notes that each individual within the diaspora has various experiences and identities, and that they are distinct from one another. Refer to Chapter 3 for more details.
36 Anderson, "The Iconic Ghetto," 8.
37 Anderson, "The Iconic Ghetto," 8.
38 Glover, "White Imitations Dropped by Acting School in Harlem," 1.
39 Woodley, interview.
40 Wesley, *The Mighty Gents*, 15.
41 Bogle, *Toms, Coons*, 5.
42 Anderson, "The Iconic Ghetto," 16.
43 Woodley, interview.
44 Bogle, *Toms, Coons*, 5.
45 Anderson, "The Iconic Ghetto," 14.
46 Cohen, "Punks, Bulldaggers, and Welfare Queens," 439.
47 Hopkins, interview.
48 Wesley, *The Mighty Gents*, 44.
49 Fleming, interview.
50 Fleming, interview.
51 Wesley, *The Mighty Gents*, 31.
52 Wesley, *The Mighty Gents*, 31.
53 "Black-on-Black" crime is a term used by the conservative right to highlight crimes in inner cities by Black people against other Black people. However, studies of the 1960s and 1970s in Harlem reveal that law enforcement agencies, such as the FBI, placed drugs in urban neighborhoods to promote such crimes. Notably, white-on-white crime is just called crime, without a racial descriptor. For more information refer to Mark Wilson's *Inventing Black-on-Black Violence: Discourse, Space and Representation*.
54 Robinson, *Black Marxism*, 9.
55 Cohen, "Punks, Bulldaggers," 445.
56 Cohen, "Punks, Bulldaggers," 446.
57 Green, interview.
58 Daniels, interview.
59 As noted in Chapter 2, Marc Primus, historian and co-founder of the Afro-American Studio, identified himself, McClintock, and Walker as twice-marginalized.
60 Neal, *Looking for Leroy*, 158.
61 Malcolm X, *Autobiography of Malcolm X*, 138.
62 Cohen, "Punks, Bulldaggers," 445.
63 Ferguson, *One-Dimensional Queer*, 9.
64 Barksdale Theatre Records, 1945–2006 (bulk 1954–2004), Library of Virgina, Richmond.
65 Toomer, "National Black Theatre Festival," 9.
66 Louis, interview.
67 Johnson, *Appropriating Blackness*, 38.
68 Cohen, "Punks, Bulldaggers,"
69 West, *Before It Hits Home*, 55.
70 Although dramaturgically, if the Baileys were Baptist, they most likely wouldn't have holy water, the symbolism is powerful.
71 Daniels, interview.
72 Marlon Riggs documented his own battle with AIDS. The film follows him as his body deteriorates. Johnson, *Appropriating Blackness*, 37.
73 Johnson, *Appropriating Blackness*, 37.

74 Sinclair, "Kudos," 24
75 Sinclair, "Kudos," 24.
76 Newspaper article from the Private Collection of Geno Brantley. Publication unknown.
77 Sinclair, "Kudos," 24.
78 Louis, interview.
79 Daniels, interview.
80 West, *Before It Hits Home,* 68.
81 Daniels, interview.
82 West, *Before It Hits Home,* 12.
83 From an advertisement for the festival. Private Collection of Geno Brantley.

Bibliography

Ambrosino, Brandon. "Why Some Black Men Prefer the Down Low and What It Says About the Black Church in America." *Washington Post,* September 4, 2015. https://www.washingtonpost.com/national/religion/why-some-black-men-prefer-the-down-low-and-what-it-says-about-the-black-church-in-america/2015/09/04/59788754-533b-11e5-b225-90edbd49f362_story.html.

Anderson, Elijah. "The Iconic Ghetto." *The Annals of the American Academy* 642 (2012): 8–24.

Bogle, Donald. *Toms, Coons, Mulattoes, Mammies, and Bucks: An Interpretive History of Blacks in American Films,* 4th ed. New York: Continuum, 2001.

Chafe, William. *The Unfinished Journey: American Since World War II.* New York: Oxford University Press, 1995.

Cohen, Cathy. "Punks, Bulldaggers, and Welfare Queens: The Radical Potential of Queer Politics?" *GLQ: A Journal of Lesbian and Gay Studies* 3, no. 4 (1997): 437–65.

Crime Bill, Title VII, Sec 7001, (1994), H.R. Res.

Daniels, Thaddeus. Interview by Elizabeth Cizmar, August 12, 2015, Jersey City, NJ.

DeGruy, Joy. *Post Traumatic Slave Syndrome: America's Legacy of Enduring Injury and Healing.* Milwaukie, OR: Uptone Press, 2005.

Deutsch, Linda. "OJ Simpson Murder Trial: 'If It Doesn't Fit, You Must Acquit.'" *NBC Los Angeles,* June 10, 2014. https://www.nbclosangeles.com/news/local/oj-simpson-20years-later-glove-fit-darden-dunne-murder-trial-of-the-century/1976992/.

Ferguson, Roderick. *One-Dimensional Queer.* Cambridge: Polity, 2019.

Fleming, J. Ron. Interview by Elizabeth Cizmar, September 9, 2015, Richmond, VA.

Foucault, Michel. *The History of Sexuality, Volume 1: An Introduction.* Translated by Robert Hurley. New York: Random House, 1978.

Gearan, Ann, and Abby Phillip. "Clinton Regrets 1996 Remark on 'Super-Predators' After Encounter with Activist." *Washington Post,* February 25, 2016. https://www.washingtonpost.com/news/post-politics/wp/2016/02/25/clinton-heckled-by-black-lives-matter-activist/.

Glover, William. "White Imitations Dropped by Acting School in Harlem." *Times-Picayune* (New Orleans, LA), December 24, 1972, 1.

Green, Joan. Interview by Elizabeth Cizmar, May 30, 2016, New Rochelle, NY.

"Hillary Clinton Campaign Speech." *C-SPAN,* January 25, 1996. https://www.c-span.org/video/?696061/hillary-clinton-campaign-speech.

Hopkins, dl. Interview by Elizabeth Cizmar, September 9, 2015, Richmond, VA.

Johnson, E. Patrick. *Appropriating Blackness: Performance and the Politics of Authenticity.* Durham, NC: Duke University Press, 2003.

Loui, Lola. Interview by Elizabeth Cizmar, September 2, 2015, Bronx, NY.

Martel, Ned. "The Media and Race in O. J. Trial." *New York Times,* October 4, 2005. https://www.nytimes.com/2005/10/04/arts/television/the-media-and-race-in-o-j-trial.html.

Malcolm X. *The Autobiography of Malcolm X, as Told to Alex Haley.* New York: Ballantine Publishing Group, 1964.

Mazzola, Jessica, and Karen Yi. "50 Years Ago Newark Burned." *NJ.com,* May 15, 2019. https://www.nj.com/essex/2017/07/what_you_need_to_know_about_the_1967_newark_iots.html.

McClintock, Ernie. "Perspective on Black Acting." *Black World* 23, no. 7 (May 1974): 79–85.

Melamed, Jodi. "Racial Capitalism." *Critical Ethnic Studies* 1, no. 1 (Spring 2015): 76–85.

Neal, Mark Anthony. *Looking for Leroy: Illegible Black Masculinities.* New York: New York University Press, 2013.

Proctor, Roy. "Stage Presence: Remembering Ernie McClintock as artist, mentor," *Richmond Times-Dispatch,* August 29, 2003, D5.

Robinson, Cedric. *Black Marxism: The Making of the Black Radical Tradition,* 3rd ed. Chapel Hill: University of North Carolina Press, 2020.

Sinclair, Abiola. "Kudos for Cheryl West's 'Before It Hits Home.'" *New Amsterdam News,* August 31, 1996, 24.

Taylor, Chloë. "Biopower." In *Michel Foucault: Key Concepts,* edited by Dianna Taylor, 41–54. New York: Routledge, 2011.

Taylor, Diana, ed. *Michel Foucault: Key Concepts.* New York: Routledge, 2011.

Toomer, Jeanette. "National Black Theatre Festival Unites Generations of Artists." *Black Masks,* February 28, 1998, 9.

Ward, Marguerite. "How Decades of US Welfare Policies Lifted up the White Middle Class and Largely Excluded Black Americans." *Business Insider,* August 11, 2020. https://www.businessinsider.com/welfare-policy-created-white-wealth-largely-leaving-black-americans-behind-2020-8.

Wesley, Richard. *The Mighty Gents.* New York: Dramatist Play Service, 1979.

West, Cheryl L. *Before It Hits Home.* New York: Dramatist Play Services, 1993.

Woodley, Sheldon. Interview by Elizabeth Cizmar, September 27, 2015, phone.

Young, Harvey. *Embodying Black Experience: Stillness, Critical Memory and the Black Body.* Ann Arbor: University of Michigan Press, 2013.

7
TO SEE ANOTHER DAY (1998–2003)

On November 30, 1999, Ernie McClintock experienced a tremendous loss when his creative and life partner of 38 years, Ronald Walker (Figure 7.1), passed away. A notebook of McClintock's in the archives contains an entry chronicling the birth and death of Walker, along with other significant dates (Figure 7.2). McClintock's heartbreaking notations of Walker's life highlights the couple's commitment to each other and their joint devotion to Black Theatre. Walker and McClintock balanced each other. Walker's deep, kind voice and slower pace ensured innovative technical direction and set/lighting designs and comforted the actors. His soothing demeanor and measured temperament sharply contrasted with McClintock's intensity. When interviewed for this project, actor Lola Louis, who was with McClintock during his last days recalled a conversation where McClintock insisted, "If anyone writes about me, make sure that they don't forget Ronald."[1] In 2001, McClintock opened the Walker Gallery in Richmond as an homage to his partner's life and legacy, the unsung hero of the Afro-American Studio for Acting and Speech, the 127th Street Repertory Ensemble, and the Jazz Actors Theatre. The gallery hosted community events featuring the artwork by the late designer as well as local artists. A 2002 *Style Weekly* article describes McClintock's expansive vision as unlimited by traditional theatrical productions. In a project known as "Studio A," he brought "together musicians poets and writers, actors, and of course, audiences."[2] Studio A was a communal space for artists to convene and share their work while surrounded by Walker's artwork and spirit. One of the last productions the couple collaborated on was Dr. Endesha Ida Mae Holland's *From the Mississippi Delta* (2005), a play based on her autobiography of the same name that follows Holland from her traumatic childhood to her time as a sex worker and through her achievement in doctoral studies. It focuses on community, not

DOI: 10.4324/9781003187448-8

188 To See Another Day (1998–2003)

FIGURE 7.1 Ronald Walker Standing in Front of His Artwork.
Credit: Private collection of Christel Temple.

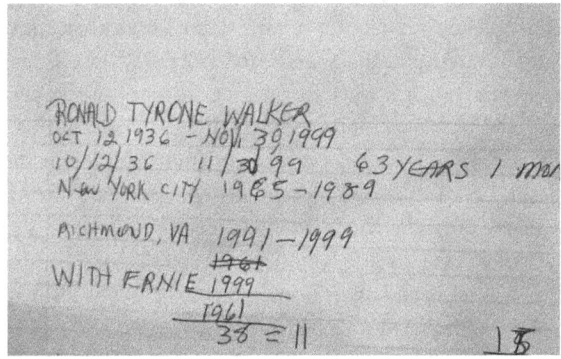

FIGURE 7.2 Entry from Ernie McClintock's Journal.
Credit: Private collection of Geno Brantley.

just in content and how Holland's community "raised her" but also production-wise, with three cis female actors playing all roles in the play.

After Walker's passing, McClintock focused on creating a Black Theatre Festival in Richmond as a legacy in which he was not the sole star of Black Theatre but part of the African continuum; he wanted his students and future generations to continue the work. He envisioned the Black Theatre Festival to be an annual event that promoted the "kaleidoscope character in the African

Diaspora,"[3] analyzed in Chapter 2. This kaleidoscope was based on preserving the Contemporary Black Classics and on responding to the lived sociopolitical moment and exploring the evolving genres of Black cultural expression.

Throughout the past five years of his life, McClintock persistently expanded his offerings at the Jazz Actors Theatre. In particular, he embarked on creating hip-hop theatre in his street theatre genre, harkening to *Where It's At* (see Chapter 2). He created two original hip-hop theatrical pieces along with his ensemble members, *Ndangered* (1999) and *The Rose that Grew from Concrete* (2001). *Ndangered* explored issues related to young Black men in Richmond, including Black masculinity, sexually transmitted infections, incarceration, and stereotypes. *The Rose that Grew from Concrete* was a collection of poems, songs, and stories from McClintock's late mentee, Tupac Shakur. Through these theatrical events, McClintock's technique and directorial aesthetic extended to a versatile array of genres, styles, and presentations yet consistently remained rooted in the Afrocentric notions of self-determination and community (Figure 7.3).

Although pieces like *Ndangered* and *The Rose that Grew from Concrete* dealt with pressing contemporary issues, McClintock never forgot the value of looking at the past to understand the present, evidenced by his last production of David Feldshuh's *Miss Evers' Boys* (1992), which examines the devastating Tuskegee Study. The "Tuskegee Study of Untreated Syphilis in the Negro Male" (1932–1972) by the United States Public Health Services and the Centers for Disease Control and Prevention intentionally neglected to treat approximately 400 Black men in Alabama for syphilis. The men were told they were being treated for "bad blood" in exchange for transportation to clinics, free meals, and burial insurance. The purpose of the experiment was to see what happened to the Black body when syphilis went untreated. Black bodies were regarded as dispensable. When penicillin was made available, the patients were left untreated and uninformed. "The deceptions meant to keep men in the study throughout

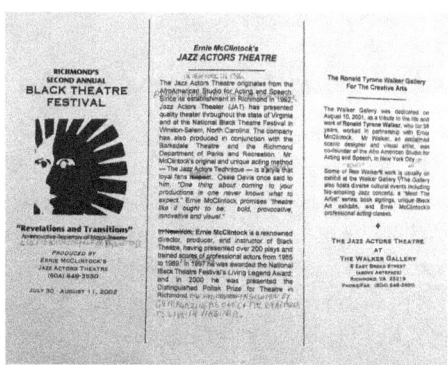

FIGURE 7.3 Clip from a pamphlet for Richmond's Second Annual Black Theatre Festival, 2002.

Credit: Private collection of Geno Brantley.

their lives and prevent them from getting actual treatments."[4] Specifically, they were told that pink baby aspirin, iron tonics, and painful spinal taps were their treatments. The study haunted Black communities for decades. To that end, McClintock's season planning and exploration of myriad experiences within Black communities provides an example for contemporary theatre artists to engage with societal issues that have faced and continue to face historically marginalized groups. By confronting these issues from the perspective of the oppressed, as opposed to the oppressor, a shift of societal consciousness can ensue.

This chapter chronicles the last five years of McClintock's life, in which he demonstrated his devotion to Black Theatre and his investment in creating theatrical spaces that were inclusive of multiple perspectives and ontological experiences across generations. It highlights four productions from this period: *From the Mississippi Delta*, *The Rose that Grew from Concrete*, *Ndangered*, and *Miss Evers' Boys*. Although these four pieces may appear divergent, they all center on individualized experiences that speak to the greater community. Through this understanding of individual experiences and obstacles, the audience can rehabilitate, echoing the beginnings of the Afro-American Studio, which Marc Primus described as "a temple of healing."[5]

Chapter 7's methodology leverages and combines firsthand interviews with McClintock's students and collaborators; archival research from newspapers, magazines, and personal papers; and contextual research to foreground his theoretical and practical connection to hip-hop. This chapter engages with womanist thinkers, such as Alice Walker, Layli Phillips, Lisa M. Anderson, and Freda Scott Giles, as well as hip-hop scholars Daniel Banks, Justin A. Williams, and Nicole Hodges Persley. Along with historical context, these theoretical frameworks aid in understanding each genre's respective political and subversive underpinnings as a part of McClintock's evolving aesthetic from 1998 to 2003.

From the Mississippi Delta: Autodrama for the Collective

From the Mississippi Delta, produced in 1998 at the Barksdale Theatre, is an autobiographical play by Endesha Ida Mae Holland. Her childhood story begins in the Deep South. The play presents an alternative Black female perspective to McClintock's earlier-produced plays like *spell #7* (see Chapter 4), which explores urban artists in Harlem. The play, based on Holland's memoir of the same name, recounts the author's story in which she attributed her transformation from a poverty-stricken child to PhD scholar to community support. The idea of community is reflected in an ensemble of three women, which mirrors McClintock's training and aesthetic. These work in tandem to create a space where they, at times, come to the fore of the stage; one actor is featured while the other two support the scene. Much like a jazz ensemble, there are different "solos" that highlight the individuality of the actor within this unified story yet also reflect the importance of community support. The structure of the play—where actors are cast in multiple roles, moving in and out of character—reflects a more circular aesthetic, rather than casting one actor per role. The circular nature of the womanist play echoes an Afrocentric model of storytelling, which McClintock integrated in the staging. Finally, near the play's conclusion, the actors recite Alice Walker's poem "Revolutionary Petunias," recognizing the fortitude, compassion, and resilience of Black women.

Alice Walker, Chikwenye Okonjo Ogunyemi, and Clenora Hudson-Weems are identified as having laid the foundation of womanism, each representing a distinct perspective. Walker coined the term "womanism" in 1979. In the mid-1980s, Ogunyemi contributed to the growing field of womanism as it relates to the diaspora by engaging with postcolonialism. In 1993, Hudson-Weems established Africana Womanism, which focuses on the struggles of Africana women and emphasizes how they should center themselves in their careers and advocate for fair treatment for themselves and their children in a phallocentric society; she also notes that Africana men and women must work together as opposed to fighting within their community.[6] As articulated by Phillips,

> While Walker's womanism clearly endorses same-sex love and relationships, Ogunyemi's African womanism takes a more polyvalent perspective, and Hudson-Weems's Africana womanism rejects homosexuality outright, the process of interpolation that shapes womanist theory and praxis beyond its original progenitors allows room for differences of opinion about sexuality, all while rejecting systematic discrimination and oppression based on sexuality on the basis of its dehumanizing consequences.[7]

Divergences in these theorists' respective philosophies further demonstrate how Black women's experiences and perspectives are not monolithic.[8]

In Alice Walker's *Coming Apart* (1979), she explains she wrote this text to bring visibility to Black women who have historically been invisible, rejected, and overlooked. Womanism aims to center the experiences of Black women in their struggles, strength, and looks at daily resistances as revolutionary. Walker acknowledges the multiplicity of experiences in womanism as well as the overlap:

> I have, as well as all have, shared a part of my life—since the day I was born—with men whose concept of woman is degraded one. I have also experienced, like the woman in this piece, Forty-second Street; I felt demeaned by the selling of bodies, threatened by violence, and furious that my daughter must grow up in a society in which the debasement of women is actually *enjoyed*.[9]

McClintock provided womanist artists with a platform, especially when considering Afrocentricity's emphasis on healing. As Phillips articulates in *The Womanist Reader*, womanism explores "problem solving in everyday spaces... restoring the balance between people and the environment/nature, and reconciling human life with the spiritual dimension."[10] Much like McClintock's productions and Phillips's assessment of womanist methods, womanists work within the realm of the everyday, which defies both "academic and ideological claims on the definition, labeling, and elaboration of women's resistance activity under the exclusive and limited label 'feminist.'"[11] However, McClintock's technique and season planning provided space for womanist perspectives outside his ontological experience, in which the "everyday" was featured in a theatrical space.

In terms of theatrical practice and scholarship, McClintock's technique and aesthetic is in conversation with pedagogue-director-playwright Glenda Dickerson and scholars Freda Scott Giles and Lisa Anderson whose practice and scholarship contributed to expanding and acknowledging womanism and Black feminism in theatrical spheres. McClintock and Dickerson had a personal friendship and had overlaps of students (i.e., Gwendolen Hardwick discussed in Chapter 2). As analyzed by scholar/dramaturg Khalid Yaya Long, "We recognize Dickerson as a Black feminist/womanist aesthetician who modeled a Black feminist theatre theory through her praxis."[12] Just as McClintock honored the creative agency of his actor, so too did Dickerson through her practice of referring to actresses as "divas" and actors as "counts" in which the divas voices took precedence and the actors co-devised blocking through connecting to the rhythm of the text.[13]

From a scholarly perspective, Freda Scott Giles and Lisa M. Anderson's research has unearthed Black women's voices in academic spaces and have identified aesthetics particular to Black cis female theatre artists. Giles defines womanist theatre as "constructed around the major precepts of feminist, Afrocentric, and post-Afrocentric theatre theory, resulting in a reshaping of dramatic form and narrative."[14] Inherently, this reshaping upends white Eurocentric forms and reveals "patriarchal misrepresentation, bias and oppression."[15] In Anderson's *Black Feminism in Contemporary Drama*, she analyzes the plays of Pearl Cleage, Breena Clarke, Glenda Dickerson, Shirlene Holmes, Kia Corthron, and Sharan Bridgforth. Not only were Dickerson and McClintock peers, he had a close relationship with Breena Clarke and her family (see Chapter 2). Anderson applies the work of Barbara Christian to the notion of a Black feminist theatre aesthetic. Rather than "invent[ing] a theory of how we out to read," one starts with the play/production itself and invites in a critical eye toward the intersection of race, class, language, and gender.[16] Similar to McClintock, Anderson's Black feminist theatre aesthetic in that what emerges in the majority of these plays is the underlying aim to unify and build community.

As mentioned in previous chapters, McClintock included Black female perspectives rooted in womanism, yet in the 1990s, the theory itself was firmly established in the lexicon of academia. In the 1970s, in many cases, Black women made an effort to distinguish themselves from the hypermasculinity often projected in Black Power spaces. Nikki Giovanni and Barbara Smith (see Chapter 3) are two significant figures who pointed out heterosexist strains within the movement. In the 1990s, the country was 20 years distanced from the height of the Black Arts/Black Power Movement, so there was a development of womanism and an exploration of various offshoots. Holland's play and McClintock's production build off the foundation of Walker's original definition with a particular emphasis on Black female empowerment. They examine the circumstances of Holland's life: born into poverty in the South, in a society that left her fewer options. However, with the support of women (as reflected in the all-female cast), her resolve prevails. Even though the cast played cis male and cis female characters, the audience was well aware that only Black women were on stage, a powerful manifestation of the womanist spirit.

As a cisgender man, McClintock's participation in womanism is best understood as akin to how Michael Awkward situates his own positionality in "A Black Man's Place in Black Feminist Criticism." Awkward evokes the words of novelist Toni Morrison in framing his own positionality as a comrade of Black feminists.[17] However, Awkward adds that "while gendered difference might be said to complicate the prospect of non-phallocentric black feminism, it does not render such a project impossible."[18] Providing space for Black women to speak from their diverse backgrounds in devising work selected by, performed by, and about Black women harkens to Barbara Smith's call in her 1977 essay, "Toward a Black Feminist Criticism." McClintock's acting technique and productions relate to Awkward's plea to decenter phallocentric practices. In effect, McClintock's theatre production and support of Black female agency relate to Awkward's analysis of his own writing. "The writing self as biologically male is to emphasize the desire not to be ideologically male; it is to explore the process of rejecting phallocentric perspectives by men which men traditionally have justified the subjugation of women."[19] As far as his studio approach in the 1990s to dealing with womanist works, he continued to invite Black women's experiences to contribute to the development of womanism, as opposed to asserting the dominance of his male gaze.

Locality and Audience Impact

The Barksdale Theatre produced *From the Mississippi Delta* in 1998, six years after it premiered at Circle in the Square Theatre in Manhattan, where it was produced by Oprah Winfrey. Although both productions were situated in the context of the 1990s, they took place in two divergent communities: one northern urban city and one small southern city. The play can impact audiences anywhere, but with a protagonist born in the South, brutally raped by a white man, and spiritually transformed during her time in the Student Nonviolent Coordinating Committee, it would have had a special kind of resonance in a small southern city. The story embodies self-determination in Holland's act of writing her autobiography into the American narrative. Her inner strength emanated from a revelatory connection to her community and, subsequently, her African ancestry.

The context of the New York production at Circle in the Square differs in terms of that city's population, especially considering the complex differences between New York's and Richmond's relationships to slavery. Richmond was also closer to still-standing plantations and active white supremacist factions. In a review of the New York production, Frank Rich mentions that, during the same week as the show, a former Ku Klux Klan member came dangerously close to winning a gubernatorial race in Louisiana.[20] Further, the play was first performed in 1992, the year after Rodney King was unjustly assaulted (see Chapter 5). Notably, prior to the play being published in 2005, McClintock received an updated version from Circle in Square, demonstrating his wide-reaching connections. In 1998, the year of McClintock's production, James Byrd Jr., a Black man in Texas, was brutally dragged to death by three white men, demonstrating that lynching was not a phenomenon of the past. Although *From the Mississippi Delta* is a single story by Holland, with the backdrop of these events, the message is ultimately one of community, perseverance, and spiritual growth. The play provides audiences an alternative perspective on the horrors of everyday American life and gives hope to younger generations amid racial injustice in contemporary society.

Jazz Acting and *From the Mississippi Delta*

The Jazz Acting technique applied to *From the Mississippi Delta* allowed the actors to stay rooted in Holland's autobiographical story while finding spontaneity in the riffs from night to night. Joan Green, part of the all-female ensemble, asserts, "Ernie's contribution helped his actors to portray real people, portray our people as we are. It's something we have to learn."[21] McClintock articulated in a 1998 interview how Jazz Acting was embodied in Holland's play: "[The actors] know the song and the music, but they hear things from other musicians [or actors] that impact how the piece is expressed. There's an openness inherent in it."[22] The openness built on trust among the ensemble struck stage manager Donna Pendarvis, who in the first few days of rehearsal kept a promptbook, exhaustively writing and erasing staging: "But then it dawned on me, this was going to change every single time until they found it which could be the day before or the night of the show."[23] Pendarvis realized that the riffs in performance were not a problem from a stage manager's perspective because "of the process and how it evolves as an ensemble."[24]

McClintock's staging of Holland's play nods to the community that "raised" the playwright and also to the ancestors in the continuum. In interviews,

Holland consistently insisted she was not a self-made person but rather a product of her community. In her play, she urges those around her to see her story not just as one of personal will but as one that shifted into a purpose-filled life, which came to fruition through the collective Black community. In the script, community is reflected in the character breakdown: Woman 1, Woman 2, and Woman 3, who all begin the play singing, one by one, "Trouble in Mind." The fact that the characters' names are all "Woman" reflects the greater womanist community, bringing attention to an overlap of experience. The song, written by Richard M. Jones, in 1924 was originally sung by Thelma La Vizzo and became popular in 1926 with a recording featuring singer Bertha "Chippie" Hill and trumpeter Louis Armstrong. Then, in 1961, Nina Simone recorded the blues song, making it popular yet again. The song offers hope in the midst of oppression: "Trouble in mind, I'm blue/ But I won't be blue always/ 'Cause I know the sun's gonna shine in my back door someday."[25]

In the play, the actors then each speak in first person as Holland. McClintock's production cast Joan Green, Helen Butler, and Tanya Tatum in these roles (Figure 7.4). These women played all characters in the play: Black and white, male and female, young and old. In his review of the New York premiere, Rich asserted that the story had "chaotic waning passages" that were "redeemed by eloquence."[26] The "chaotic waning passages" suggest that the structure of the play does not follow the typical form of scenes and dialogue, as well as the beginning, middle, and end model prescribed in Aristotle's *The Poetics*. For Aristotle, the plot is of utmost importance, followed by character, thought, diction, music, and spectacle. The heart of Holland's play is character, what she experiences, and how she defies the odds and is raised by her community. Therefore, *From the Mississippi Delta* falls sharply outside the western Aristotelian structure, connected to Eurocentric storytelling, on which critics like

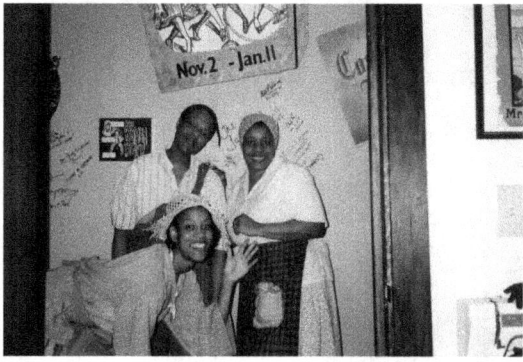

FIGURE 7.4 Helen Butler, Joan Green, and Tanya Tatum backstage at the Barksdale Theatre.

Credit: Private collection of Elizabeth M. Cizmar.

Rich base their assessment of "good" theatre. Therefore, Holland's play in the Black Aesthetic tradition disrupts the content and form of the white aesthetic.

McClintock built upon the community aspect of the play in the powerful ending that moved the audience but remains curiously absent from reviews. A local stage manager/dramaturg, Matt DiCintio, filled in one night for Pendarvis, calling the show. He recalls the audience's tears and joy at the end of the production, moving the cast on stage and the crew backstage. From the audience perspective, in the archives, there is a letter from Renate S. Brandt describing the show as marvelous in which, "It was just exhausting to experience the tremendous level of energy your three ladies brought to their parts. A very satisfying and thought-providing theatre evening..."[27] The play's circular structure is notable in the ending when the three women say, in unison, "I remain—awaiting the call to sisterhood, Dr. Endesha Ida Mae Holland," and then sing "Trouble in Mind" again. In McClintock's production, the women exited the stage and then reentered, placing shoes, one by one, in the middle of the stage.[28] The powerful conclusion to McClintock's production is not part of the scripted text. By the end of the song, shoes filled the center of the stage, signifying all who had contributed to Holland's life. Although Richmond-based critic Roy Proctor applauded the play in many respects, his Eurocentric bias became apparent when he suggested the play "would be better at Barksdale if McClintock provided more quiet interludes to puncture and articulate the fevered pace of the production."[29] The pace of the show and cadence of the play represented Holland's urgency and passion. Measured, quiet interludes dictated by a director for the sake of it would not serve the organic nature of Jazz Acting. Additionally, in a glowing review, S. Edwards Stuart described the production as "an unforgettable experience"[30] yet noted how the chronological play skirts logic. All of the reviews in the archives neglect the symbolic conclusion, which punctuated Holland's journey and McClintock's vision: a balancing act highlighting self-determination and community building.

The Hip-Hop Connection

Although hip-hop theatre may seem contrary to works like *From the Mississippi Delta*, they are similar in terms of the notion of reaching the collective. According to Daniel Banks, hip-hop theatre emerged in the 1990s when British dancer/poet/emcee Jonzi D coined the term to describe a blended performance style.[31] Hip-hop developed as a form of political and social resistance in many urban centers across the United States by youth of color and their allies. As Banks notes, hip-hop itself is much more than just a musical genre; it is a multiethnic, grassroots, global culture leveraging self-expression to combat social justice. The theatrical genre was "born out of [a] struggle to own both content and form and, in that way, owes a direct debt to the activist and resistance culture of Hip Hop."[32]

Hip-hop theatre has recently become a popular topic for courses, festivals, conference panels, and youth camps. Several aspects of the performance genre distinguish hip-hop theatre. One of the most important is community engagement, which resonates with McClintock's acting technique and aesthetic (see Chapter 2). The other identifiable components include voicing the political and social concerns of youth, challenging mainstream theatrical forms, reflecting popular culture, engaging with dialogue on class disparities, and telling stories of marginalized members of society who are not usually visible on the mainstream stage.[33] Through McClintock's teaching and directing, *Ndangered* and *The Rose that Grew from Concrete* challenged the status quo, a characteristic of hip-hop theatre identified by scholar Nicole Hodges Persley.[34] Hip-hop theatre is a theatrical form that addresses ethnicity, class, culture, gender, sexuality, and generation.[35] Challenging the status quo was certainly part of McClintock's agenda, and each of the productions discussed in this chapter reflect that commitment to upending hegemonic systems. This radical inclusion further speaks to McClintock's values and efforts to work against the mainstream to create a socially conscious space. Another way McClintock connects to this form is through the notion of Nommo (see Chapter 5). Nommo considers the human body and mind as being one with the force of life and intimately connected with the earth and the first ancestors. Nommo informs theatrical performance with an emphasis on vocality: "... the power of the *word*, that Nommo force which manipulates all forms of raw life and conjures images that not only represent his biological place in Time and Space, but his spiritual existence as well."[36] As Banks notes, many hip-hop theatre practitioners were artistically raised on the concept of Nommo, demonstrating that McClintock was perhaps one of the early facilitators of the genre. He provided space for youth to express their social and political concerns in a nonlinear story with a poetic vernacular.

Prior to 1999, McClintock was a formidable influence on one of the most well-known hip-hop artists of the twentieth century, Tupac Shakur. Hip-hop as a cultural form is often understood as a misogynistic and homophobic genre, much like the Black Arts Movement. However, the rise of hip-hop scholarship has opened up pathways to understanding the nuances and subversive ways the form challenges the status quo. As Justin A. Williams notes, the "'big bang' moment for the birth of hip-hop music was when DJ Kool Herc threw his first party on August 11, 1973."[37] At the same time, supposing a "big bang" moment runs the risk of reducing the development and nuances of how the form evolved from various cultures. However, as Williams's anthology demonstrates, the roots of hip-hop are deep and the connection to a diverse array of artists is complex. Specifically, hip-hop's origins lie in many cultures; the pioneers in the Bronx were African American, Puerto Rican, Cuban, Dominican, Jamaican, and Bajan, along with white allies.[38] McClintock was primarily concerned with the agency of the Black artist, especially in the 1960s and 1970s, and as the company evolved in the 1990s, actors across races learned under him.

McClintock's connection is not just his mentorship of Tupac Shakur but the development of his collectively-authored works into the twenty-first century. To understand McClintock's synergy with hip-hop theatre, it is critical to contextualize the ever-evolving form situated by contemporary hip-hop scholars.

As explored by scholars like Alice Pryce-Styles, the origins of hip-hop can be directly linked to the Black Arts Movement from a political and practical standpoint. Pryce-Styles identifies the development of hip-hop from the Harlem Renaissance, which "embraced and elevated African American modes and styles of expression," [39] developing into the radical ideas and strategies of the Black Arts Movement. Notably, jazz and other art forms of the Harlem Renaissance were political in their own right and in their own cultural moment. The most well-known figure of the Black Arts Movement, Amiri Baraka (discussed at length in Chapter 4), was a playwright, poet, and activist who implemented early iterations of spoken word, a form of hip-hop theatre that surged in the 1990s, at his Black Arts Repertory Theatre/School in 1965.[40] Jazz Acting, as an acting technique, is a nimble approach that can be applied to many genres and styles, including hip-hop theatre. At its core, it is tied to self-determination and community building, which are consistent in hip-hop performance.[41]

Just as McClintock was inclusive in his practice, hip-hop is rooted in African and Latino cultural aesthetics and speaks to and pushes against a broad audience. Hodges Persley references a critical point articulated by Danny Hoch in his 2004 manifesto

> hip-hop theatre is not solely an African American form—it's part of the continuum—if it were not for African Americans, there wouldn't be hip-hop, but neither would hip hop exist if not for the polycultural social construct of New York in the 1970s.[42]

The elements of hip-hop are breaking, graffiti, MCing, and DJing, [43] which McClintock did not necessarily apply element for element in his own work. However, the sociopolitical underpinnings of the art form, as well as the genres of hip-hop performance, can be connected with McClintock's hip-hop productions *Ndangered* and *The Rose that Grew from Concrete*.

The form of these productions evolved from McClintock's first street theatre performance, *Where It's At* (see Chapter 2), which was consistently tethered to self-determination and community building. As Marc Primus noted,

> *Where It's At*. He did that over and over again and different every time. He came back to New York after years of being in Virginia. It was hip hop.... He was interested in converting hip hop to theatre.[44]

The conversion took all those elements, including the social and political concerns of his young company members, engaged with the community, and subverted mainstream theatrical practices in form and content. These works were not typical plays with distinct characters in a cohesive narrative. Rather, they were pieces of poetry, stories, music, and dance, and they gave voice to Black performers from varying experiences and backgrounds. Therefore, since the inception of the studio in 1996 until 2003, McClintock was committed to developing soul-infused, poetic, and interactive performance. This echoes Hodges Pressley's assertion that "hip-hop theater's newness, self-reflexivity, and ambition allows it to be conscious of when it needs to move forward as it pays homage and respect to its rich past."[45] McClintock did not stay stagnant in the script or social issues addressed in these pieces; in other words, as the world shifted and changed, so too did *Where It's At*.

The Rose that Grew from Concrete

Ernie Claude McClintock, a gay theatre director and teacher, and Tupac Amaru Shakur, a rap artist who exuded heteronormative masculinity and "thug life," [46] had a profound relationship from the first time Tupac walked into the 127th Street Repertory Ensemble until the young artist's death in 1996. McClintock's homage to the late rapper in 1999, three years after his murder, shows the synergy and spiritual connection between the two. In September 1983, Tupac's mother, Afeni Shakur, a former Black Panther and activist, enrolled Tupac in the 127th Street Repertory Ensemble. Hip-hop scholar James Spady published an article in 2015 based on an interview conducted with Tupac at least 20 years prior. Spady noted, "In addition to being a gifted and learned poet/philosopher, Tupac was a superb dramatist with over five years of formal training."[47] Twelve-year-old Tupac was cast as the understudy as Travis Younger in Lorraine Hansberry's *A Raisin in the Sun*, where he learned as much from watching and being an ensemble member as he did on stage.

McClintock's production of *A Raisin in the Sun* at the Apollo Theatre in 1984 was part of a fundraising effort for Jesse Jackson's presidential campaign. According to longtime friend and Studio member Hazel Rosetta Smith, during rehearsals, she would watch Tupac mouthing the words of the play as the actors worked on scenes.[48] She was unsure whether he was imitating, marking, or memorizing. The young actor initially cast in the production left because he was not keeping up with his schoolwork. Tupac stepped in and knew every word of the play. According to actors who had witnessed Tupac in the rehearsal space—including Levy Lee Simon, who played Walter Lee, and Hazel Rosetta Smith, a swing in the production[49]—the young Tupac was magnetic on stage and viscerally connected to language, foreshadowing his own career and fame as a poet and hip-hop artist. In reflecting on his own performance, a twenty-something Tupac was humbled: "I didn't know what I was doing back then even though I was good at everything, I wish I had them now [Hazel Smith and Ernie McClintock] because they were both great actors."[50]

During Tupac's residency with the 127th Street Ensemble, he developed a bond with actor Hazel Rosetta Smith. She contends that she really listened when he was speaking, something she believes adults should do: listen to young children, specifically young Black boys who, in economically depressed neighborhoods like Harlem, can be led astray into violence and harmful behavior that quell their spirits and potential.[51] Smith's support and his mother's care influenced Tupac as a protector and caregiver who revered Black women. In the interview with Smith, she expressed with much joy that Tupac and her were kindred spirits. Smith further posits that she and McClintock influenced Tupac's understanding of the value of words and the impact on audiences. She states:

> [Tupac] was a young, a curious mind and loquacious. You could see it in his eyes and face. When you spoke to Tupac, he would look right at you with such an intense gaze, like laser beams. You knew he was hearing you. So because you felt he was hearing you, you realized it was important what you were saying.... So you have this young boy sitting there watching Ernie directing this group of people. Seeing him bringing these things out of us. And it was so obvious, this thing Ernie did to us even in rehearsals. We were being creative and being creat*ed* by Ernie so I think that Tupac was seeing that, understanding what Ernie was describing, and I think that played a big part in his rapping. I think he realized what you are saying is a serious message.... He knew that words really mattered and if you said it a certain way, people are going to get it and they're going to remember it.[52]

This description connects to what actor Levy Lee Simon identifies as one of the crucial elements of the Jazz Acting technique: word value. This also calls to mind the idea of Nommo: "the power of the *word*, that Nommo force which manipulates all forms of raw life and conjures images that not only represent his biological place in Time and Space, but his spiritual existence as well."[53] Word value can be defined as how much emphasis or weight an actor gives to any given word.[54] Consideration of word value can mean focusing on pronouns as opposed to verbs, which diverges from the western Stanislavsky-based acting method specifically, as explored in Chapter 5. Mainstream acting techniques focus on verbs moving the text and action of the play along and emphasizing a character's motivation. In McClintock's productions, pronouns were more prominent and imbued performances with Nommo, yielding a more poetic connection to language.

Years later, after McClintock and Walker had settled in Richmond, Tupac traveled to Virginia with his entourage to see the Jazz Actors Theatre's revival of N. R. Davidson's *El Hajj Malik* and reconnect with his early mentor. dl Hopkins recalled, "One day [Ernie] called me: 'dl, I need you to go to the

Holiday Inn and pick up Tupac Shakur.'"[55] This sort of incident was typical when working with and studying under McClintock: his network was wide and reached all levels of the social stratosphere. Hopkins reflected that "Tupac was a lot smarter than people thought, and he was a regular guy."[56]

Tupac and McClintock kept in touch over the years. Even though McClintock's connections and network extended to Hollywood, Broadway, and the music industry, he did not just cultivate a slew of celebrities. He was interested in these actors as individuals and in what they contributed to their communities. Jazz Actor Derome Scott Smith drove McClintock to Atlanta to visit Afeni Shakur and her son. Smith notes,

> We went to the house, and Ernie didn't realize who Tupac was. Tupac was downstairs working on music, and Ernie sees the gold, platinum albums. Ernie said, 'I knew he was a rapper but I didn't know about all this.'[57]

During this trip, Smith and Tupac read a scene together from Charles Fuller's *Zooman and the Sign*, in the rapper's living room. Ernie repeated loudly, "AGAIN, AGAIN."[58] No matter the context or the star status, McClintock treated his actors equally.

As with all his students, the connection between Tupac and McClintock extended beyond performing in a play or McClintock teaching acting. An image of Tupac, Ronald Walker, and McClintock standing in front of a poster for *El Hajj Malik* is a powerful visual representation of McClintock's legacy (Figure 7.5). At the height of Tupac's fame, he returned to Richmond to visit his mentor, who was philosophically aligned with Black Power. Many of Tupac's lyrics focused on healing the community, self-determination, and connecting generations. For example, his 1993 song "Keep Ya Head Up," on the album

FIGURE 7.5 Tupac Shakur, Ronald Walker, and Ernie McClintock Stand Before a Poster for a Production of N.R. Davidson's *El Hajj Malik*.
Credit: Private collection of Geno Brantley.

Strictly 4 My N.I.G.G.A.Z., was dedicated to his godson Elijah and "a little girl Corinne," the future generations in the African continuum in which he states the importance of women and queries why women are so mistreated in society. He calls for the collective to take an active role in healing past traumas, including sexual assault. The notion of healing as a community effort appeared in his song "Changes," one year earlier. As explored in Chapter 1, McClintock's training for Black actors developed the skills to self-define through healing, with the intention of then healing these actors' communities.

In terms of the structure and form of "Changes," it lives in the jazz tradition because it revises Bruce Hornsby's 1986 hit "The Way It Is." It echoes Harris's definition that identifies a jazz aesthetic as a transformational process, "a procedure that uses jazz variations as paradigms for the conversion of the white poetic and social ideas into black ones."[59] Hip-hop is a descendant of jazz and often appropriates the hook of a song as a point of departure to convert white western storytelling and music into a piece rooted in Black culture and rhythms. Tom Breihan summarizes Hornsby's 1986 number-one hit as such: "'The Way It is,' the gentle and florid soft-rock jam, is unambiguously a song about racism and about people with money doing everything in their power to keep their place atop the societal pyramid."[60] Breihan notes that Hornsby came from a wealthy family himself, "atop the societal pyramid." The song explicitly references the Economic Opportunity Act and the Civil Rights Act of 1964, highlighting the class inequities. Although the song's title suggests apathy, Hornsby insists that we should not lose hope or believe that nothing can change. Tupac revised the title and the content to "Changes." He reflects on the responsibility of individuals and the system that is stacked against young Black men. He provides a personal, firsthand account of daily discrimination, police brutality, and systemic issues in, for example, the prison system. Tupac also revised the hook, suggesting that a breaking point has been reached: daily discrimination, institutional racism, and targeting of Black bodies, urging change.

One of McClintock's last productions was *The Rose that Grew from Concrete*, offered a portrayal of Tupac, the slain artist, beyond a one-dimensional, stereotypical rap star. This is not a traditional scripted play with distinct characters, plot, rising action, climax, and falling action, as the Aristotelian structure dictates. The theatrical piece "combined a mix of modern and African dance and poetry, hip-hop themed soliloquies and some R&B musical selections."[61] As part of the Second Annual Black Theatre Festival, McClintock asserted that "*The Rose* shows another side of Tupac, which is important for people to see—the side that we saw before he died."[62] Smith also attests to that "other side" of Tupac: the curious, compassionate artist. McClintock's piece highlighted how hip-hop and Tupac's contribution to music and art can reach multiple generations and audiences. Presumably, the show was inspired by Tupac's posthumously released 2000 album of the same name.

The production was performed in early August 2002 at the Firehouse Theatre on West Broad Street, to a full audience. The cast included six women from Richmond's City Dance Troupe, five male actors, and a two-man percussion and guitar ensemble. Reviewer Holly M. Rodriguez reported that "the production created an experience that carried the audience through a roller coaster of emotions from happiness and excitement to fear and loneliness, and in the end, peace."[63] The peace was reflected in a final dance routine by five couples, choreographed by Rodney Williams, wavering between modern dance and ballet. This wavering also reflects a subversion of what is considered "high art" melded with folk dance. The notion of peace is important because hip-hop can often reflect a community's outrage, yet there is a way to leverage that outrage into better living and working conditions, creating a more productive and equitable society. As Williams noted in an interview, "Rodney Williams, choreographer for the City Dance Troup and 'The Rose' said producing black theater in Richmond is a struggle, but there is strong potential for growth here. 'It's always hard—the arts have to struggle for a voice,' he said. 'But I thank God for people like Ernie McClintock, because it takes someone like him, someone with persistence and dedication to the craft, to make it work.'"[64] Williams's description of McClintock's work ethic and "dedication to the craft" was undoubtedly passed along to Tupac, echoing Ron Karenga's 1968 assertion that Black art should be "revolutionary. In brief, functional, collective, and committing."[65]

Ndangered

Part of the festival included a collectively-authored hip-hop piece titled *Ndangered* that focuses on issues facing young African American men, including incarceration, absence of a father in family life, peer pressure, sexually transmitted infections, and racism. This production, modeled after *Where It's At* in terms of approach and process, was first produced in 1999. Similar to *The Rose that Grew from Concrete*, *Ndangered* is not considered a play per se but a theatrical piece that foregrounds the concerns of young Black men. It was a way to give artistic agency to actors and provide space for them to share their individualized and collective experiences with audiences. The premise was that these men are endangered species. The topics the cast and McClintock tackled are connected to Foucault's notions of sovereign power, biopower, and disciplinary power, identified in Chapter 6. Whereas *Before It Hits Home* connects with biopower, *Ndangered* can be filtered through the lens of biopower *and* disciplinary power, which works through institutions and population regulation, when looking at the imbalance of incarcerated Black men and the impact of sexually transmitted infections and racism.

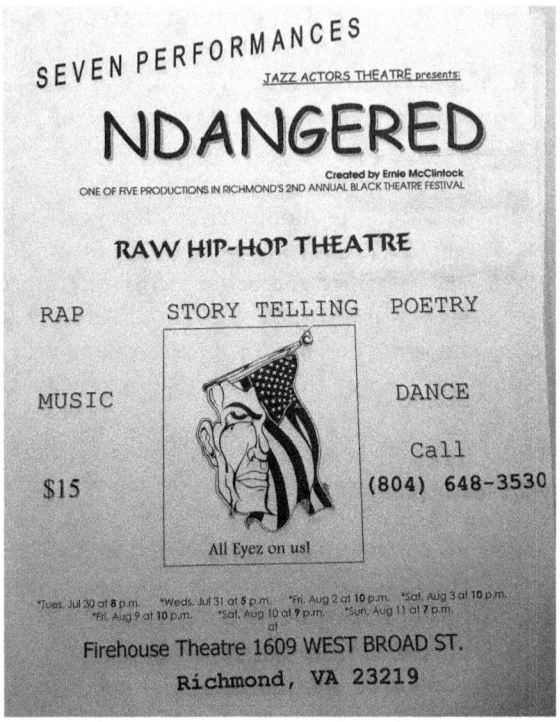

FIGURE 7.6 *Ndangered* Flyer.
Credit: Private collection of Geno Brantley.

In 1999, *Ndangered* toured Richmond, New York, and Winston-Salem. It received mixed reviews. Michael J. Venable described the opening moments of the piece:

> The auditorium was dimly lit and spooky; a nervous audience sat hushed. The ringleader appeared first, cracking his whip while his booming voice introduced the circus. Crew members then wheeled out animals under the red light—endangered black creatures clad in loin cloths, howling, screeching and pawing through the bars that confined them. A few creatures then displayed their magnificence by standing upright and even talking! Concocting amazing speech patterns, they angrily lashed out at demons inhabiting hip-hop culture—snakes that have slithered into what once was their creative social protest, living art, and poetry in motion to insert their venom, reducing it to egotistical commercial babble.[66]

The 1999 cast included Haige Brown, Charles Green, Brother Juarez, Iman Shabazz, Kenya Gadson, Naadir Studevent, and Jeffrey Page, who choreographed the piece. In an influential article in *American Theatre* in 1999 about hip-hop theatre, Holly Bass acknowledged the striking images of the piece but wrote that the show "fails to draw a clear connection between the many forms of black arts represented in the vignettes and their contribution to hip-hop."[67] Although this critique may be valid, Bass did not indicate what those connections should have been and why in a theatrical piece it is necessary to specify the contribution to hip-hop. I assert the point of McClintock's piece was as an authentic theatrical staging of these young actors responding to their immediate environment, just as *Where It's At* was in the late 1960s and early 1970s. Artists responding to and confronting their respective environments and inequities is a common theme and approach in hip-hop theatre. Therefore, I argue *Ndangered* engaging with these issues is inherently a contribution to hip-hop theatre. Further, although Bass critiqued *Ndangered*, she nonetheless established McClintock and his company as part of the initial phase of hip-hop theatre's development.

McClintock charged each of the actors to "bring something real and significant to this piece that helps tell the contemporary story of young black men in America."[68] The piece included free verse, songs, dramatizations, comic moments, and audience participation. Venable asserted, "*Ndangered* combined emotions and thoughts that all young black men have once confronted in some capacity. It is fresh, fast-paced, dynamic, daring, and very, very real."[69] The vulnerability of these young actors, steered by McClintock, demonstrates that the notion of McClintock's studio as a "temple of healing," declared in 1966 and explored in Chapter 2, persisted into the twenty-first century.

When *Ndangered* was presented at the 10th National Black Theatre Festival in Winston-Salem, reviewer Linda Armstrong applauded the production's content and form, in particular how it "looked at the young Black man's desperate need to be encouraged and loved by Black women and it touched on how Black men must take care of each other."[70] She further highlighted the smooth and well-thought-out production value, with an emphasis on "a young man's spiritual development."[71] A subsequent Jazz Actors newsletter acknowledges audience reactions to the piece: "Youth audiences and the media have found this show particularly interesting. Numerous McClintock fans were blown away by this totally unexpected event from the theater veteran, in spite of his reputation for innovation and excellence."[72] The level of vulnerability and intensity in the *Ndangered* series came as a result of McClintock demanding excellence and challenging his actors to create and perform beyond their comfort zones. Notably, McClintock's observation that audiences were surprised by the caliber of the performance demonstrates that even a few years before his passing, preconceived notions about him persisted, arguably due to his queer positionality and the content of his work. An out-gay man facilitating the creative process of a hip-hop production with topics that are usually associated with Black masculinity ruptured the notion that queerness and hip-hop are antithetical.

These individual stories and commitment to self-determination in a theatrical space extended to community building among the actors themselves, as well as audiences. Jazz Actor and activist Iman Shabazz, who performed in *Ndangered*, asserted that he does not like performing outside of the context of the Jazz Actors Ensemble because good is not good enough. McClintock's influence on Shabazz extended beyond a performance context:

> What became apparent to me was that while you can shine in an ordinary crowd, that wasn't good enough for him but also we shouldn't accept that in terms of our own standards.... The idea was beyond just helping me become a better actor. It was helping me to become a better man who understood our culture and the connections of that culture to the work we were doing and then how it impacted the rest of the community.[73]

Shabazz's words echo the foundational principles that remained consistent throughout McClintock's career: self-expression as self-determination and ensemble as community. Additionally, the primacy of the actor in these collectively-authored works underlines and privileges the actor's creative input to a production. These nonlinear pieces, emanating from the Black Power principles of self-determination and community building, are clearly implementing an Afrocentric worldview, where Black bodies are subjects rather than objects. The structure and content fall outside the Aristotelian structure, which emphasizes plot over character. These pieces are not even really about the characters in a fictional play. Rather, self-determination and community building necessitate the primacy of the ontological experiences of the actors. Moreover, they are speaking in their own idioms and of their own experiences and subverting stereotypes that saturate the media and entertainment industries.

Richmond's Black Theatre Festival

McClintock's efforts to establish an annual Black Theatre Festival underscore his desire to fill the lacuna of Black theatre in Richmond for future generations. From his experience as vice president of the Black Theatre Alliance in 1971 (chronicled in Chapter 2) and as a frequent guest of honor at the National Black Theatre Festival, he observed the importance of Black artists across the country communing and celebrating each other's work. Richmond's Black Theatre Festival, much like his Black repertory theatre analyzed in Chapter 4, produced provocative and socially conscious theatre.

Prior to the inaugural Black Theatre Festival in 2001, McClintock organized a conference in Richmond on March 10, 2001, called "Hold Fast to Your Dreams," sponsored by the Tupac Amaru Shakur Foundation, Amaru Entertainment, and the Barksdale Theatre. Featured speakers included former students such as Helmar Cooper and Christel Temple, longtime friend and novelist Breena Clarke, director Woodie King Jr., and Afeni Shakur. Three panels addressed equity, diversity, and emerging genres: "Fairness in the Arts: Advocacy,

Activism and Recourse," "Diversity Programs that Work: Performance Training Opportunities," and "New Trends in Black Theater: Hip Hop Theater and More." The issues that predominantly white universities and training programs are confronting in 2022 in terms of equity, diversity, and inclusion were being addressed in this format under McClintock's leadership in 2001.

The event program details the Jazz Actors Theatre's mission within the context of African American theatre history. It states, "Black theatre has historically been a vehicle for social consciousness, and that is as important to Jazz Actors Theatre's mission as the work it puts on stage."[74] McClintock, therefore, situated his life and career as part of the larger African theatrical diaspora, which reflects his whole way of functioning as an artist, without the goals of capitalist success. The greater cause was to empower Black artists and audiences, raise social consciousness, and create theatre that impacted the community. In this program, McClintock further identified the mission of the Jazz Actors Theatre (Figure 7.7). From the first days of the Afro-American Studio for Acting and Speech in 1966, he never deviated from his aim of producing historically and socially significant plays, creating a technique geared toward accessing the individuality and cultural identity of his students, and providing the community with an education.

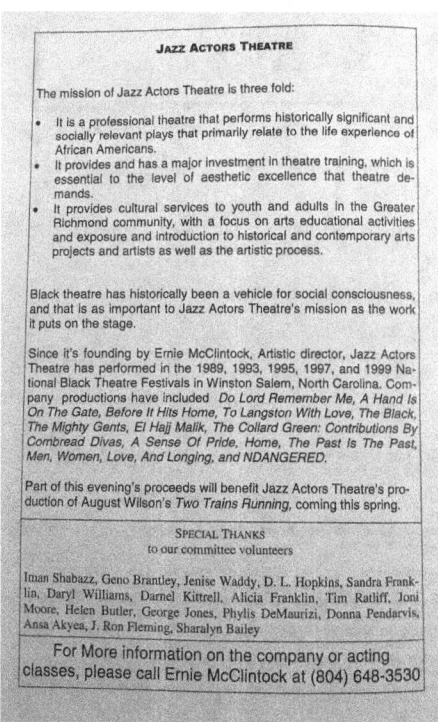

FIGURE 7.7 Back of Program for "Hold Fast to Your Dreams," March 10, 2001.
Credit: Private collection of Geno Brantley.

Each Black Theatre Festival in Richmond had a particular theme connected to the mission of the Jazz Actors Theatre. In 2001, the inaugural year, "Theatre à la Carte: From Harlem Renaissance to Hip Hop," showcased five productions: Roscoe Lee Brown's *A Hand Is on the Gate* (1966), James de Jongh's *Do Lord Remember Me* (1978), Ernie McClintock's *Ndangered* (1999), Anna Deavere Smith's *Fires in the Mirror* (1992) , and the collected poetry of Tupac Shakur, *The Rose that Grew from Concrete* (2001). The versatility of material ranged from Contemporary Black Classics (see Chapter 3) to new collectively-authored pieces, and included solo performances and ensemble-driven pieces.

Richmond's Second Annual Black Theatre Festival was titled "Revelations and Transitions." In it, McClintock revived *Ndangered* (retitled *Ndangered 2002*) and *The Rose that Grew from Concrete*, and produced *Before It Hits Home* (see Chapter 6). McClintock also directed John Henry Redwood's *The Old Settler* (1998), described by the director as "two lonely middle-aged sisters become enlivened by the appearance of a handsome young stranger who stirs up more than memories."[75] Redwood's heartfelt play laced with humor gives voice to two older women in Harlem in the 1940s, a population whose story is often untold. The poetic text presumably appealed to McClintock's fascination with words and the Black idiom of a particular era, and yet again extended his inclusion of middle-aged Black women who do not often appear in mainstream theatrical storytelling. When middle-aged Black women appear in the mainstream, they are often relegated to iterations of the Mammy stereotype. As McClintock wrote in the Director's Note in the play's program, "I've never been satisfied with the simple 'let's put on a play attitude' prevalent in most theatres but rather have been absorbed in traveling proven avenues of excellence that support realization of specific artistic concepts and visions."[76] The festival also presented the City Dance Troupe, an award-winning Richmond-based company known for "theatricality, diversity, and technical execution."[77] The addition of the troupe and *The Old Settler* alongside hip-hop theatre and a story of queer sexuality during the early 1990s exemplifies how McClintock was constantly seeking new material and modes of presentation, making efforts to be ever more inclusive of experiences and perspectives in the diaspora.

The third and final Black Theatre Festival was called "To See Another Day," which brings to mind McClintock's lifelong commitment to providing a model of acting and theatrical production for future generations to carry forward. Derome Scott Smith, directed *Langston Is My Man* (1999), a musical inspired by and centered on Langston Hughes's poetry. Harlem Renaissance writer and activist Langston Hughes was one of the most prolific poets of the twentieth century to apply the notions of jazz aesthetics in his writing. The City Dance Troupe returned to the festival to perform. McClintock revived his children's theatre piece, *A Sense of Pride* (see Chapter 5), reflecting that idea of educating the next generations. Two scripted pieces were Ramona King's *Steal Away* (1982) and David Feldshuh's *Miss Evers' Boys* (1992). The festival ran from July

17 to August 3, 2003. Roughly three weeks after the festival closed, on August 26, McClintock died in Richmond.

Miss Evers' Boys

Feldshuh's *Miss Evers' Boys* was McClintock's last production. The final performance was on August 3, 2003, and twenty-three days later, McClintock passed away. Right to the end he was fully committed to his mission of training Black actors and producing stories centered on Black experiences. Granted, *Miss Evers' Boys* was written by a white heterosexual playwright and physician, but the story sheds light on a traumatic event in American history that resulted in yet another example of historical trauma done to Black bodies.

To call the Tuskegee Study a historical trauma is not hyperbole. The loss of faith and trust in public health officials that resulted had major impacts on public health crises such as the AIDS epidemic in the 1980s and, most recently, the COVID-19 pandemic. The US Department of Health and Human Services defines historical trauma as follows:

> Multigenerational trauma experienced by a specific cultural, racial or ethnic group. It is related to major events that oppressed a particular group of people because of their status as oppressed, such as slavery, the Holocaust, forced migration, and the violent colonization of Native Americans. While many in such a group will experience no effects of the historical trauma, others may experience poor overall physical and behavioral health, including low self-esteem, depression, self-destructive behavior, marked propensity for violent or aggressive behavior, substance misuse and addiction, and high rates of suicide and cardiovascular disease.[78]

The impact of the Tuskegee Study inflicted even more trauma on Black bodies and communities because it underlined the blatant disregard for Black life and access to public health.

According to historian James H. Jones, author of a 1981 book that inspired Feldshuh's play, "No scientific experiment inflicted more damage on the collective psyche of black Americans than the Tuskegee study."[79] This historical nuance is critical in understanding Black communities' responses to public health crises and mistrust of health authorities, a fact that, according to Jones, many white folks have difficulty understanding. Mistrust has a long history and is tied to deep-rooted historical traumas. In 1992, *Newsweek* published an article on conspiracy theories claiming that AIDS was a genocidal effort to eliminate Black folk. The majority of Black politicians, academics, and civic officials did not subscribe to such theories in a literal sense; however, the neglect of communities of color who suffered gravely at the hand of epidemics and pandemics "smacked of racism."[80]

Although the play is fiction, the story is based on a nurse who was involved in the Tuskegee Study. The play follows the lives of four men who were part of the experiment: Willie Johnson, Hodman Bryan, Caleb Humphries, and Ben Washington. In the author's note, Feldshuh writes, "The characters (including the nurse), the context, and the incidents of the play are products of the playwright's imagination, and any quotations from primary sources have been rearranged, reassigned or paraphrased."[81] In the play, Eunice Evers, a nurse, cares for these men; initially, she is hopeful the study will cure their ailments. However, the study takes a turn, and she is faced with deceiving them to see the study through. She puts her trust in the doctors and honors her duties as a medical professional, yet when she sees her patients' health deteriorate, she can no longer go along with the study's deception. The play reveals moments where Evers gives testimony, reflecting on the shameful stain on American history. After the play premiered in 1989 at Center Stage in Baltimore and was produced in regional theatres with directors, such as Irene Lewis, Kenny Leon, and D. Scott Glassera, it was adapted into an HBO film and won the 1997 Emmy for Best Television Movie.

Jazzing *Miss Evers' Boys*

The Jazz Actors Theatre production featured Christel Temple (Miss Evers) Sheldon Woodley (Caleb), Wali Brandon (Ben Washington), Brandon Fobbs (Willie Johnson), J. Ron Fleming (Hodman Bryan), Tony Scott (Dr. Eugene Brodus), and Joe Inscoe (Dr. John Douglas). One of the most memorable and difficult scenes is when Dr. Douglas and Miss Evers perform a spinal tap on Caleb Humphries. Douglas has trouble finding the spinal canal, poking and prodding Caleb in the process. When he finally finds the canal, Caleb's pain is excruciating:

> CALEB. (*He resists moving and, trying to ignore the intermittent bursts of pain which occur only when the needle is pushed in, automatically falls into his preaching voice; his anger is stronger than the pain and it is this anger that makes his words clear and resonant, despite the procedure.*) Ahhh.... That needle is the work of the devil... it's sharp and burning and greedy gold in color... ahhh.... (*A catechism.*) What color was Job? Black. What color was Jeremiah? Black. Who was Moses' wife? An Ethiopian. David said he became like a bottle in the smoke. What's natural? It's as natural to be black as the leopard to be spotted.... Ahhh.[82]

Textually, there is something happening here: what the character is saying and then the subtext. The audience is aware that this study is bogus, and Caleb's words and "anger," as described by the playwright, also speak to the greater outrage of the Tuskegee Study and the historical trauma inflicted on Americans of African descent.

As actor Christel Temple, who played Miss Evers, notes, in 2003, the internet did not have such a breadth of information available to the actors for research as it would today, so they relied on Jazz Acting habits and gestures. Temple states,

> I remember asking Ernie what a spinal tap was supposed to look like on stage and if the audience would know that we were just making it up.... We had a huge needle and lot[s] of squinting and needle-shy choices among our habits and gestures.[83]

This application of Jazz Acting's use of the physical, repeatable choices known as habits and gestures (analyzed in Chapter 5) remedied the question whether an actor should have to go through physical pain or recall a traumatic physical event to achieve convincing portrayals.

As a result of this physicality, the actors were able to reach heightened emotion, not as a result of what they were feeling but of what they were doing. From the 1960s to 2003, McClintock rejected "gimmicks" as a method of bringing raw emotion to performance. In the play, Miss Evers and Caleb are romantically interested in each another. On one night of the production, Sheldon Woodley, who played Caleb, kissed Temple on stage, which was not written in the script but was another manifestation of Jazz Acting in performance. Temple recalls,

> I think [Ernie] appreciated the way Sheldon went with the flow and made a decision as an actor... that might have been the same night that I was able to muster up a tear on stage as Sheldon's character was walking away... we were able to pull off a fantastic emotional moment for the play with really incredible follow-through.[84]

Another Jazz Acting moment occurred in one performance when Woodley decided not to wear undergarments during a scene. When he jumped off the examining table, he "showed the audience his rear end."[85] Apparently McClintock rolled his eyes, but presumably appreciated those bold choices that were indicative of a Jazz Actor.

Miss Evers' Boys was part of the final Black Theatre Festival produced in Richmond in 2003 and McClintock's last show. McClintock's health was failing, and although he would often lie down on a lavish antique red chaise (Figure 7.8), Temple recalled, "I did not have any idea of how sick Ernie was at that time or that this would be his final production."[86] During this period, McClintock would lie on his chaise, surrounded by the late Ronald Walker's artwork. At times, he would have to miss rehearsals, but he knew this cast would be able to realize his vision in the Jazz Acting aesthetic (Figure 7.9). As far as the design, Geno Brantley, who apprenticed for Ronald Walker for decades, designed the

FIGURE 7.8 Ernie McClintock's Red Chaise.
Credit: Private collection of Christel Temple.

FIGURE 7.9 Cast Photo of *Miss Evers' Boys*.
Credit: Private collection of Christel Temple.

lights and set. Therefore, in many ways, the torch of the Jazz Actors Theatre was passed, in terms of Walker's legacy and McClintock's trust in his ensemble.

To cast the title role, McClintock called Temple, who was living in Baltimore and working in a tenure-track position at the University of Maryland, Baltimore County. Commuting two-and-a-half hours while balancing her book project, publications, teaching, and maintaining her personal life was a challenge. However, as she said, "It's difficult to say 'No' to Ernie because any request coming from him is a compliment (which is very, very rare. Ernie makes sure to keep his actors humbled, even keeping positive newspaper reviews of our performances from us)."[87] She refused to watch the film of *Miss Evers' Boys* because as a practice, McClintock insisted that the watching previously recorded performances was irrelevant to their process. Temple further recalls there was a positive review of the production that especially noted the dynamic between her and Sheldon Woodley. But McClintock refused to let the actors see it to keep their focus on the work and the process, as opposed to the result.

Despite this positive review, audiences did not fill the seats of Pine Camp's Theatre in August 2003. However, even though the audiences were small, they were meaningful. Temple articulated McClintock's vision and process on this show:

> Ernie's work was often attentive to Black masculinity in its many forms, and we had many emotional moments during rehearsals and the production during which we just could not forget the gravity of this actual historical tragedy that Feldshuh translated into dramatic form. Ernie was pushing us to do it right. He wanted us to do it right for the ancestors who experienced the tragedy and to pay homage to them. This production had a unique sincerity and even sadness about it because of the historical Tuskegee experiment.[88]

Paying homage to the ancestors and establishing a production where the actors knew their history was a consistent practice in McClintock's teaching and directing. It connects back to Marc Primus's Black History classes, taught at the inception of the Afro-American Studio for Acting and Speech (see Chapter 2). Ronald Walker had died four years earlier; three weeks after the last performance McClintock died; within a couple of years, Wali Brandon, who played Ben Washington, passed on. In the play, Ben loses his battle with syphilis at the hands of government neglect. Therefore, according to the cast, the show's theme of death particularly resonated with the performers after its closing.[89]

Conclusion

McClintock's passing was a devastating loss for the Jazz Actors family and the American Theatre, but the complex legacy he left challenges incumbent systems, subverts hegemonic powers, and expands notions of what it means to be a queer Black Nationalist in the American theatre. His efforts to continue the mission of the Black Arts Movement to create Black theatrical institutions that are about, for, and near Black communities remained steadfast throughout his 40-year career. Perhaps the term "career" is limiting in this context, because to McClintock, Black Theatre was not just his job but his calling and his life. He was consumed by theatre, waking up in the middle of the night with a notebook across his chest so he could write down ideas for his next production.[90] As a result of this unsatiated hunger for new Black theatre, he produced hip-hop theatre, a natural next step in Black artists developing an artistic genre that spoke to the current moment and daily lives of Black folk. The productions based on scripted plays—*From the Mississippi Delta* and *Miss Evers' Boys*—featured Black history and served not just as entertainment but as education for the Richmond community.

In the end, Richmond's Black Theatre Festival did not survive after McClintock's passing, but he and his legacy have not been forgotten in the lives and careers of his students. In 2011, the Richmond Theatre Critics Circle Awards renamed its Best Ensemble Award the Ernie McClintock Best Acting Ensemble Awards.[91] Even eight years after his passing, the professional theatre in Richmond acknowledged the caliber of ensemble work in his productions and the high standards he established in regional theatre. Although the festival only lasted three seasons, his students continue to carry the torch of Jazz Acting in a host of professions as actors, playwrights, educators, scholars, producers, and activists. Without fail, each of the Jazz Actors interviewed attest that Ernie McClintock was their mentor. He was invested in the development of their craft as actors and also in their development as individuals, their connection to each other, and ultimately in their legacy as proud descendants of their ancestors in the African Diaspora.

Notes

1 Louis, interview.
2 "Live Art."
3 Harrison, "Praise/Word," 7.
4 Lynch, "Lawsuits and Legacies," 43.
5 Primus, interview. Refer to Chapter 2 for a comprehensive understanding of healing in the 1960s.
6 Hudson-Weems, "Africana Womanism," 53.
7 Phillips, "Introduction," xxxvii.
8 Phillips, "Acknowledgments," xiv.
9 Walker, "Coming Apart," 3.
10 Phillips, "Introduction," xx.
11 Phillips, "Introduction," xx.
12 Long, "The Black Feminist Theatre of Glenda Dickerson," 180.
13 Long, "The Black Feminist Theatre of Glenda Dickerson," 180.
14 Giles, "In Their Own Words," 28.

15 Giles, "In Their Own Words," 28.
16 Anderson, *Black Feminism in Contemporary Drama*, 3.
17 Awkward, "Black Man's Place," 71.
18 Awkward, "Black Man's Place," 69.
19 Awkward, "Black Man's Place," 69.
20 Rich, "Defeating Racism."
21 Green, interview.
22 Timberline, "Footlights," 36.
23 Pendarvis, interview.
24 Pendarvis, interview.
25 Donna Pendarvis's promptbook, *From the Mississippi Delta*, script with notes. From the private collection of Geno Brantley.
26 Rich, "Defeating Racism."
27 Letter from Renate S. Brandt to the Barksdale Theatre, March 22, 1998, from the Private Collection of Geno Brantley.
28 DiCintio, interview.
29 Proctor, "Storytelling Is Front and Center," E3.
30 Stuart, "Triumphant Triumvirate," 36.
31 Banks, "Introduction," 1.
32 Banks, "Introduction," 1.
33 Banks, "Introduction," 17–18.
34 Hodges Persley, "Hip-Hop Theater," 86.
35 Banks, "Introduction," 18.
36 Harrison, *The Drama of Nommo*, xvi.
37 Williams, "Introduction," 1.
38 Banks, "Introduction," 9.
39 Pryce-Styles, "MC Origins," 17.
40 "Interactions between BAM poets and contemporary hip-hop artists have tended to be potent, natural, and numerous." Pryce-Styles, "MC Origins," 17.
41 Daniel Banks's introduction to *Say Word! Voices from Hip Hop Theater* provides a thorough overview of hip-hop theatre. He identifies self-determination and community engagement as two identifying features.
42 Hodges Persley, "Hip-Hop Theater," 87.
43 For a more exhaustive analysis of hip-hop theater and performance, see Williams's *The Cambridge Companion to Hip-Hop*.
44 Primus, interview.
45 Hodges Persley, "Hip-Hop Theater," 95.
46 Among Shakur's many tattoos was a sizable "Thug Life" tattoo across his abdomen. Thug Life was the name of his hip-hop group before he left the group to pursue a solo career.
47 Spady, "Tupac Amaru Shakur," 7. Spady's article does not include the date of his interview with the hip-hop artist. Spady was a leading scholar in hip-hop studies. For more in-depth information, refer to his books *Nation Conscious Rap* (1991), *Twisted Tales: In the Hip Hop Streets of Philly* (1995), and *street Conscious Rap* (1999). These works include interviews with over 60 artists including Tupac Shakur.
48 Hazel Smith, interview.
49 In the 127th Street Repertory Company, even if an actor was not cast in a production, they would serve the process. This could be as an understudy, backstage crew, costumes, and/or wherever the show needed support. Therefore, even if one wasn't cast, they were still integral to the production and learned by doing as well as watching McClintock's rehearsal process.
50 Spady, "Tupac Amaru Shakur," 7.
51 Hazel Smith, interview.

52 Hazel Smith, interview.
53 Harrison, *The Drama of Nommo*, xvi.
54 Simon, interview.
55 Hopkins, interview.
56 Hopkins, interview.
57 Derome Smith, interview.
58 Derome Smith, interview.
59 Harris, *Poetry and Poetics*, 13.
60 Breihan, "Number Ones."
61 Rodriguez, "Listening to Black Voices."
62 Rodriguez, "Listening to Black Voices."
63 Rodriguez, "Listening to Black Voices."
64 Rodriguez, "Listening to Black Voices."
65 Karenga, "Black Nationalism," 33. For a more extensive explanation, refer to Chapter 3.
66 Venable, "Ndangered Acts," D3.
67 Bass, "Blowing up the Set," 19.
68 Venable, "Ndangered Acts," D3.
69 Venable, "Ndangered Acts," D3.
70 Armstrong, "10th Anniversary," 1.
71 Armstrong, "10th Anniversary," 1.
72 Letter dated October 21, 1999, private collection of Geno Brantley.
73 Shabazz, interview.
74 *Hold Fast to Your Dreams* program, from the Private Collection of Geno Brantley.
75 *Transitions and Revelations* program, from the Private Collection of Geno Brantley.
76 *The Old Settler* program, from the private collection of Geno Brantley.
77 *Transitions and Revelations* program.
78 "Trauma: What Is Historical Trauma?"
79 Jones, "The Tuskegee Legacy," 38.
80 Jones, "The Tuskegee Legacy," 40.
81 Feldshuh, *Miss Evers' Boys*, 5.
82 Feldshuh, *Miss Evers' Boys*, 50.
83 Temple, email correspondence.
84 Temple, email correspondence.
85 Temple, email correspondence.
86 Temple, interview.
87 Temple, email correspondence.
88 Temple, email correspondence.
89 Temple, interview.
90 Brantley, interview.
91 "Richmond Theatre Critics Circle."

Bibliography

Anderson, Lisa M. *Black Feminism in Contemporary Drama*. Urbana: University of Illinois Press, 2008.

Armstrong, Linda. "10th Anniversary of Black Theater Fest Boasts Pride." *New York Amsterdam News*, August 12, 1999, 27:1.

Awkward, Michael. "A Black Man's Place in Black Feminist Critique." In *The Womanist Reader*, edited by Layli Phillips, 69–84. New York: Routledge, 2006.

Banks, Daniel. "Introduction: Hip Hop Theater's Ethic of Inclusion." In *Say Word! Voices from Hip Hop Theater*, edited by Daniel Banks, 1–23. Ann Arbor: University of Michigan Press, 2011.

Bass, Holly. "Blowin' Up the Set." *American Theatre* 16, no. 9 (1999): 18–20.
Brantley, Geno. Interview by Elizabeth Cizmar, September 9, 2015, Richmond, VA.
Breihan, Tom. "Number Ones: Burce Hornsby & The Range's 'The Way It Is.'" Stereogum, January 21, 2021. https://www.stereogum.com/2113715/the-number-ones-bruce-hornsby-the-ranges-the-way-it-is/columns/the-number-ones/.
DiCintio, Matt. Interview by Elizabeth Cizmar, October 10, 2016, Boston, MA.
Feldshuh, David. *Miss Evers' Boys*. New York: Dramatists Play Service, 1995.
Giles, Freda Scott. "In Their Own Words: Pearl Cleage and Glenda Dickerson Define Womanist Theatre." *The Womanist: Theory and Research* 2, no. 1 (Fall/Winter 1996–1997): 28–35.
Giovanni, Nikki. "Black Poems, Poseurs, and Power." In *Call and Response: Key Debates in African American Studies*, edited by Henry Louis Gates Jr. and Jennifer Burton, 711–15. New York: W.W. Norton & Company, 2001.
Green, Joan. Interview by Elizabeth Cizmar, May 30, 2016, New Rochelle, NY.
Harris, William J. *The Poetry and Poetics of Amiri Baraka: The Jazz Aesthetic*. Columbia: University of Missouri Press, 1985.
Harrison, Paul Carter. *The Drama of Nommo*. New York: Grove Press, 1972.
Harrison, Paul Carter. "Praise/Word." In *Black Theatre: Ritual Performance in the African Diaspora*, edited by Paul Carter Harrison, Victor Leo Walker II, and Gus Edwards, 1–12. Philadelphia: Temple University Press, 2002.
Hodges Persley, Nicole. "Hip-hop Theater and Performance." In *The Cambridge Companion to Hip-Hop*, edited by Justin A. Williams, 85–98. Cambridge, UK: Cambridge University Press, 2015.
Holland, Endesha Ida Mae. *From the Mississippi Delta*. Woodstock: The Dramatic Publishing Company, 2005.
Hopkins, dl. Interview by Elizabeth Cizmar, September 9, 2015, Richmond, VA.
Hudson-Weems, Clenora. "Africana Womanism." In *The Womanist Reader*, edited by Layli Phillips, 44–54. New York: Routledge, 2006
Jones, James H. "The Tuskegee Legacy AIDS and the Black Community." *The Hastings Center Report* 22, no. 6 (November–December 1992): 38–40.
Karenga, Ron. "Black Nationalism." In *The Black Aesthetic*, edited by Gayle Addison Jr., 32–38. Garden City, NY: Doubleday & Company, 1971.
"Live Art: By Gathering Artists of All Kinds at His 'Studio A' Series, Ernie McClintock Brings Art to Life." *Style Weekly*, March 2, 2002. https://www.styleweekly.com/richmond/live-art/Content?oid=1375445.
Long, Khalid Yaya. "The Black Feminist Theatre of Glenda Dickerson." In *The Routledge Companion to African American Theatre and Performance*, edited by Kathy A. Perkins, Sandra L. Richards, Renée Alexander Craft, and Thomas F. DeFrantz, 180–85. New York: Routledge, 2018.
Louis, Lola. Interview by Elizabeth Cizmar, September 2, 2015, New York.
Lynch, John. "Lawsuits and Legacies: Competing Memorializations of the Tuskegee Syphilis Study." In *The Origins of Bioethics: Remembering When Medicine Went Wrong*, 43–77. East Lansing: Michigan State University Press, 2019.
Mayfield, Julian. "You Touch My Black Aesthetic and I'll Touch Yours." In *The Black Aesthetic*, edited by Gayle Addison, 24–31. Garden City, NY: Doubleday & Company, 2017.
Pendarvis, Donna. Interview by Elizabeth Cizmar, September 9, 2015, Richmond, VA.
Phillips, Layli. *The Womanist Reader*. New York: Routledge, 2006.
Primus, Marc. Interview by Elizabeth Cizmar, August 25, 2015, Atlanta, GA.

Proctor, Roy. "Storytelling Is Front and Center." *Richmond Times-Dispatch*, March 16, 1998, E3.

Pryce-Styles, Alice. "MC Origins: Rap and Spoken Word Poetry." In *The Cambridge Companion to Hip-Hop*, edited by Justin A. Williams, 11–21. Cambridge, UK: Cambridge University Press, 2015.

Rich, Frank. "Defeating Racism, Violence, and Want." *New York Times*, November 12, 1991. http://www.nytimes.com/1991/11/12/theater/review-theater-defeating-racism-violence-and-want.html.

"Richmond Theatre Critics Circle: Celebrating Excellence in Richmond-Area Theatre." *Richmond Theatre Critics Circle*, n.d. Accessed August 1, 2021. http://www.artsies.org/the-2011-rtcc-artsies-awards/.

Rodriguez, Holly. "Listening to Black Voices." *Style Weekly*, August 14, 2002. https://www.styleweekly.com/richmond/theater-listening-to-black voices/Content?oid=1367803.

Shabazz, Iman. Interview by Elizabeth Cizmar, September 9, 2015, Richmond, VA.

Shakur, Tupac. "Changes." *AZ Lyrics*, n.d. Accessed January 21, 2017. https://www.azlyrics.com/lyrics/2pac/changes.html.

Shakur, Tupac. "Keep Ya Head Up." *AZ Lyrics*, n.d. Accessed January 21, 2017. https://www.azlyrics.com/lyrics/2pac/keepyaheadup.html.

Simon, Levy Lee. Interview by Elizabeth Cizmar, September 18, 2015, phone.

Smith, Barbara. 2001. "Toward a Black Feminist Criticism." In *Call and Response: Key Debates in African American Studies*, edited by Henry Louis Gates Jr. and Jennifer Burton, 723–33. New York: W.W. Norton & Company.

Smith, Derome. Interview by Elizabeth Cizmar, September 9, 2015, Richmond, VA.

Smith, Hazel. Interview by Elizabeth Cizmar, August 11, 2021, Zoom.

Spady, James. "Tupac Amaru Shakur: Lights Dimmed, Drama. Epistemologies, Cultural Transformations and the Rights/Rites of Memory." *SCOOP U.S.A.*, July 17, 2015, 7.

Stuart, S. Edward "Triumphant Triumvirate." *Style Weekly*, March 17, 1998, 36.

Temple, Christel. Interview with Elizabeth Cizmar, August 10–12, 2021, email.

Timberline, Holly. "Footlights." *Style Weekly*, March 17, 1998, 36.

"Trauma: What Is Historical Trauma?" *Administration for Children & Families*, n.d. Accessed August 8, 2021. https://www.acf.hhs.gov/trauma-toolkit/trauma-concept.

Venable, Michael J. "Ndangered Acts in Mysterious Ways." *Richmond Times-Dispatch*, August 10, 1999, D3.

Walker, Alice. "Coming Apart." In *The Womanist Reader*, edited by Layli Phillips, 3–11. New York: Routledge, 2006.

Williams, Justin A. "Introduction: The Interdisciplinary World of Hip-Hop Studies." In *The Cambridge Companion to Hip-Hop*, edited by Justin A. Williams, 1–8. Cambridge, UK: Cambridge University Press, 2015.

Witherspoon, Jimmy. "Trouble in Mind." *Lyrics.com*, n.d. Accessed August 1, 2021. https://www.lyrics.com/lyric/29245360/Best+of+the+Blues%2C+Vol.+1+%5BExcalibu%5D/Trouble+in+Mind.

CONCLUSION

Beyond the Biography

In 2015, when I started this research as part of my doctoral studies, I became interested in Ernie McClintock because of my career and training as an actor. In the nascent stages of researching and tracking down people who worked directly under his tutelage, I primarily saw this project as a historical excavation of a glossed over but significant figure in the Black Arts Movement. However, the revival of McClintock's legacy—in terms of his performance aesthetic and acting technique—has the potential to be so much more than a history lesson. Jazz Acting, in addition to shaping my scholarship, has reshaped my approach in the rehearsal hall as a director, on stage as an actor, and in the classroom as a teacher. In academic circles, I am considered a scholar of Ernie McClintock, which I am proud to be. However, through this journey I consider myself a student of Ernie McClintock, at my core. My white cis positionality as "the McClintock scholar" runs the risk of looking like an attempt to "save" McClintock from the ashes, privileging my white gaze; in thinking about myself as a student of McClintock's, I allow the research to guide me and his students to teach me. Ultimately, by viewing marginalized historical figures as teachers rather than names in books, as theatre artists and educators we can honor and apply the work of artists of color that many teachers at PWIs want to do but do not necessarily have a roadmap for. Thus, I consider this book a starting point for artists and teachers to investigate and query their own methodologies and artistic endeavors.

Historical Significance

The historical significance of Ernie McClintock is apparent in his contribution to the Black Arts Movement and his mentorship of hundreds of actors across the country. His pupils went on to become groundbreaking academics, dynamic actors, inspired directors, and revolutionary activists in a plethora of genres and mediums. His Afrocentric aesthetic does not stand alone but rests on the shoulders of his ancestors, including scholar Alain Locke, poet Langston Hughes, actor Charles Gilpin, actor Ira Aldridge, actor-activist Paul Robeson, and actor Frank Silvera. His Black Nationalist activism is also in conversation with thinkers of the Black Arts Movement, including Amiri Baraka, Larry Neal, and James Baldwin.

Leaders within the Black Theatre Movement—including those of the Black Arts Repertory Theatre and School, the National Black Theatre, the New Lafayette Theatre, the Negro Ensemble Company, and the Urban Arts Corps—had their own philosophies on how to promote the movement's principles to create a more equitable and just society for people of African descent (see introduction). At the core of the Black Arts Movement is this idea of community: the Black Theatre Movement community comprised various people and theatres that did not always see eye-to-eye but came together to unify, subvert mainstream practices, and celebrate Afrocentricity. Thus, the term "community" is not simply meant to suggest an idealistic image of arts leaders logrolling. Rather, it also means divergences in opinions and approaches. The inclusivity of these perspectives and the ability to remain part of that community despite differences is what promotes change.

Among the important organizations and milestones of the Black Theatre Movement, McClintock was not just an artist but a leader. Specifically, he was the first vice president of the Black Theatre Alliance, which aimed to unite Black Theatres to pool funding and appeal to governmental programming to get more financial support and resources for the Black Theatre. In the introduction I shared an anecdote about McClintock's 1972 speech in a New York City town hall, where he wore a denim suit and spoke out against prejudice against Black Theatres, which observers considered the "highlight" of the evening. His unorthodox style and outspoken nature as a leader set him apart. McClintock co-organized the first AUDELCO awards in Harlem at the Afro-American Studio for Acting and Speech in 1973. To this day, the AUDELCOs are an important awards ceremony that honor Black Theatre performers and artists. McClintock worked alongside leaders in these organizations like Vivian Robinson (founder of the AUDELCOs), and Delano Stewart, Hazel Bryant, and Roger Furman (playwrights who established the Black Theatre Alliance).

McClintock's contribution to the Black Theatre Movement presents the legacy and practice of an artist countering narratives of the Black Arts Movement and Black Power, which included hypermasculine militant figures. He was a Black Nationalist who revered Malcolm X; he was also a gay Black man in a long-term partnership with Ronald Walker. His life and legacy shows that the philosophies of Black Power and the personal lives of gay folk can coexist. His leadership in the Black Theatre Movement profoundly shifts perceptions of who helped shape the movement itself.

McClintock did not fit within traditional ideas of heteronormative Black masculinity, which was a factor in his erasure in Black Arts Movement histories. McClintock's erasure can be attributed both to his sexuality and to his unorthodox way of working. He ruptured gay stereotypes and did not fit into tidy hegemonic definitions of straight versus gay folk. Yet, due to his vantage point as a queer artist, part of his conception for his theatre was the inclusion of Black actors from various backgrounds and experiences, and programming across genres and styles. As was fully unpacked in Chapter 4, he "quared" the Black Theatre Movement, acknowledging "difference within and between particular groups."[1] His strategies promoted a kaleidoscopic view of Blackness, countering assumptions that there is a singular Black experience. His sexuality and his partnership with Walker were not the entirety of his identity, but these were certainly part of his lived experience. In McClintock's theatre, authenticity required actors to embrace all parts of themselves to assert their creative agency.

McClintock's Application of Community and Self-Determination

Within the Afro-American Studio for Acting and Speech, the 127th Street Repertory Ensemble, and the Jazz Actors Theatre, "community" translated on stage to the notion of ensemble but also related to the company of actors collaborating together. Just like those committed to Black Power, in McClintock's theatre one could not commit 50 percent or even 99 percent. Commitment to the ensemble meant 100 percent devotion: showing up at rehearsals despite blizzards, injuries, and family emergencies. He expected everyone involved in his company to be as devoted to the temple of theatre as he was. By embracing this level of discipline and a "no excuses" policy, the ensemble trusted one another, created electric moments on stage, and formed a bond to the point where, to this day, they all refer to themselves as the "Jazz Actors Family." Those not cast in a show would be stage managers and stage hands; they would paint sets, assist McClintock, and otherwise contribute to the production both on and off stage. This devotion was not just to acting as an art form but to theatre as a sacred space. And yet, even though McClintock was a disciplinarian with a temper, all the actors interviewed for this book attest to his healing power and ability to nurture Black actors.

The other foundational aspect of his technique was self-determination, which can be linked to Alain Locke's concept of self-expression, fully explored in Chapter 2. Self-expression emphasizes the actor's role and potential to propel social change. Self-expression requires teachers or directors honor the unique identity and perspective of an individual. In his programming, he invited in voices from across the diaspora, including Black Power activists, womanists, queer folks, those from lower socioeconomic statuses, immigrants, historical figures, middle-class families, and hip-hop artists. As inclusive as he was, the stories remained cis and solely included able-bodied actors. Yet, his model, employed from the 1960s to the first decade of the twenty-first century, could be implemented by educators and artists. If McClintock were alive today, based on his evolutionary approach of including genres based on the pulse of society at certain times, I venture to say that he would include these voices in his repertoire and company. We can recognize the shortcomings of his inclusion but also acknowledge the potential his legacy offers.

His inclusivity extended to his thoughts on drama criticism by establishing the Contemporary Black Classics. Similar to how Jazz Acting developed over 40 years, McClintock put forth the concept of an ever-evolving canon to respond to the cultural and political context of a moment, necessarily expanding inclusion of multiple Black perspectives. And, as explained in Chapter 3, based on his openness to allowing the Contemporary Black Classics to be a subject of healthy debate among experts in Black Theatre, he likely viewed the Black Aesthetic as an ever-evolving concept rather than a fixed definition. Thinkers involved with the Black Aesthetic asked for Black writers to "[re-evaluate] Western aesthetics, the traditional role of the writer, and the social function of art."[2] McClintock and his contemporaries knew the shortcomings of mainstream education and commercial theatre, where white, western standards relegated Black Theatre and artists to a second-tier status.

Just as McClintock considered the inclusion of queer works like *Equus* and *Before It Hits Home*, womanist theatre like *Spell #7* and *From the Mississippi Delta*, and hip-hop drama like *Ndangered* and *The Rose that Grew from Concrete*, educators and producers need to meet the moment and actively include stories outside mainstream narratives. While this has not been a priority for PWIs or white-run theatres, there are always pockets of resistance within these institutions and companies that can look to McClintock to teach them. He often butted heads with administrators and, as a Black queer man, lived in a world that discriminated against him. McClintock, therefore, can be a teacher to us all, from various backgrounds, gender identifications, ethnicities, and socioeconomic classes.

Practical Application of McClintock's Legacy in the Contemporary World

How can McClintock be a teacher posthumously? How can we apply his lessons and approach in our own classrooms and theatres? A significant takeaway from the development of McClintock's technique—from the Theatre of Common Sense to Jazz Acting—is that actors should allow their processes to be nimble and ever-evolving. In acting circles, especially in educational spaces, there is often a culture of being faithful to only one technique, such as the Method, the Meisner Technique, the school of Stella Adler, and so forth. Rather, because culture shifts and genres are emerging all the time, actors will be better equipped by staying open to and inclusive of different ways of approaching their art. Many of the more western methods were based in creating a technique for plays written by white western cis males. For example, Stanislavski and the Moscow Art Theatre were tied to Anton Chekhov's oeuvre. However, if one is working on a play by a playwright of color or a queer writer, perhaps this linear way of approaching character creation will not be as beneficial as approaching a character from a subaltern perspective. The more skills an actor acquires from various approaches, the more flexible they will be when approaching different characters and stories. Practically speaking, the more versatile an actor is, the more acting gigs they will land.

Concurrently, the principles of McClintock's work—self-determination and community building—remained steadfast because they were grounded in his Afrocentric worldview. Therefore, actors considering their own nonnegotiable principles, based on who they are rather than who a director wants them to be, will ground themselves while allowing for an organic development of their craft. As someone who studied Method acting, Practical Aesthetics, and now Jazz Acting, I offer units on various techniques in my own classroom to expose students to different ways of finding an entry point to character. Similarly, Monica White Ndounou, in her article "Encountering Black Culture in Acting Classrooms and Beyond," identifies her acting pedagogy as one that integrates Afrocentric cultural practices and traditions "alongside Western acting methodologies in the American theatre."[3] In my Acting I class, after being introduced to a sampling of various techniques, the actors exercise artistic autonomy and decide which approach will serve their chosen monologue or scene. This strategy is designed to encourage self-determination and artistic agency.

In terms of season planning at both professional theatres and university campuses, McClintock actively pursued the inclusion of perspectives from across the diaspora. He brought forward the narratives of those often overlooked within his own community, such as people from lower socioeconomic classes in *The Mighty Gents* and gay men grappling with the AIDS epidemic in *Before It Hits Home*. In womanist pieces, he did not necessarily have that lived experience but through the virtue of the self-expression embedded in the technique, he required actors to be fully prepared with characterization as well as physical and vocal choices, and he would then shape the production. He denounced the idea of the director as puppeteer and actors as marionettes solely living out the director's vision. This approach can privilege the perspective of the director rather than inviting in individual actors' ontological reality and creative agency. Just as McClintock did in encountering works outside his own lived experience, directors can unearth actors' creativity and lived experiences and shape a production from there.

224 Conclusion: Beyond the Biography

Directors can look to McClintock to teach them how to integrate an actor's self-expression and creative input into the process while still running a tight ship. In a recording on acting technique, McClintock tells his actors that "[the] director is always the final voice.... Some things you can add in that no one will notice, but you can't change anything to alter a performance or the intention. This is to keep the performance from going off the rails when someone has a whim."[4] The Jazz Acting approach is not about chaos or random choices. The melody, the characterization, and the text are the foundation, and when that is achieved, the sophistication of riffs creates the quintessential McClintock electricity on stage.

Through McClintock's technique, actors can consider finding variations, or riffs, in performance, yet remain rooted in their character development achieved during the rehearsal process. In a 1972 lecture, McClintock stated that "[actors] must bring the play to the director."[5] That is, adjustments and compromises occur in the rehearsal hall but preparation in terms of characterization is the actor's responsibility. As far as riffs, theatre is ephemeral and that should be embraced, rather than trying to repeat a precise performance night after night. Theatre is not a static medium; audiences come to the theatre to see something happen for the first time. As I often tell my students, your character does not know how the play is going to end. Leaning into the riffs and new moments that can occur in live theatrical performance rather than aiming for rigidity and perfection will provide actors space to assert their artistic agency and find new moments night after night. Additionally, much like call and response, audience reactions that vary from night to night should be taken into account in the performance. Within the Afrocentric worldview, in the context of live performance, call and response acknowledges the collective experience of the participants onstage and in the audience. Actors find a melody, something to truly ground them and ensure consistency as stipulated by a director or stage manager, but still find moments of variation that can be in conversation with the audience.

In my own process of becoming a student of McClintock through studying his archive and conducting interviews with his pupils, I have discovered the necessity for acting teachers as well as actors to evolve their craft and pedagogy through training, which can come in various forms. An archive of an overlooked figure can be a form of training in itself. For most acting teachers, it has been a while since we have been in the classroom at a conservatory, graduate program, or undergraduate institution. Therefore, I encourage all of us to broaden our minds and engage with methods of acting that, although they have been in practice for decades, are only now being discussed in scholarship and at academic theatre conferences. As an undergraduate and a Master of Fine Arts student, I attended PWIs, where Afrocentric acting methods and histories were rarely mentioned. Mainstream acting is traditionally tied to Stanislavski. Thus, so many educators, including myself, are primarily trained in Stanislavski and that is what we teach. Not until my graduate studies at Tufts University, when I was in Monica White Ndounou's class The Historical and Theoretical Development of African American Theatre, did I encounter Black plays beyond *The Dutchman* and *A Raisin in the Sun*. Although western methods can be effective, they are limiting. If teachers want more inclusion and diversity in the classroom, they need to stop focusing solely on mainstream acting. Becoming a student again provides the opportunity to rethink how we structure our classes, provide more options for students, and decolonize western acting methods. Furthermore, in the spirit of decolonizing, subaltern acting methods should not have to be defined according to or in comparison with Stanislavsky or any other western approach.

McClintock's life and legacy can be a transformative model for educators of all backgrounds to actively pursue inclusivity. Most educators agree that equity, diversity, and inclusion (EDI) initiatives are an important part of rethinking curricula, but that they often fall short. The truth is that many students of color at PWIs still feel marginalized and not included in programming for theatre seasons. Specifically, an examination of PWIs' season programming shows that white playwrights still get top billing. Decolonizing the Eurocentric ways of teaching and creating art must start in the classroom but also in season selections; the voices of the historically marginalized should be privileged and white fragility no longer managed. One way teachers do this is by including a more diverse range of plays in a syllabus. This is a great start, but there is more work to be done at PWIs. Moreover, the cherry-picking approach can often border on cultural appropriation as opposed to cultural appreciation. There is a distinct difference between culturally appropriating the work of a figure like McClintock and taking the time to listen, learn, and *know that you don't know*. Bringing in artists, guests, and teachers from a plethora of backgrounds and traditions and positioning the professor as a student models to a class that the teacher is learning and expanding their knowledge base. There are incremental yet effective ways to increase representation in the classroom, even if one's home institution is slow on the uptake. Do the work and actively pursue learning about cultural modes of theatrical expression outside your comfort zone. Above all, maintaining a humble attitude and admitting shortcomings in one's own education or process is a powerful example of how artists are forever students. McClintock's teachings can be a portal to considering other figures from various backgrounds and gender identities, demonstrating the practical use of history in the classroom. Despite history being a traditionally white, cishet enterprise, the excavation of these historical figures as game changers can counter those traditional narratives. By looking at a figure like McClintock, we can reposition history as an applied learning tool in academic-based and practically focused classes.

I sit in a privileged position as a Vanderbilt professor with white skin and three degrees in theatre. It is not lost on me that the efforts for actors, artists, scholars, and teachers who live in a different reality than I do may not have access or the time and space to excavate overlooked figures. I think it is up to educators—not just in Historically Black Colleges and Universities or only professors of color at PWIs—to pursue these excavations and include figures and paradigms outside of our own training. With the support of mentors and teachers, I have been pursuing this excavation for seven years; just as McClintock was not alone in his approach, I too am contributing to a greater conversation with scholar-artists like Sharrell Luckett, Monica White Ndounou, Nicole Hodges Persley, E. Patrick Johnson, and La Donna Forsgren, who have all laid the groundwork for my research on McClintock. Thus, this book, adding as it does to the work of those scholars and artists who came before me, is an offering to broaden the conversation and hold universities and theatres accountable for actively rather than passively instituting diversity and inclusion, beyond the simple mention of EDI in meetings. McClintock's Jazz Acting privileges the notion of artistic agency and demands individuals create from a place of authenticity, all while providing space for a multiplicity of voices to be heard in the room where, like a piece of jazz music, moments of dissonance and harmony emerge. Above all, these jazz conversations can sometimes be congruous and sometimes uncomfortable and have the power to upend previous modes of creating and teaching that have historically privileged white cishet bodies into a paradigm that is truly inclusive.

Notes

1 Johnson, "'Quare' Studies," 135.
2 Neal, "The Black Arts Movement," 29.
3 Ndounou, "Encountering Black Culture in Acting Classrooms and Beyond."
4 McClintock, "Acting Technique."
5 McClintock, "Acting Technique."

Bibliography

Johnson, E. Patrick. "'Quare' Studies, or (Almost) Everything I Know About Queer Studies I Learned from My Grandmother." In *Black Queer Studies: A Critical Anthology*, edited by E. Patrick Johnson and Mae G. Henderson, 124–57. Durham, NC: Duke University Press, 2005.
McClintock, Ernie. "Acting Technique Lecture, the Afro American Studio for Acting & Speech." From the Private Collection of Geno Brantley, February 2, 1972. Magnetic Reel.
Ndounou, Monica White. "Encountering Black Culture in Acting Classrooms and Beyond," *Theatre Topics* 19, no. 1 (March 2009): 95. https://doi.org/10.1353/tt.0.0056.
Neal, Larry. "The Black Arts Movement." *Drama Review* 4, no. 12 (Summer 1968): 28–39. https://doi.org/10.2307/1144377.

INDEX

Note: *Italic* page numbers refer to figures and page numbers followed by "n" refer to endnotes.

12 Years a Slave 11
127th Street Repertory Ensemble 2, 9, 21, 58, 66, 81, 83, 87, 89, 94, 101, 109–10, 120, 124, 128, 151, 215n49; AUDELCO award nominations (1982) *112*; company members of *82*; season poster (1982) *111*; *see also* Harlem Jazz Theatre

absolutes, significance of 40, 150
actor self-acceptance 9
Actors Studio Drama School 77n34
Actors Studio of New York 37
Addison, Gayle, Jr. 104n13
Advanced Theatre Workshop 66, 81
African American collective history, significance of 57–58
Africana Womanism 191
African Collage, Epitaph to the Coagulated Trinity (McClintock) 45
Afro-American Studio for Acting and Speech (Harlem) 2, 12, 20–21, 42, 46, 47, 51, 151; brochure of *59*, 60; character analysis at 64; character center of gravity at 64–65; character rhythm at 65; community observations at 65–66; healing and self-expression at 58–63, 66–70; logo of *52*; physical warm-up exercises at *62*; sign hung in *53*; *see also Hajj Malik, El* (Davidson); *Where It's At*

Afro-American Studio Theatre Center 81, 89
Afro-American Total Theatre 1
Afro-Caribbean representation 119–21
Afrocentricity 11, 154; Asante on 53–54; community principle in 12–13; rhythm as core in 65; self-determination principle in 13–14
Aldridge, Ira 220
Alexander Technique 76–77n18
Allen, Debbie 140
Altria Theatre 152
Amen Corner, The (Baldwin) 90
American Society for Theatre Research 102
American Theatre 204
Anderson, Elijah 169
Anderson, Lisa M. 190, 192
Angelou, Maya 42, 140
Angels in America (Kushner) 177
Apollo Theatre 199
Armstrong, Louis 195, 205
"Art or Propaganda?" (Locke) 14
Asante, Molefi Kete 11, 53, 154
Association for Theatre in Higher Education 102
Atreus Aegyptus 57
Audience Development Committee, Inc. (AUDELCO) 84, 87, 89, 104n10, 220

228 Index

Awkward, Michael 193

"Babylon Revisited" (Baraka) 10
Bailey, Peter 71, 88–89, 91
Baker, S. Allison 144, 146, 147
Baldwin, James 30, 31, 56, 61, 90, 115, 131, 220
"Ballot or the Bullet, The" (X) 46
Banks, Daniel 190, 196, 215n41
Baraka, Amiri 4, 7, 8, 10, 13, 20, 21, 22n34, 38, 42, 56, 83, 84, 85, 90–94, 115–16, 131, 178, 198, 220
Barksdale Theatre 190, 193
Barnes, Clive 72, 75, 124
Barton, Melissa 27
BART/S *see* Black Arts Repertory Theatre and School (BART/S)
Bass, Holly 204–205
Bates, Jerome Preston 60, 89, 109, 123, 128–29, 139, 151
Before It Hits Home 151, 156, 161, 167, 168, 175–82, 203, 208
Big White Fog (Ward) 41
biopower 163, 169
Birth of a Nation (Griffith) 66
Black Aesthetic 5, 84, 85–87
"Black Arts Movement, The" (Neal) 4, 10, 85, 86
Black Arts Movement: Black women's role in 104n13; contemporary Black classics and 83–85, 87, 88, 90, 93, 97, 100–101; Harlem and 55, 58, 61, 66, 71, 75, 76n13; homophobia in 104n15; misogyny in 104n15, 114; quaring of Black Theatre Movement and 113–15, 117; Richmond and 136, 141, 144, 156; significance of 10, 13–15, 19, 21, 22n17, 38, 168, 175, 176, 182, 197, 198, 214, 219–21; theatre emergence in 2–8
Black Arts Repertory Theatre and School (BART/S) 4, 5, 7
Black authenticity 115, 122, 130
Black Consciousness 104n17, 155
"Black Cultural Nationalism" (Karenga) 86
Black Drama (Loften) 60
Black Feminism in Contemporary Drama (Anderson) 192
Black feminist theatre aesthetic 192
Black habitus 167–68, 173, 176, 179, 182
Black image abuse antidote 121–24
"Black Man's Place in Black Feminist Criticism, A" (Awkward) 193

Black masculinity 10, 20, 176, 179, 180, 189, 205, 221; Harlem and 55, 70; quaring of Black Theatre Movement and 115, 131
Black Mass (Baraka) 7
Black nationalism 30, 42, 46, 71, 214, 220; contemporary Black classics and 93, 105n45; quaring of Black Theatre Movement and 113, 115, 121, 122, 130
Black Nativity (Hughes) 90
Blackness 13, 61, 66, 116, 121, 175, 176, 179; inauthentic representation of 56; as not monolithic 8, 18, 56, 131, 221; racial 115
Black Odyssey (Huggins) 60, 61, 90
Black-on-Black crime 174, 184n53
"Black Poems, Poseurs, and Power" (Giovanni) 86
Black Power Movement 26, 27, 72, 75, 88, 118, 162, 164, 174
Black queer sexuality 9–10, 103, 110, 124, 125; *see also* queer sexuality
Black queer theatre, in Richmond 175–82
"Black Revolutionary Theatre, The" (Baraka) 85
Blacks, The (Genet) 152–55
Black subversion in twentieth-century performance 47–48n28
Black Theatre Alliance (BTA); disbanding of 117; importance of 1, 6, 22n22, 83, 84, 87–88
Black Theatre Alliance magazine 74, 83
Black Theatre History 62, 63
Black Theatre in the 1960s and 1970s (Williams) 15, 54–55
Black Theatre Movement 12, 68, 70, 83, 84, 109–13; Afro-Caribbean representation and 119–21; Black image abuse antidote and 121–24; jazzing of western narrative and 124–30; quare framework for 113–16; Reaganomics affecting 116–19
Blaine, Vivian 35
Blight, William 98
Bogle, Donald 76n12, 133n76, 165
Bourdieu, Pierre 167
Boys Choir of Harlem 139
Bradley, Sara 105n32
Brandon, Wali 210, 213
Brandon, Wally 173
Brantley, Geno 15, 118, 119, 142, 151, 211, 215n25
Breihan, Tom 202

Bridgforth, Sharon 106n74, 192
British National Theatre 125
Broaddus, Ed 100
Brown, Haige 204
Brown, Roscoe Lee 208
Brown v. Board of Education (1954) 30
Bryant, Hazel 1, 87, 220
BTA *see* Black Theatre Alliance (BTA)
Buchanan, Pat 164
Bullins, Ed 7–8, 38, 56, 66, 131, 140, 166, 178
Burleigh, Henry T. 106n60
Butler, Helen 195
Butler, Judith 113–14
Byrd, James, Jr. 194

call and response 23n43, 33, 48n30
Calloway, Cab 29
Canaan, Gareth 28
capitalism 174, 175
Carroll, Vinette 8, 87, 140
Carter, Woody 61, 94
Ceremonies in Dark Old Men (Elder III) 140
CETA *see* Comprehensive Employment and Training Act (CETA)
Chafe, William 4, 27, 29, 118, 161, 166, 167
Chekhov, Anton 57
Cherry Orchard, The (Chekov) 57
Chicago Black Renaissance 27
Chicago Paramount Pictures 34
Chicago Tribune 37
Chitlin Circuit 152–53
Christian, Barbara 192
churches, in Black Christian circles 178
Circle in the Square Theatre 193, 194
City and the Pillar, The (Vidal) 31
City Dance Troupe 208
Clarke, Breena 54, 70, 71, 192, 206
Cleage, Pearl 192
Clinton, Hillary 165
Clinton, William Jefferson 164
Cochran, Johnny 166
Cohen, Cathy 16, 162, 163, 169, 175, 176
Collard Greens and Cornbread Divas, The 155, 156, 180
collectively-authored definition of 8n47
collective memory 20, 96, 98, 174
Coming Apart (Walker) 191
Common Sense approach 139, 143, 148
community building 6, 10, 17, 161, 196, 198, 205, 206, 223; contemporary Black classics and 87, 97; Harlem and 53, 75, 76; quaring of Black Theatre Movement and 115, 121, 123, 131; Richmond and 141, 142, 157
community healing 53, 66–70, 100
Comprehensive Employment and Training Act (CETA) 117
Confessions of Nat Turner, The (Styron) 99
Contemporary Black Classics 18, 81–85; Black Aesthetic and 85–87; community efforts to unify 87–89; definition of 78n68, 82; discrimination in 1970s and 100–101; *Do Lord Remember Me* and 97–100; framing of 89–91; *Slave Ship* and 91–97
Cooper, Helmar 54, 63, 70, 71, 72, 89, 94, 155, 206
Cornacher, Karen 121
Corthron, Kia 192
Cosby Show, The 115
Coward, Noel 34
"Creation, The" (Johnson) 37
critical memory 97, 167, 184n35
Cuffee, Paul 105n45
cultural capital 104n12
cultural hegemony 33, 48n32
cultural trauma 11, 58, 94

Daniels, Thaddeus 40, 150, 151, 156, 175, 178, 179, 181
Davidson, N. R. 46
Davis, Ossie 140
Day of Absence (Ward) 7
Death of a Salesman 90
Dee, Ruby 140
dehumanization 3, 42, 58, 62, 92, 94–96, 99, 120
de Jongh, James 84, 90, 97
Delaney, Martin 105n45
democratic history 60, 77n23
De Priest, Oscar 29
Dexter, John 124
DiCintio, Matt 196
Dickerson, Glenda 57, 192
"Different Fight, 'Same Goal'" (Yurcaba) 43
Dogwood Dell Productions 144
Do Lord Remember Me (de Jongh) 84, 90, 97–100, 141, 167, 208
domestic colonialism 33, 48n32
Don't Bother Me, I Can't Cope (Carroll and Grant) 8
double consciousness 13
Douglass, Frederick 106n60

Drama of Nommo, The (Harrison) 149
Dream on Monkey Mountain 65, 103, 109, 119–20
Du Bois, W. E. B. 11, 13, 14, 76n2, 85
Dunnaville, Shantell 118, 137
Dutchman, The (Baraka) 7, 91

EAD *see* Expansion Arts Division (EAD)
Ebony magazine 56
Edwards, Bolanyle 9, 65, 72, 109, 122
Elam, Harry, Jr. 27, 41
Elder, Lonnie, III 140
Electra 37
Electronic Nigger, The (Bullins) 7
"Encountering Black Culture in Acting Classrooms and Beyond" (Ndounou) 223
Enelow, Shonni 11, 55
English repertory model 76, 109, 110, 116, 119, 121
Enrico IV 37
Equus (Shaffer) 9, 10, 103, 109, 110, 124–30, *128*, 139, 176
Espie, Helen 40, 150
Etwaroo, Indira 90, 180
Expansion Arts Division (EAD) 117
Experimental Death Unit #1 (Baraka) 7, 81
Eyerman, Ron 11

Fame 115, 131
Fanon, Frantz 10
Federal Violent Crime Control and Law Enforcement Act (1994) 164–65
Feldshuh, David 189, 208, 210
Ferguson, Roderick A. 162, 177
Firehouse Theatre 203
Fires in the Mirror (Smith) 208
First Word 150–51, 172–73, 180
Firth, John 125, 126, 130
Fleming, J. Ron 118, 154, 168, 173, 174, 210
Fobbs, Brandon 210
Forsgren, LaDonna 104n13
For the Love of Freedom (Simon) 159n74
Fort Riley Theatre Company 39
Foucault, Michael 163, 169
Four Black Revolutionary Plays (Baraka) 8
fourth wall 12
Franciosa, Anthony 34
Frankel, Gene 37
Freedman, Doris 67, 68
Freeman (Hayes) 139
Freeman, Morgan 109

From the Mississippi Delta 187, 190–93; Jazz Acting technique in 194–96; locality and audience impact of 193–94
Fugard, Athol 140
Fuhrman, Mark 166
Fuller, Charles 201
Fumed Oak (Coward) 34
Furman, Roger 87, 220

Gadson, Kenya 204
Garvey, Marcus 105n45
Gates, Henry Louis, Jr. 85, 102, 152, 153
Gazzara, Ben 34
Gazzo, Michael V. 34
Genet, Jean 152
Giles, Freda Scott 190, 192
Gilpin, Charles 220
Giovanni, Nikki 84, 85, 114, 122, 193
Glassera, D. Scott 210
Glass Menagerie, The 90
Glover, William 169
God-conscious art 56
Goin' A Buffalo (Bullins) 7, 66
Gorn, Elliott J. 29
Gossett Academy of Dramatic Arts (GADA) 43
Gossett, Louis, Jr. 43–46
Gramsci, Antonio 33
Grant, Micki 8
Great Depression 28
Great Goodness of Life (A Coon Show) (Baraka) 81, 94
great homosexual trial 16
Green, Charles 204
Green, Joan 109, 178, 179, 195
Griffin, Zaria 181
Griffith, D. W. 66
Grigg, Flo 147
Guardino, Harry 35
Guillory, John 85, 102, 104n12
Guys and Dolls 35

habitus 167; *see also* Black habitus
Hajj Malik, El (Davidson) 46, 55, 70–75, 82, 84, 200; Martin on 73–74; Primus on 72–73
Hall, Arsenio 140
Haller, Mark H. 27
Hamilton (Miranda) 60
Hamlin, Larry Leon 139–40, 141
Hand Is on the Gate, A (Brown) 208
Hansberry, Lorraine 41–42, 89
Happy Ending (Ward) 7

Hardwick, Gwendolen 57
Harlem Jazz Theatre: invitation for 137; mission of 140; significance of 138–41; *see also* 127th Street Repertory Ensemble
Harlem Renaissance 141, 198
Harper Theatre 37
Harrison, Paul Carter 8, 67, 149
Harris, Rosemary 140
Harris, William J. 14, 129
HARYOU Act 5
Hatch, James 15, 88
Hatful of Rain, A (Gazzo) 2, 34–36
Hayes, Phillip Dean 138–39
healing: contemporary Black classics and 99, 100; Harlem and 53, 54, 58–63, 66–70; quaring of Black Theatre Movement and 121, 123, 124; significance of 6, 14, 17–18, 20, 192, 201, 202, 221
Helen Espie Dramatic Arts Studio 37, 40
Helen Espie Fine Arts Institute 2
Henry V 38
heteronormativity: Afrocentric roots and 30, 31; contemporary Black classics and 84, 86, 101; Harlem and 56, 70, 76n8; quaring of Black Theatre Movement and 110, 113, 115, 131; significance of 10, 15, 17, 20, 21, 163, 165, 175, 176, 178, 199, 221
Hill, Bertha "Chippie" 195
Hill, Errol 15
hip-hop theatre 196–99, 215nn41, 43; Nommo and 197; origins of 198
historical trauma 209
historio-drama 60
History of African American Theatre, A (Hatch and Hill) 15
History of the American Nation (McLaughlin) 11, 93
Hoch, Danny 198
Hodges, Mary 149, 151, 153
Hodges Persley, Nicole 190, 197, 198, 199
Hold Fast to Your Dreams conference 206–207
Holland, Endesha Ida Mae 187, 190, 193–96
Holmes, Shirlene 192
Hooks, Robert 38, 140, 144
Hoover, J. Edgar 3
Hopkins, dl 99–100, 153, 171, 172–73, 200–201
Horne, J.W. Robinson 100, 145, 154

Hornsby, Bruce 202
Hudson-Weems, Clenora 191
Huggins, Nathan 60, 61, 62, 90–91, 95
Hughes, Langston 90, 208, 220
Hunter, Vicky 87, 89–90
hypermasculinity 113–15, 131, 193, 220; contemporary Black classics and 84–86, 94, 97, 101; resistance for 71–72

"Iconic Ghetto, The" (Anderson) 169
impressionistic style, in literary theory 91, 96
Inscoe, Joe 210
In Search of Our Mothers' Gardens (Walker) 9
internal colonialism *see* domestic colonialism
In the Wine Time (Bullins) 7
Island, The (Fugard, Kani, and Ntshona) 140

Jackson, Michael 150
Jazz Acting 2, 12–13, 40, 53, 94, 122, 142; character analysis and 64; in performance 70–76; physicality and 64; technique of 148–51, 170, 194–96, 210–13
Jazz Actors Theatre 2, 136, 137–38, 145, 148
"Jazzing It", concept of 151
jazzing, of western narrative 124–30
Jazz Theatre of Harlem 2
Jazz Theatre of Richmond 136, 144–45
J-E-L-L-O (Baraka) 7
Jenkins, Bruce 101, 109, 123
John, Errol 103, 120, 146
Johnson, E. Patrick 10, 15, 18, 56, 58, 71, 113–14, 125, 130, 179
Johnson, James Weldon 37
Johnson, Marsha P. 43
Jones, James Earl 43
Jones, James H. 209
Jones, Omi Osun 106n74
Jones, Rhett 61
Jones, Richard M. 195
Jonzi D 196
Joseph, Peniel 3, 27, 42
Juarez, Brother 204

Kalb, Madeleine G. 41
Kani, John 140
Karenga, Ron 21, 85–86, 104n17, 203
Kasa-Vubu, Joseph 41

Kennedy, John F. 41
Kennedy, Robert F. 3–4
King, Martin Luther, Jr. 3
King, Ramona 208
King, Rodney 142, 166, 194
King, Woody, Jr. 87, 140, 144, 206
Kramer, Larry 177
Kushner, Tony 177

Langston Is My Man 208
Larson, Jonathan 177
La Vizzo, Thelma 195
Lawson, Mark 124
Lee, Don L. 10, 92
Leon, Kenny 210
Lewis, Irene 210
Library of Congress 98
Locke, Alain 11, 13, 14, 54, 76n2, 220
Long, Barry 98
Long, Khalid Yaya 192
"Look at the Contemporary Black Theatre Movement, A" (Bailey) 88
Looking for Leroy 115
Louis, Lola 120, 178, 181, 187
Luckett, Sharrell D. 106n74
Lumumba, Patrice 3, 41, 42

Mabley, Moms 46
Macbeth, Robert 6, 7, 56
Madheart (Baraka) 7, 81, 164
Martin, Gottfried 73
Martinique Theatre 73
Matthew, Pat 123
McBride, Dwight A. 115
McClintock, Ernie Claude: Afrocentric framework in works of 11–14; as apolitical 71; application of community and self-determination 221–22; and Baraka compared 13; on Black Theatre Alliance (BTA) 88; breathing and articulation exercises of 122; on capitalism 175; early life of 2, 27–34; on ensemble-building 129–30, 151; historical significance of 219–21; inclusive approach of 8–11, 71, 110, 111–12, 147, 182, 222; leadership quality of 1–2; legacy, practical application in contemporary world 222–26; Living Legend Award for 162, 177–78, 183n2; as mistreated 146, 147; on music and rhythm in character development 98; Nommo and 197; parents of 27–28; quareness and 113, 115; reevaluation of art 86–87; theatrical vocation (1950s–1960s) 34–39; training with Gossett, Jr. 43–46; Tupac and 200–201; in US Army 38–39; womanism and 193
McConachie, Bruce 27, 33
McLaughlin, Andrew C. 93
McQueen, Steve 34
Method acting 11, 51, 76nn8, 18, 77n34, 98, 99
Middle Passage 18, 32, 60, 61, 90, 91, 92, 95, 96
Mighty Gents, The (Wesley) 66, 156, 161, 165, 168–75
militarism and art 86
Milner, Ronald 91–92
Miranda, Lin-Manuel 60
Miss Evers' Boys (Feldshuh) 167, 189, 208, 209–13
Mitchell, Al Suavae 89
Mitchell, Lionel 120
Mitchell, Loften 43, 60
Mohammed, Elijah 105n45
Moon on a Rainbow Shawl (John) 120, 146, 147
Moore, Lisa L. 106n74
Moreau, Joseph 93
Morrison, Toni 193
Mosque Theatre 146
Moynihan, Daniel Patrick 171
Mpolo, Maurice 41
Murray, Bill 40
My Fair Lady 35

National Black Theatre 6, 8, 56
National Black Theatre Festival 138, 140, 141, 162, 177, 179, 205
National Endowment for the Arts (NEA) 5, 117
National Endowment for the Humanities 5
nationhood 86
Nation of Islam 105n45
Native Son (Wright) 41
naturalism 23n46
Ndangered 189, 197, 203–205, 208
Ndounou, Monica White 106n74, 138, 223, 225
NEA *see* National Endowment for the Arts (NEA)
Neal, Larry 4–5, 10, 21, 84, 85, 86, 220
Neal, Marc Anthony 58, 71, 115, 125

"Negro and the American Theatre, The" (Locke) 13
Negro Ensemble Company 6–7, 38, 141
New Amsterdam News 66
New Lafayette Theatre 7, 8, 15, 56
Newsweek 209
Newton, Huey P. 78n60
New York Amsterdam News 119
New Yorker magazine 63
New York Shakespeare Festival *see* Public Theater
New York Times 66
Nixon, Richard 4, 5, 67
Nixon, Ruth 139
Nommo 149, 150, 197, 200
Normal Heart, The (Kramer) 177
North Carolina Black Repertory 140
Ntshona, Winston 140

Ogunyemi, Chikwenye Okonjo 191
OJT *see* on-the-job-training (OJT)
Okito, Joseph 41
Olaniyan, Tejumola 121
Olaye, Shola Gabby 123
Old Settler, The (Redwood) 208
One-Dimensional Queer 162–63, 177
on-the-job-training (OJT) 138, 139, 143

Page, Jeffrey 204
Pantagleize 37
Paper, The 87
Papp, Joseph 1, 37, 38
Pendarvis, Donna 146, 194, 196, 215n25
Perkins, Kathy 85, 102–103
Perry, Tyler 153
Personal Responsibility and Work Opportunity Reconciliation Act (PRWORA; 1996) 165
Peterson, Louis S. 41
Philips, Layli 9, 22n27
Phillips, Kimberly L. 38
Phillips, Layli 190, 191, 192
Pine Camp 146, 147
Pinkney, Mikell 85, 103, 121
"Poem for Willie Best, A" (Baraka) 42
Pollard, Cherise 114
Primus, Marc 10, 16, 18, 21, 47, 57, 58, 60–61, 77n23, 116, 119, 126, 184n59, 213; on Baraka 93; on *El Hajj Malik* 72–73; on *Equus* 124; on Malcolm X 70; on *Where It's At* 67, 198
Prison Notebooks (Gramsci) 33
Proctor, Roy 196

pronouns, significance of 40, 150, 171, 200
Pryce-Styles, Alice 198
Public Theater 37
"Published Criticism and its Positive Effect on Black Theatre" (McClintock) 74, 83
"Punks, Bulldaggers, and Welfare Queens" (Cohen) 163, 172
"pure coon", stereotype of 171
"Pussy Poem" (Edwards) 9

queering 114, 131–32n11
queer literary culture, in 1940s and 1950s 30–31
queer sexuality 9–10, 97, 103, 110, 124–26, 128, 177, 183n2, 208

racial blackness 115
racial capitalism 162, 163, 176, 182
racial divide, as center of American politics 163–68
radical political consciousness 40–43
Raisin in the Sun, A (Hansberry) 37, 41–42, 89, 90, 199
Ray, Gene Anthony 115
Reaganomics 116–19, 136
Redwood, John Henry 208
Regal Theatre 33, 34
Rent 177
Republican National Committee (RNC) 164
Rethinking the Gay and Lesbian Movement (Stein) 43
"Revolutionary Petunias" (Walker) 191
"Revolutionary Theatre, The" (Baraka) 92
Richards, Sandra L. 85, 102–103
Rich, Frank 194
Richman, Mark 35
Richmond 142–43, 147; Black queer theatre in 175–82; collectively-authored performance in 155–56; Department of Parks and Recreation 144, 145, 146, 147
Richmond Afro-American and The Richmond Planet, The (Horne) 145
Richmond Black Theatre Festival 20, 182–83, 188–89, 206–209
Richmond Free Press 146
riffs 12–13, 53, 62, 64, 65, 72–74, 96, 123, 151, 179, 194, 224
Riggs, Marlon 179, 184n72
Riley, Clayton 7
River Niger, The (Walker) 140
RNC *see* Republican National Committee (RNC)

Robertson, Pat 164
Robeson, Paul 220
Robinson, Cedric 162, 174
Robinson, Vivian 89, 104n10, 220
Rodriguez, Holly M. 203
Rose that Grew from Concrete, The 189, 197, 199, 202–203, 208
Rustin, Bayard 43

Salaam, Yusef A. 122
Samalenge, Lucas 42
Sanchez, Sonia 4, 114
Schechner, Richard 88
Schoolbook Nation (Moreau) 93
Schumann-Heink, Ernestine 146
Scott, Spencer 41
Scott, Tony 210
Seale, Bobby 78n60
Second City 48n60
Sedgewick, Eve 114, 132n11
self-determination: Afrocentric roots and 27, 42; contemporary Black classics and 86, 87, 94, 97, 99, 100; Harlem and 55, 57, 63, 64, 70–72, 75, 76; importance of 3, 11, 13–14, 157, 161, 176, 178, 179, 189, 194, 196, 198, 201, 205, 206, 215n41, 221–23; quaring of Black Theatre Movement and 109, 121, 131
self-expression 58–63, 66–70, 221, 223
Selwyn Theatre 34
Semmes, Clovis, E. 27, 33, 48n32
Senghor, Leopold 104n17
Sense of Pride 155, 208
Sewer, Ed 123
Shabazz, Iman 155, 204, 205–206
Shaffer, Peter 9, 103, 109, 124
Shaffer, Tia M. 106n74
Shakur, Afeni 199, 201, 206
Shakur, Tupac 189, 197, 199–202, 215n46
Shange, Ntozake 56, 70, 103, 109, 121, 122
Shango de Ima (Carril) 139
Shewey, Don 133n62
Showalter, Elaine 85, 102, 104n12
Silvera, Frank 2, 21, 34, 35–37, 46, 220
Simon, Levy Lee 10, 101, 109, 126, 139, 156, 159n74, 199, 200
Simone, Nina 195
Simpson, O. J., trial of 166
Sinclair, Abiola 126, 180
Sirens, The (Wesley) 140
Slave Ship (Baraka) 84, 90, 91–97
Smethurst, James Edward 104n15
Smith, Anna Deavere 208

Smith, Barbara Harris 85, 102, 104n12, 193
Smith, Derome Scott 149, 150, 168, 201, 208
Smith, Hazel Rosetta 199, 200
social abandonment 163, 169
Souls of Black Folk, The (Du Bois) 130
sovereign power 163, 169
Spady, James 199, 215n47
Spell No. 7 (Shange) 103, 109, 121–24
Stanislavski-based techniques 21, 51, 55, 76n8, 77n34, 98, 149, 150
Stanislavski, Konstantin 11
Steal Away (King) 208
Stein, Marc 43
Stewart, Delano 87, 220
St. Marks Playhouse 152
street life 7
street poetry theatre 70
Stretching Out 62, 63
Structural Amnesia 98
Stuart, S. Edwards 196
Studevent, Naadir 204
"Studio A" project 187
Style Weekly 187
Styron, William 99
Sweet Tea 125

table read 180–81
Take a Giant Step (Peterson) 41
Taming of the Shrew, The 38
Taste of Honey, A 37
Tatum, Tanya 195
Taylor, Chloë 163
Teer, Barbara Ann 6, 20, 56, 87, 144
Temple, Christel 138, 142, 146, 206, 210, 211, 213
text, musicality of 171
Theatre Renny 119, 121, 130
Thompson, Garland Lee, Jr. 36
Thorne, Robin 123
Till, Emmett 29–30
Tisch School of the Arts (New York University) 57
Tongues United (Riggs) 179
"Toward a Black Feminist Criticism" (Smith) 193
Trask, Michael 30
Tri-State Defender 81
Truman, Harry 38
Tshombe, Moïse 41
Turnbull, Walter 139
"Tuskegee Study of Untreated Syphilis in the Negro Male" 189–90, 209

Two Rooms (McClintock) 45
Two Thousand 180

Umbra Writers' Workshop 4
United States Armed Forces Institute 2
Urban Arts Corps 8
urban ghetto 171–72
US homophile movement 42–43

Vaughan, Sarah 46
Venable, Michael J. 204, 205
Victoria Five Theater 180
Vidal, Gore 31

Walcott, Derek 56, 109, 119
Walker, Alice 9, 190, 191
Walker, George 47n28
Walker, Greta 63
Walker, Joseph 87, 140
Walker, Ronald 2, 15, 42, 43, 46, 47, 53, 58, 70, 71, 81, 95, 100, 118, 138, 141, 156, 163, 178, 187, 213, 221
Wallace, Gregory 89, 109, 126, *127*, 128, 139
Ward, Douglas Turner 7, 38, 178
Ward, Marguerite 165
Ward, Theodore 41
Washington, Booker T. 105n45
Washington, Denzel 126, *127*
Washington, Dinah 46
Watson, Jamantha Williams 38
Watts Rebellion 142, 157n20
welfare queen, stereotype of 171, 182
Wesley, Richard 56, 66, 140, 156, 161, 167, 168
West, Cheryl L. 156
West, Cornel 127
When the Chickens Come Home to Roost (Holder) 126

Where It's At 55, 189, 198; affecting audiences 68, 70; flyer of 66–67, *67*; newspaper clippings about *69*; Primus on 67
"White Imitations Dropped by Acting School in Harlem" (Glover) 169
whiteness 6, 51, 55, 61, 119, 174, 175
white western theatre 12
Wilbur Theater 133n62
Williams, Bert 47n28
Williams, Justin A. 190, 197
Williams, Mance 16, 54–55, 68, 76n13, 152
Williams, Rodney 203
Wilson, August 152, 153, 178
Wilson, Mark 184n53
Wilson, Robert 46, 88
Winfrey, Oprah 193
Winters, Shelley 34
womanism 9, 20, 22n27, 103, 110, 114, 155, 191–93, 223
Womanist Reader, The 192
women poets, views of 114–15
Women's Wear Daily 73
Woodley, Sheldon 150, 158n49, 170, 171, 210, 211
word value 132n52, 200
Wright, Richard 41

X, Malcolm 3, 13, 46, 55, 63, 70–71, 83, 105n45, 175

Yancy, George 99
Young, Harvey 91, 97, 167, 168, 184n35
Yurcaba, Jo 43

Zinn, Howard 77n23
Zola, Émile 23n46
Zooman and the Sign (Fuller) 201